Seasons of HOPE

Also by James Bartleman

Exceptional Circumstances (2015)

The Redemption of Oscar Wolf (2013)

As Long as the Rivers Flow (2011)

Raisin Wine: A Boyhood in a Different Muskoka (2007)

Rollercoaster: My Hectic Years as Jean Chrétien's Diplomatic Advisor, 1994–1998 (2005)

On Six Continents: A Life in Canada's Foreign Service, 1966–2002 (2004)

Out of Muskoka (2004)

Seasons of HOPE

Memoirs of Ontario's First Aboriginal Lieutenant Governor

James Bartleman

DUNDURN
A J. PATRICK BOYER BOOK

Editor: Michael Carroll
Design: Laura Boyle
Cover design: Laura Boyle
Cover image: © Andrew Stawicki, Photosensitive
Printer: Webcom

Library and Archives Canada Cataloguing in Publication

Bartleman, James, 1939-, author
Seasons of hope : memoirs of Ontario's first Aboriginal Lieutenant Governor / James Bartleman.

Includes index.
Issued in print and electronic formats.
ISBN 978-1-4597-3306-0 (paperback).--ISBN 978-1-4597-3307-7 (pdf).--
ISBN 978-1-4597-3308-4 (epub)

1. Bartleman, James, 1939-. 2. Lieutenant governors--Ontario--Biography. 3. Ambassadors--Canada--Biography. 4. Chippewas of Mnjikaning First Nation--Biography. I. Title.

FC636.B37A3 2016 971.064092 C2015-908471-7
C2015-908472-5

1 2 3 4 5 20 19 18 17 16

We acknowledge the support of the **Canada Council for the Arts** and the **Ontario Arts Council** for our publishing program. We also acknowledge the financial support of the **Government of Canada** through the **Canada Book Fund** and **Livres Canada Books**, and the **Government of Ontario** through the **Ontario Book Publishing Tax Credit** and the **Ontario Media Development Corporation**.

Printed and bound in Canada.

VISIT US AT

Dundurn.com | @dundurnpress | Facebook.com/dundurnpress | Pinterest.com/dundurnpress

Dundurn
3 Church Street, Suite 500
Toronto, Ontario, Canada
M5E 1M2

For Marie-Jeanne, Anne-Pascale, Laurent, Alain, Sebastien, Nicholas, Henry, Marie-Anne, Thomas, and future generations. And to the selfless donors who have supported Frontier College since 2005 in running Summer of Hope Literacy Camps in up to 100 First Nations across Canada, spreading the love of reading and books to cumulative totals of some 40,000 children and youth, 10,000 involved parents and community members, and 1,500 Indigenous and non-Indigenous camp counsellors, as well as distributing close to 200,000 books to the children.

You can't know what a life has been until it is over.

— André Alexis, *Fifteen Dogs*

Contents

Preface

This memoir is a book of stories. Drawn from all four seasons of my life, some are brief vignettes, others are based on diary entries and family trees, and still others are full-fledged accounts of developments that shaped the latter part of the twentieth century. Some are stories of coming of age, adventure, encounters with great men and women, accomplishment, and failure. Others bear witness to Third World misery, First World wealth, international terrorism, great loss of life, civil war, heroism, cynicism, generosity, and meanness. Necessarily selective for reasons of space, they extend back more than seventy years, tracing my unlikely journey from a tent in the Muskoka village of Port Carling in the 1940s to the vice-regal suite as Ontario's twenty-seventh lieutenant governor at Queen's Park a half century later and beyond.

They demonstrate that my life, like those of everyone else, was largely shaped by chance. If I hadn't lived for a time near a dump with a supply of comic books, learned to read at an early age, and met a benefactor who sent me to university, perhaps I would never have left the village where I was raised. If I hadn't sought shelter from the cold in St. Paul's Cathedral in London on December 6, 1964, and listened to a sermon by Reverend

Martin Luther King, maybe I wouldn't have been inspired to write the exams to join the Foreign Service. If I hadn't taken an early-morning flight in the spring of 1974 from Brussels to Vienna on North Atlantic Treaty Organization (NATO) business, I wouldn't have met my wife and the mother of our three children and five grandchildren. If I hadn't become foreign-policy adviser to newly elected Prime Minister Jean Chrétien in 1994, he wouldn't have appointed me Ontario's lieutenant governor in 2002. And if I hadn't become lieutenant governor, I wouldn't have been able to finish my career giving back to society by establishing libraries in Indigenous-run schools across the province, a book club for 5,000 Indigenous children, creative-writing awards, and most important of all, summer reading camps for marginalized Indigenous children in Northern Ontario.

James Bartleman
Perth, Ontario
November 5, 2015

Part One

Muskoka: 1946–1966

The Indian Village of Obagawanung, now Port Carling, consisted of some twenty log huts, beautifully situated on the Indian River and Silver Lake with a good deal of cleared land about it used as garden plots, and the Indians grew potatoes, Indian corn, and other vegetable products. They had no domestic animals but dogs and no boats but numerous birch bark canoes.

The fall on the River there, being the outlet of Lake Rosseau, was about eight feet, and fish and game were very plentiful. When Mr. Hart and I were encamped there, Musquedo brought us potatoes and corn and we gave him pork and tobacco in return.

— Vernon B. Wadsworth *Reminiscences of Indians in Muskoka and Haliburton, 1860–64*

1

Sunshine Sketches of a Little Town

One quiet Sunday afternoon in June 1946 a truck delivered my mother, brother, two sisters, and me, together with rucksacks and an assortment of pots and pans, to a tent near the village dump in the small Muskoka village of Port Carling. Bob was eight, I was six, Janet was four, and Mary just two months. My father was white and my mother Indian,* a distinction we children never noticed. Always having had a roof over our heads and plenty to eat, we didn't know our family was dirt-poor and at the bottom of thc social scale. All of this would change when school started in the fall.

My father greeted us with a large, welcoming smile. He had come to Port Carling a month earlier to visit his Indian father-in-law, who lived at the small Indian reserve known locally as the Indian Camp, and had decided to stay — at least for a while. His ambition was to go north to look for work near an Ojibwa reserve on Georgian Bay where my mother had relatives. In the interim he had found work shovelling gravel and loading rock on trucks by hand for a local trucker for 60 cents an hour. Not being Indian, he wasn't allowed to remain with his father-in-law at

* My late mother, her family, and friends from the Chippewas of Rama First Nation were proud of their Indian heritage and always referred to themselves as Indian or Indians. I use the terms *Indian*, *Native*, *Aboriginal*, or *Indigenous* interchangeably according to the context throughout this memoir.

the Indian Camp, so he constructed a rough shelter from rusty pieces of corrugated iron at the village dump, and saved his money until he could buy a tent and send for his wife and children.

My family had spent the war years in a tough, multi-ethnic area of Welland, Ontario, where my father was a steelworker. Our neighbours included Canadians of French, Hungarian, Jewish, Polish, and Italian origin, a mix that Aboriginal kids fitted into easily. Everyone was working-class and described themselves as such. Literally on the other side of the tracks, the quarter was boxed in by railway spur lines. The sound of locomotives shunting boxcars was part of our lives, as were the shouts and laughter of drunks on Saturday nights. Bob and I revelled in this classless rough-and-tumble world. We regularly skipped school to play with our friends along the railway tracks. We engaged in petty vandalism, slipping into the sheds of neighbours to open cans of paint and splatter their contents on the walls or simply mix them together for malicious pleasure. When our parents weren't looking, we even helped ourselves to my father's homebrew; it tasted terrible.

My father enjoyed life. He prepared enormous quantities of homemade raisin wine and invited his steelworker buddies over to drink. A natural storyteller, he held court in the living room, recounting the dramatic events of his life. Bob and I shared his pride in dropping out of school at the age of fourteen and dodging the truant officer who wanted to send him to the reformatory for delinquent boys. He would also describe his adventures as a hobo during the Great Depression, riding the rails across Canada, hiding from the railway police, knocking on doors to ask for food in exchange for doing chores, working as a lumberjack and farm labourer, and begging on street corners.

Inevitably, he would produce well-worn newspaper clippings describing an incident some years earlier that had provided his fifteen minutes of fame. My white grandmother had obtained a job as cook, and one of my aunts as maid, for Stephen Leacock, whose summer home was in Orillia, my father's hometown. My father had taken his canoe out on Lake Couchiching just as an enormous storm blew up. When my grandmother appealed to Leacock to save him, Canada's best-known humorist rode his motorboat to the rescue and hauled my father from the water against his will. The story was picked up by the wire services and carried in the international press. What follows are the *New York Times* and *Toronto Daily Star* versions of the story.

New York Times, Orillia, Ontario, July 9, 1939

Dr. Stephen Leacock, noted Canadian author and lecturer at McGill University, played a prominent part in the rescue of Percy Bartleman, 21, of Orillia, whose sailing canoe capsized on Lake Couchiching. A sudden squall upset the canoe along with several other small craft. Residents say they never had seen higher waves on the lake. Dr. Leacock, whose summer home is on Brewer's Bay, was about to set out on a fishing trip in his motor launch with the caretaker of his place, Jack Kelly, and Mrs. Kelly when the storm broke. They had not lifted anchor and were about to make for a dock when they saw Bartleman clinging to his overturned canoe a half mile from shore.

As the Leacock boat headed into the high waves, Mrs. Kelly fainted. The motor launch headed back for shore, but when Mrs. Kelly recovered momentarily, it headed out to the youth's aid again. Mrs. Kelly was overcome again and the launch took her ashore, where she was put in a doctor's care. Dr. Leacock and Kelly headed into the lake again. After almost turning back within 100 yards of the canoe, as waves broke over them, they reached Bartleman's side. Kelly lassoed Bartleman with a rope as Dr. Leacock manned the wheel. Bartleman was taken in to a motor camp, where other persons, blown across the bay in boats, were receiving shelter. The camp was littered with fallen limbs and broken branches ripped from the surrounding trees by the wind. William K. Bartlett, Orillia newspaper man, was one of those caught in the squall.

"The force of the waves knocked the rudder off my sailboat," he said. "I let down my sail immediately, but just the same I went scudding across the lake before the wind. I passed not far from Bartleman's boat and threw a life-buoy toward him. It didn't get near him."

Toronto Daily Star, July 10, 1939

Stephen Leacock, famous Canadian humorist and economist, played the leading role Sunday in a dramatic rescue. To Prof. Leacock's knowledge of the boats and Lake Couchiching's waves, Percy Bartleman, 21, of Orillia, owes his life. It was a rope tossed to him by Prof. Leacock that saved him as he clung to his overturned canoe.

Mostly disclaiming any heroism today, Prof. Leacock spoke of the storm and Bartleman. "I really didn't have any part in the rescue: the young man really saved his life," he said. "I don't know how he managed to stick to that canoe," said Prof. Leacock. "A couple of times he went under while we were coming towards him, but he held on."

As for his part in the rescue, Prof. Leacock said, "I'm used to boats. We weren't in any danger, but Bartleman was. The waves were tremendous.

"All we did was take him off the canoe, put him in the motor boat, and eventually ensconce him in a chair in my living room. So far as our saving him from drowning goes, this is twaddle. If he hadn't been cool he would have drowned long before we got to him. But he was cool. As we approached him we could see him sitting calmly on the bottom of his canoe. First above water, and then under water. He was as cool as a cucumber. I never saw anything like it. When we took him off his dripping perch he grinned. The boy has a sense of humour, too."

"The storm was a terrible one," Mr. Leacock said. "It was like a sudden cyclone."

Prof. Leacock, his caretaker, Jack Kelly, and Mrs. Kelly were prepared to set out in their motor launch for an afternoon's fishing when the storm broke. They decided to remain in the safety of Brewer's Bay, in front of Mr. Leacock's home just outside Orillia, till the storm passed over. A little while after the onset they saw Bartleman's overturned canoe with its small sail.

At the time, Kelly, six-foot Irishman, was steering the twenty-six-foot launch, Prof. Leacock told him to make for Bartleman. Mrs. Kelly, who had been in bed all week under the doctor's care, fainted as the launch struck the huge waves and the full force of the cyclonic wind.

"When I left the wheel to pick her up off the floor of the boat the waves and wind turned us round and almost capsized us," Kelly related. "When she recovered we went back for another try and she fainted again. We took her to shore, tied a rowboat on behind and picked up some extra rope, and, then, Prof. Leacock took the wheel and we went out again into the teeth of it."

Kelly stated, "once the engine began to stall, and I figured we would have to take to the rowboat, but, somehow, we made it. I don't know how."

When the engine began to sputter, Prof. Leacock shouted at Kelly, "We can't turn back now. We'll have to go on."

"If Prof. Leacock had not got in so close to the canoe as he did, there is no telling what would have happened, because it would have taken us about an hour to come about and to have come up to him again," said Kelly, "and we would have been lucky to keep upright ourselves."

"It was one of those terrible storms that come up suddenly with the wind, "Prof. Leacock said, adding that he feels none the worse for his experience.

Bartleman had been out paddling with his wife and baby in the morning. At the time of the accident he had fitted a small sail to the craft. The terrible squall caught him unawares.

My father's version of the "rescue" is different. He claimed he had been in greater danger from being run over by Leacock's launch than from drowning. He also said the *New York Times* was wrong in saying he had been taken to a motor camp afterward. Leacock had taken him to his Brewer's Bay home where to my father's satisfaction the famous author poured two water glasses full of whiskey and they toasted their adventure. Then, as my father dried himself off, he heard Leacock on the telephone telling his story to the press. But then again, my father would likely have tried to make the story sound better each time he told it.

My father, Percy Bartleman, in 1939, about the time Stephen Leacock "saved" him from drowning. *Courtesy Bartleman Family.*

But these are just quibbling details. What counts, as far as I'm concerned, is that I was born a few months later on December 24, 1939, in a house on the shore of Lake Couchiching not far from where Leacock hauled my father into his launch. And I would like to believe I wouldn't have had a father to raise me if Leacock hadn't persevered in his rescue attempts. When I told this story in June 2003 at a McGill University convocation ceremony awarding me an honorary doctorate, I think the crowd thought I was quoting from Leacock's famous book *Sunshine Sketches of a Little Town* — but I didn't care.

2

The Dump Road

Port Carling's reputation in postwar Ontario as one of Canada's leading tourist centres meant nothing to me at the time. I had no idea that it constituted a microcosm of what would become the globalized world of the twenty-first century, with its winners and its losers squeezed into one small village of no more than 500 permanent residents and several thousand summer residents within a block of a few square miles. Nor did I suspect that it would have been difficult to find in Canada a place where the contrasts between rich and poor, sophisticated and rude, city and country, Gentile and Jew, American and Canadian, descendants of original settlers and newcomers, were more pronounced. The Indians were the invisible brown minority at the bottom of the heap. I only knew that an exciting summer was in store for the Bartleman children, living outdoors with our family in a tent on the side of the gravel road that wended its way over a large hill from the main street of the village to the dump. There was also the prospect of spending time with my Indian grandfather, my Indian uncle, and various Indian great-uncles and great-aunts who, as always, were spending the summer at Port Carling in their ghetto at the Indian Camp.

My father had put up the tent on the property of an aged former prospector named Pat Paddington, who had drifted to Port Carling with his Indian wife, Violet, and her adult daughter, Stella. Pat was eking out an existence as a casual labourer and had built a small cabin with a leaky tin roof that sounded like a drum when it rained. Pat and Violet were kind to the Bartleman brood. We spent long afternoons in their cabin drinking in the scent of sweetgrass and listening to my mother and her two Indian friends murmuring in Chippewa while they fashioned baskets from strips of white ash and transformed porcupine quills, beads, and birchbark into fancywork, the local term for handicraft. Stella had tuberculosis, like so many thousands of Indians at that time, and died shortly after we arrived in Port Carling.

We were proud of our large tent and considered that our location close to the village dump presented opportunities rather than disadvantages. Granted, the dump had its own distinctive fragrance, and the permanent black cloud of smoke from burning orange crates, cardboard, scrap lumber, and discarded furniture wasn't to everyone's taste. But where else could one find treasures such as slightly soiled but usable toys and sometimes torn but still readable comic books, and see wildlife (including raccoons and skunks) in profusion, not to mention flocks of seagulls and crows, which constantly circled over their culinary delights? The comic books, especially *Dick Tracy*, *Terry and the Pirates*, *Superman*, and *Little Orphan Annie*, I particularly treasured and would rush back to the tent to show them to my mother and to whine until she relented and helped me decipher the words in the bubbles over the characters. By the end of the summer, I was well on my way to learning to read, the first step out of a life of poverty.

Fire from the burning garbage spread that summer into the bush, causing an enormous forest fire. We had first-row seats as the villagers fought it to a standstill in the meadow below the rocky outcrop on which our tent was located. Ferndale House, a large resort on Lake Rosseau two miles from the village, also went up in flames that summer. From our campsite high above the village, we heard the frantic pealing of church bells late one evening summoning the men of the village to assemble at the fire hall, and then, somewhat later, the sirens of the venerable fire truck as it hastened, followed by a convoy of firefighters and the curious, to the hopeless fight with the inferno. My father's employer was later engaged, with every other trucker in the area, to haul the debris to the dump. Fire-blackened cans of pineapples, pears, peaches, and a variety of vegetables and soups were dropped off at our tent. With the labels on the cans burnt off, Bob and I played a game guessing the contents before opening them. We were winners when the reward was pineapples or peaches rather than pork and beans.

Pat Paddington shared the Dump Road with two other families. The neighbour at the base of the hill, who lived with his wife and daughter in an old log cabin, was well known to my mother, since he had often accompanied her father on visits to the owner when she was a child. By the summer of 1946, however, the house was collapsing. The end was in sight when a grossly overweight lady who had had too much to drink started to dance a jig during a party and fell through the floor. Then the daughter was hit by a car and killed, demoralizing the family, after which they abandoned house and village to begin their lives again elsewhere. This was my first encounter with death. The day before she was killed, we had played among the weeds and the long grass behind the cabin, our legs wet from morning dew and our bare feet sticky from stepping in the soft droppings of the free-ranging chickens. We had searched for eggs among the straw, almost overwhelmed by the pungent odour of ammonia in the airless chicken coop. The next day she was dead, the first of three village children who would die violent deaths from accidents in my Port Carling years.

I would see much death in my Foreign Service career: corpses lying among the crowds on the sidewalks of Dhaka, Bangladesh; Mother Teresa carried in great pomp and dignity on an open bier at her funeral in Calcutta; a Russian drug lord, victim of a gangland killing, powdered and laid out in ostentatious splendour in an Orthodox church in Moscow; a beautiful Israeli woman being lowered without a coffin into a grave among the orange groves of the Judean hills while the mourners chanted Kaddish; and the mummified bodies of Lenin and Ho Chi Minh in their mausoleums in Moscow and Hanoi. They would all look like my dead schoolmates in their open coffins at the village churches in Port Carling — just sleeping.

The other neighbour, an ancient villager, lived on the other side of Pat Paddington in an unpainted shack with a pigsty and an outhouse in the backyard. He spent his days sitting in a rocking chair, corncob pipe clamped between the blackened stumps of his few remaining teeth, watching loads of garbage go by. From time to time he would wander up to the dump to collect a supply of rotting fruits and vegetables for his pig before resuming his inactivity. A highlight of our day was to watch our neighbour feed his pig, an enormous beast with four-inch tusks that gobbled down its food with much grunting and evident pleasure. A granddaughter lived in the shack but refused to speak to Bob and me, even though she didn't seem to have any friends and we tried to convince her to come with us to the dump.

Social position was the last thing on my mind that summer of 1946. I remember the burning heat of the day and the incessant chirping of crickets in the evenings, a setting I was to be reminded of years later when travelling in southern France along the Mediterranean coast. Bob and I (our sisters being too young to join in) kept ourselves busy with cow-dung fights, using dry manure collected in a nearby pasture as ammunition. We gathered wild strawberries among the weeds and grass near a fenced-off water hole, which always smelled fresh and humid even on the hottest days. As the berry picker of the family, I would disappear into the bushes on the side of the dusty road to collect baskets of raspberries in July and blackberries in August, seeking out a spot where I could sit undisturbed for hours among the brambles to daydream and watch birds, insects, and the clouds in the Muskoka sky. I would return to the tent, hands and mouth red from juice, legs and arms scratched from thorns, looking forward to praise from my mother for a job well done.

3

The Haunted House

My education in the realities of Muskoka village life began when my parents decided to spend the winter in Port Carling. The only place they could afford to rent was an uninsulated two-bedroom summer cottage on the Indian River, with cracks in the outer walls, defective electrical wiring fashioned from discarded telephone cables, and an outhouse. My father had to agree to purchase all his firewood from the owner and vacate the premises before the first tourist arrived in May of the following year.

Winter came early that year. The sky was lit up at night by the northern lights and stars, clouds of freezing mist hung over the river, and the snow crackled underfoot. After we went to bed, the fire in the wood stove would go out, a dusting of snow would penetrate the cracks in the walls, ice a quarter inch thick would build up on the single-pane windows, and a covering of frost would form over everything, including the blankets on our beds. We three older children would make our way to our parents' bed to sleep with them and the baby to keep warm.

Each morning my father would get up well before dawn to light the fire. One day, out of kindling, he searched for dry branches along the banks of the river, which a strong current kept ice-free except along the shore. Spotting a dry branch on the ice, he took a chance and left the safety of the shore to get it, but broke through. Despite the minus-35-degree temperature, he pushed on to seize the branch, aware that the only way to avoid death from hypothermia was to go home and start a fire as soon as possible. His clothes quickly froze, and icicles formed on his hair and eyebrows as he returned to the cottage. My mother assumed control, lighting a fire and giving him dry clothing as Bob and I sat watching. He then went to work that morning as if nothing unusual had happened.

During the winter, my mother took the family's future in her hands, perhaps sensing that my father was simply too impractical to make major domestic decisions. She went looking for a better house, paying no attention to my father's talk about moving away from the village once spring arrived. She fixed her attention on a two-storey shack, with one room downstairs and two bedrooms upstairs, on a one-acre lot overgrown with brush and bramble on the side of a hill on the main street. My mother knew the house well — at least from the outside. As a child and adolescent in the 1920s and 1930s, she had spent her summers at the Indian Camp, where her family sold fish, quill boxes, toy birchbark canoes, and other trinkets to tourists. She told us that in those days she used to cross the street whenever she went by that shack since it was inhabited by a ghost. Two large windows, their glass broken by stone-throwing kids over the years, stared down at passersby on the street like the Windigo, the sinister eater of human flesh and evil spirit in Chippewa mythology — at least that was what my mother said. She also said she was deathly afraid in those early days that the ghost would float out of one of the black and eyeless sockets to grab her and do her in. She never dreamed, she said, that one day the house would become her home.

The years hadn't treated it well. Known in the village as "the old haunted house on the hill," it had neither indoor toilet nor electricity. Rainwater leaked through the tarpaper roof, the posts that served as foundations were rotting away, and the house leaned scarily to one side. A water pipe protruded from a hole in the floor in one corner, and the sawdust insulation packed into the walls in the 1890s had long since disappeared. But the unpainted, weather-beaten exterior boards that had turned barn-wood-black with age were solid, the interior walls of the ground-floor room were clean, and the partitions of deep brown hemlock studs covered by thin boards separating the two upstairs bedrooms were spotless and dry.

Abandoned for years, the house had been occupied in the 1920s by a poor black family. The villagers had shunned them, even though they had been long-standing residents. The family had moved to Parry Sound where they did well, but as a result of their treatment in Port Carling, they refused to sell their house to anyone from the village. My mother went to see the owners and told them she didn't have the money for a down payment but offered to sign over her family allowance cheques to pay for it. Remembering their own tough days in the village and prepared to help someone poor and Indian, they agreed to sell for $275.

We took possession in May 1947, which made our landlord happy, since he was able to rent the cottage to better-paying tenants for the summer season. My parents scrubbed clean our new home, throwing out newspapers and broken pieces of furniture that had lain undisturbed for years. They whitewashed the walls and ceilings before moving in our possessions, delivered to the front door by my father's trucker employer. And to my delight, I found a natural history encyclopedia which, despite lacking half its pages, remained one of my prized possessions for years. My father installed a wood stove purchased by mail order from Simpson's department store in Toronto, and with the help of my mother, he strung stovepipes horizontally along the ceiling across the downstairs room (which served as living room, kitchen, dining room, and clothes closet) to an opening in an old brick chimney. The theory was that heat from the stove would pass through the stovepipes to warm the room. But as far as I could tell this arrangement made it hard to keep the fire going and made the periodic cleaning of soot and creosote from the pipes that much more difficult and dirty.

Our house, the only one in the village in those early years without electricity, was lit by kerosene lamps. We would laugh whenever the power failed and our neighbours, scrambling to find lanterns and candles, were reduced to our level. Toilet facilities consisted of an outdoor privy with doors scavenged at the dump nailed together to form walls, an often-missing fourth door for an entrance, pieces of discarded plywood for a roof, and a seat some 50 feet behind the house. We children thought it hilarious to see visitors try all four doors before gaining entrance to the odorous inner sanctum. An old copy of an Eaton's catalogue, which in later years Bob dubbed the Poor Boy's *Playboy*, provided paper. Visits to the outhouse were no fun in the winter, when we had to struggle through snow up to our bums (the path was never shovelled). We never lingered, given that we would usually find ourselves sitting on the seat, as in the Dogpatch of Al Capp's *Li'l Abner* comic strip, amid snow blown in through the open door.

Nothing, however, can match the hold our old house has held over me down through the years. I can still picture every nook and cranny, see the crawl space under the stairs where my father kept his home brew and where I stored my growing collection of books, smell the old unpainted lumber, experience the disorientation of walking over a floor six inches lower on one side of the room than on the other, and feel the cold from the heavily frosted single-pane windows in winter.

4

Rage

In early July 1948, a telegram from my mother's uncle on the Rama Reserve arrived at the old house: "Your father dead. Wake tomorrow night. Funeral Friday. Come home. Uncle Jack."

My grandfather Simcoe had been in declining health for years. Like other Indigenous people of the time, he had spent his life on the outside of Canadian society, not recognized as equal under Canadian law and not even allowed to vote in federal elections. Never one to complain, he had accepted this way and rhythm of life. As a young man, he first worked as a guide and canoeist for survey parties mapping the boundary between Ontario and Manitoba. Later he was a logger in bush camps where he made a name for himself in the wrestling matches organized for the entertainment of the men during the long winter months. Then followed a stint during the Great War in an ammunition plant at Nobel, Ontario, during which he was so badly injured in an industrial accident he had to return to the reserve. There he married my grandmother, Edna Benson, who had just spent five years in the Gravenhurst tuberculosis sanatorium.

The early years of their marriage, my mother told me, were good ones. His father-in-law, Fred Benson, who had returned from the Great War with his lungs ravaged by mustard gas during fighting on the Western Front, received a small pension from the Canadian government that he shared with his daughter and her family. Each spring Ed and Edna took the train from Rama to Muskoka Wharf at the bottom of Lake Muskoka where they stored their canoe over the winter months. Then, after an easy six-hour paddle, they reached the Indian Camp in Port Carling to spend their summers with friends and family from the reserve.

My grandmother, Edna Benson Simcoe, at Couchiching Park in Orillia in the late 1930s. *Courtesy Bartleman Family.*

Shortly afterward, my grandparents' marriage fell apart. Edna, it turned out, loved drinking hard liquor and quarrelling and fighting with fist and foot. Her war-hero father died after years of coughing up blood from his damaged lungs. With his death the disability pension payments stopped coming, ending the family's economic safety cushion. Frittering away her inheritance on drink, Edna saw her family go from one of the better off on the reserve with a comfortable house and large sugar bush to one of the poorest. Worse, she turned on her daughter, beating her mercilessly and keeping her out of school for lengthy periods.

When they broke up in the mid-1930s, Ed and Edna had six children, the youngest being Scotty, a boy of six months. Edna took one child and went to live with a white man in a shack beside the scrapyard in Orillia, another child was adopted by a family at Moose Deer Point Indian Reserve on Georgian Bay, Uncle Jack took in one boy, and Ed inherited Scotty. After persuading a doubtful United Church minister that she was eighteen rather than fourteen, the oldest child, who would become my mother, married Percy Bartleman, a nineteen-year-old Orillia man who would become my father.

By marrying a white man, my mother lost her status as a Registered Indian, her membership in the band, and her right to live on the reserve. But that was a sacrifice she was prepared to make; like Ruth in the Bible, her husband's family became her family and his people became her people, or at least were supposed to be. But my mother's loss of status extended to her children, who were likewise denied access to their Indian heritage.

Although I was only a kid, this bothered me. I had one good white friend to hang out with in Port Carling until he dropped out of school and we drifted apart, but I sensed I belonged to neither the white nor to the Indian world, and I wanted to fit in somewhere. And if I had a choice, I wanted to be an Indian. It was perhaps for that reason I began spending time in the summers at the Indian Camp, where I felt at home, where the kids accepted me as one of theirs, shared their comic books with me, took me along as they dived for coins tossed into the river by summer residents from their motor launches, and included me in their expeditions to the Muskoka Lakes Golf and Country Club to make a little money carrying the bags of golfers. (It was a defining moment of my life years later when the law denying Indian rights to the children of Indian mothers and white men was changed and I was accepted as a Registered Indian and a member of the Rama Reserve.)

* * *

My mother wouldn't see her father again until the spring of 1948 when a neighbour with a car in Port Carling who was travelling to Orillia took her to his home on the reserve. Bob and I went with her. I had expected Rama to look like the Indian Camp where the people lived in neat shacks doubling as handicraft shops that smelled of sweetgrass and birchbark, where well-tended footpaths connected the homes, where pine needles several inches thick carpeted the ground and muffled the sound, and where families sat in the evenings around their campfires telling stories.

But as we passed the sign welcoming visitors to the reserve, the paved road turned into a dusty, potholed, gravel track. Bloated bodies of dogs and cats killed by speeding cars lay uncollected in the ditches. I saw the friends I had made at the Indian Camp dragging their feet as they walked along the roadway, devoid of the love of life they had displayed in their Muskoka setting. The weed-filled yards were littered with yellow-stained mattresses; rusted car bodies; old magazines; shattered bottles that had once contained cheap wine, perfume, and patent medicines; chewing tobacco packages, cigarette butts, and wrappings; and broken household equipment. Only a handful of buildings were connected to the electric grid, and outhouses were standard features in all backyards. Most homes were the dilapidated cabins and tarpaper-roofed shacks of the rural slums I would become familiar with in the Third World postings of my future diplomatic career. The house of my grandfather was no different from the others.

The neighbour from Port Carling glanced at Ed's house, dropped us off, and sped away, saying she would be back to pick us up in half an hour. Scotty, now twelve years old, his front teeth rotted away and the others black from decay after a lifetime diet of candy and sugar, gave us an enthusiastic welcome. His face was grimy, his bare feet were dirty, and his tattered trousers were held up with a piece of string. I felt ashamed of myself for flinching when he hugged me. Visibly aging and malnourished, Ed struggled to his feet to greet us. Although only in his mid-fifties, he looked like an old man in his eighties. My mother looked as if she wanted to cry.

Ed had suffered a stroke and was blind, but was, in his own words, "getting by." Scotty had dropped out of school and was doing his best to keep the house in order. Each week he went to the Indian agent for money for tea, canned milk, lard, flour, and baking powder to prepare rudimentary if unhealthy meals. He had also strung a rope from the back door of the house to the privy to allow his father to grope his way to and from the toilet.

It was a return to the unhappy past for my mother who knew her father didn't have long to live. Indeed, she wanted to take Ed and her little brother home, but that was out of the question. Her husband wouldn't like it, she assumed, since he could barely feed his family as it was. And with six family members already stuffed into the three rooms of the old house, another two people couldn't be accommodated. She shoved a handful of change, all the money she had on her, into his hands and hurried us to the waiting car.

Now, just a few months later, Ed was dead and my mother was feeling guilty. Looking back, I am sure that deep down she knew her husband wouldn't have objected if she had brought her father and brother back to live at the old house. Ed could have slept on the couch and Scotty could have squeezed in between Bob and me in our bed on the upstairs hallway. Ed and Scotty could have shared our food, and Ed would have received better medical care and lived longer. To add to her torment, she knew that everyone back on the reserve expected her to attend the wake and funeral — after all, she was the oldest child. But that was impossible. She didn't have the money to pay the taxi and bus fares and couldn't in any case leave her children alone.

The trucker then laid off my father, forcing him to set off on foot to look for work elsewhere carrying a change of clothes and his empty lunch box in a shopping bag. Eventually, a passing motorist picked him up and dropped him off at Orillia. While he was away, with no money, my mother nervously ran up a bill at the general store, hoping her good record in settling her accounts since her return to Port Carling would stand her in good stead. The kind-hearted owner, who had known her father for years, didn't object.

At this time, like an episode in a melodrama, the village clerk came repeatedly to the old house and demanded my mother pay $2 for a tag for my dog, threatening to seize and put him down if she didn't comply. Guilt-stricken, unable to grieve her father's death properly, deeply worried at the growing debt at the grocery store, not having $2 and not wanting to let the clerk take my dog to be killed, she didn't know what to do. Pushed by the grim town clerk's relentless bullying and psychologically damaged by the life of hopelessness and deprivation she had endured as a child on the reserve, she fell into a deep depression and did away with my dog herself. I was heartbroken and filled with rage and bitterness for years, not against my mother but against the clerk and people like him who abused the poor. My mother and I were both crying at the injustice of it all half a century later.

In the driveway of my Bartleman grandparents' house in Orillia in 1941, my mother holds my hand while Bob clutches kittens. *Courtesy Bartleman Family.*

Despite her pain, my mother did her best to take care of us. But at times, when she could bear her illness no longer, she would take her corncob pipe, tobacco, and matches, tell us she intended to kill herself, and as we sobbed and appealed to her not to leave, disappear into the bush behind the old house to fight her death wish by herself, always returning when the love of her children penetrated the fog of her depression. She eventually went to the village doctor for help, promising to pay him for his services when she could. In that era before anti-depression medication, he could do little other than to offer her his sympathy.

5

Peace of Mind

After we moved into the old house in the spring of 1947, my father gave Bob the job of lighting the fire each morning, but took it away when he was discovered tearing boards off the back of the house to make kindling. To Bob's satisfaction, he then gave the chore to me. Two or three years later when I was eight or nine, my father started taking me with him to help cut firewood in the bush. After taking all we could from our land behind the old house, we began scouring the wasteland back of the dump road for trees that had been killed by insect infestations or lightning strikes. The wood belonged to someone else, but my father had persuaded himself that it was a crime against man and nature to let potential fuel rot unused in the bush. In any case, he had no money to pay anyone for their dead trees nor did he intend to let his family freeze to death. He also knew that, since the village garbage truck was the only vehicle to use the road in winter, there was little chance anyone would see him scrounging around on the private property. Even if the owner were to find out and complain to the police, my father was prepared to take his chances. He could expect little pity from the provincial police should they be called in, but should it be the local constable who handled the case, he'd be let off. The genial village constable was a good friend and often came to the old house for dinner on Sundays, particularly when baked beans were on the menu.

By then we had two malamute huskies that accompanied us on our foraging expeditions, pulling a sleigh as we made our way up the dump road past the place where the family had lived during our first summer in the village. We would leave the road and range over the land until we found a dead tree. With his experience in the lumber camps, my father was an expert woodsman and a master with a crosscut saw. He would take one end of the saw and I'd take the other. I lacked the strength to do anything other than hold the saw level as my father did the heavy work, pulling and pushing it through the wood. With the tree on the ground, I would take hold of a trimming axe and do my share in removing the branches. Then, using the saw again, we'd cut the trunk into manageable lengths and load them onto the sleigh.

When the snow was wet and deep, when the wind whipped and stung my face with ice pellets, the going was pure misery. With my father in the lead, we'd force ourselves through heavy snow up to my hips. My rubber boots, open at the top, would fill with snow that would turn to water on contact with my feet and grow cold. But when there was a strong crust, when it was so cold there wasn't a cloud in the sky, when the hoarfrost on the trees sparkled and the smoke from chimneys throughout the village rose straight up to disappear into an azure sky, the work was easy and even fun. I would run and play with the dogs, my best friends, on rough land transformed into a level playing field. Then, aided by our dogs, my father and I would drag our loads home on the sleigh, going back time and again until the wood was safely stored in our backyard.

Every evening after school the following week, I'd manoeuvre the rough logs up onto a sawhorse and use a small bucksaw to cut them into stove lengths, afterward splitting the larger pieces into sizes to fit the firebox. After carrying in armloads of wood to fill the box beside the stove, I'd return to sit outside, paying no attention to the weather. Alone except for the reassuring company of the huskies, I'd think over the events of the day, enjoying my thoughts and cherishing the silence of the village in winter. Sometimes, if I was lucky, the night sky would erupt with the breathtaking spectacle of the northern lights shimmering and crackling above the mist rising from the fast-moving waters of the nearby Indian River. Other times I'd sit quietly in the falling snow and watch as snowflakes drifted soundlessly through the light of street lamps in front of the old house and blanketed the silent highway, disturbed rarely at that time of the day and year by passing cars and trucks. I would never, I thought, find greater peace of mind no matter how long I lived; I think I was right.

6

Springtime in Muskoka

I loved Muskoka in the winter, but I preferred spring when the sounds, sights, tastes, and smells of the melt were in the air. The daytime temperatures rose, the hours of daylight lengthened, the snowbanks shrank, and the black asphalt of the highway became visible. The giant icicles hanging from the eaves of the old house softened, dripped furiously, and came crashing down, and the sodden, greasy snow on the roof slipped off with a whisper. In the soft, humid heat of the day, water droplets formed within the heavy snowpack on the hillsides, coalescing and percolating down to puddle on the ground, to seep out onto the shoulders of the highway, and from there to run down to the Indian River. At night, when the temperatures fell, a crust formed over the waterlogged snow, and ice materialized on the meltwater.

In the mornings, on the way to school wearing knee-high rubber boots, I climbed over the rock-hard snowbanks to run on the crust before returning to the road to jump from frozen puddle to frozen puddle. After school I splashed my way home through the streams of surface runoff water smelling of melting snow, sand, gravel, crushed rock, dust, bark, twigs, dead leaves, and the pollution from distant smokestacks that blended together to leave an unforgettable metallic aftertaste in my mouth. And like generations of village children before me at the time of the thaw, I stopped from time to time to shove sand and dirt into the rivulets with my foot to create new channels and build mini-dams to create mini-lakes that held back the flood, however briefly.

As March became April, the creeks swelled and burst their banks, the fish moved upriver to spawn, and frogs emerged from hibernation to lay their eggs and to sing. The dead grass, as it dried, changed from black to dark brown and then to tan. In backyards throughout the village, boys lit grass fires and the men of the volunteer fire brigade were kept busy extinguishing the ones that spread out of control. Tourists, who hadn't been to the village all winter, arrived from the big cities to inspect their properties and hire local tradespeople to put their cottages in order. An aging Simcoe cousin from the reserve, who had lost a leg in the war and who was spending the spring at his shack down at the Indian Camp trapping muskrat and beaver, pushed his canoe out into the Indian River. And whooping out a cry of delight in Chippewa, he rode it like a bucking horse through the flood waters pouring over the stop logs in the dam, just as he did every year at this time, daring the gods of the river to do their worst.

The four Bartleman kids in 1946 with our mother have fun swimming in the Indian River, Port Carling. *Courtesy Bartleman Family.*

7

The Hammer

We were different and were treated as strangers in that first year in the village. Our parents were closest to the Indians at the Indian Camp, but only one, Sam Williams, a former chief of Rama Indians, wintered over in his shack. Sam radiated a sense of inner peace, impressing me enormously with his innate wisdom. He was to serve me as a role model. I spent a lot of time with Sam that first winter and was well aware, even at that early age, that if your lot in life was likely to be poverty and hard, poorly paid work, as I expected mine to be, then it was important to have peace of mind and wisdom to cope. Sam, unaware of my developing philosophy of life, gave me a .22 rifle and a box of shells to hunt rabbits and an old rowboat to fish for bass.

My father, rejected as a soldier because of a bad heart, hadn't served in the war like most of the men his age in the village (and on the Rama Indian Reserve), setting him apart from the veterans. As for the rest of us, Bob and I had to endure racial taunts from older boys who called us "dirty half-breeds." Just as hurtful, we had to listen to racist banter in the schoolyard and in the streets about lazy, uneducated, and inferior Indians, talk that we couldn't help but take personally. We had to fight a lot and didn't always win. Bob, older and more recognizably Indian, had to bear the burden of the name-calling and bullying but was never intimidated.

One Saturday afternoon in the spring of 1947 we were set upon by a group of teenagers twice our size. They called my brother a "black bastard" and told both of us in a message laced with invective that Indians and half-breeds weren't wanted in the village and that the time was overdue for us to go back to where we had come from — wherever that was. Bob and I fought fire with fire, providing our opinion on the ancestry of their mothers before fleeing to what we thought would be the refuge of our home, the aroused bullies on our heels.

To our surprise, the big kids didn't stop at the property line, but chased us up the path to our front door, which they kicked and yanked in an effort to get at us. Neither of our parents was at home to protect us, and it looked as if we were in for a beating, since the flimsy screen door fastened only with a lightweight lock wouldn't resist for long. I cowered in one corner of the room, but Bob didn't hesitate. He grabbed the rifle Sam Williams had given me, loaded it in front of our attackers, pulled back the hammer, and thrust the barrel into their astonished faces. He would have fired had our tormentors managed to open the door, and they knew it. They backed away, calling Bob a "crazy Indian" and vowing to get their revenge in the schoolyard.

Even my mother wasn't spared. Late one afternoon she was waiting for us on the veranda when my brother and I returned home from school. Suddenly, a big raw-boned kid about sixteen years old started braying from the sidewalk, "Filthy squaw! Filthy squaw! Go back to your filthy reserve! You're not wanted here!" I could see how hurt my mother was, but she said nothing to my father. She wanted desperately to fit into village life and was afraid of causing trouble. She did, however, tell us that the land Port Carling was built on was our ancestral home in a way it could never be for the other villagers whose grandparents and great-grandparents came from the Old Country. Most villagers had no idea of the origins of their families before the generation that had immigrated to Muskoka in the nineteenth century. Even fewer were aware, at least when I was growing up, that Port Carling had been built on the site of a thriving Indigenous community called Obagawanung, whose people had been chased from their homes as recently as the 1860s to make way for settlers coming from the Old Country.

My mother, however, was born on Lake Joseph within the traditional hunting grounds of her people. Her family, with other people from Rama, began spending their summers in the late nineteenth century on an island beside the locks in Port Carling, unofficially asserting their right to a small part of the land taken from the people of Obagawanung. At the turn of the century, the government set aside a few acres of land on the shore, near the island called the Indian Camp, for the use of the Rama people and their friends, the Mohawks of Wahta. She told us these roots, this relationship between her children and the land, rock and water, could never be taken from us. (The island was renamed James Bartleman Island Park in 2007, when I retired as lieutenant governor.)

8

Indigenous Roots

Several years ago the late Margaret Aldridge, a genealogist, sent me a copy of a detailed Nanigishking-Benson family tree on my grandmother's side of the family. A precious gift, for which I remain most grateful, it traces this branch of the family back ten generations to Chief Nanigishking, born in 1756, when the Chippewa of Lake Simcoe and Lake Huron still led a nomadic lifestyle. I then checked the historical record and discovered that Chief Nanigishking's descendants were also chiefs who played prominent roles in the lives of the people as they moved to settled life on the Rama Indian Reserve in the nineteenth century.

Nanigishking-Benson Family Tree

GENERATION NO. 1

Chief Nanigishking, born about 1756 in Upper Canada (sources: 1834, 1851 censuses). Married Fanny (Nanigishking), born about 1771 (sources: 1834, 1851 censuses).

Notes

If I were magically able to journey back in time to meet any one of my ancestors, I would choose my great-great-great-great-great-great-grandfather Nanigishking, who lived at the end of a golden period in the history of the Chippewa. There were individuals alive when he was a child who would have remembered the great migration of the Chippewa from Northwestern Ontario to the future Southern and Central Ontario. The battles the Chippewa fought to drive the Iroquois from their new homeland would have been fresh in everyone's memory. In the wilderness between Canada and the Thirteen Colonies, the Chippewa were fighting alongside the French, against the British, in the Seven Years' War. He was three years old when Wolfe captured Quebec City in 1759, seven years old when the warriors of his community left to take part in Pontiac's war against the British in 1763, and eight years old when they returned home after peace was restored in 1764.

I would ask him whether his father had joined the war party that left to fight alongside Pontiac, and whether he had taken part in the famous June 4, 1763, attack on Fort Michilimackinac, when Chippewa and Sauk warriors, pretending to play lacrosse outside the walls of the fort to celebrate the birthday of the king, had rushed in through the open gate, seizing tomahawks and clubs hidden under their wives' blankets, and overwhelmed the unprepared British garrison. I would ask him to tell about his mythic universe, in particular the following aspects that ring true to me, metaphorically, hiding deeper truths: all things, animals, stones, water, everything visible and invisible, are alive with Manidos or spirits; Kiche Manitou is the Great Spirit whose life energy runs through all things and binds them together in a divine world; the first humans emerged from the carcasses of animals, who are relations and not inferior beings; humans are composed of three parts: a body that rots in the dirt after death, a shadow that watches over the grave of the corpse, and a soul that travels westward over the Milky Way to reside in the Land of the Spirits; Mother Earth is Turtle Island and it came into being from a grain of sand carried by a muskrat to the surface of the sea without beginning or end; and, most beautiful of all, the

Milky Way is the handle of a bucket holding up Turtle Island — if the handle breaks, Turtle Island will be destroyed.

Change came gradually and then accelerated in my ancestor's lifetime. By 1800 settlers and missionaries had begun moving into the Lake Simcoe and Georgian Bay region, and by 1830 Chief Nanigishking and most of the Lake Simcoe and Georgian Bay Chippewa had adopted Christianity and abandoned many of their ancient spiritual beliefs.

Generation No. 2

Chief Thomas Nanigishking, born between 1779 and 1781 (sources: 1851, 1871 censuses). Died in 1872, age ninety-six (source: *Orillia Packet*, December 6, 1872). Married Mary (Nanigishking) on March 13, 1832, in Orillia.

Notes

- According to the genealogist, "the name of Chief Thomas Nanigishking (with pictograph signature of a deer totem) appears on many Indian documents from the 1830s to the 1860s."
- In August 1858, Thomas Nanigishking's authority was transferred to his son Joseph Benson Nanigishking, often known as Joseph Benson.
- In the census of 1851, Thomas Nanigishking is listed as a seventy-year-old widower. In the census of 1871, Thomas Nanigishking is listed as a ninety-two-year-old Indian chief. His death is mentioned in the *Orillia Packet*, December 6, 1872.
- Chiefs Thomas and Joseph Nanigishking were subordinate to Head Chief William Yellowhead. Joseph Benson Nanigishking succeeded William Yellowhead as principal chief of the Chippewas of Rama upon the latter's death in 1864. He was the last hereditary chief of the Rama Indians (see Generation 3 below).
- By treaties made in 1798, 1815, and 1818, the Chippewa surrendered the ancient country of the Huron lying north and

west of Lake Simcoe. From this area, grants were made in fulfillment of earlier pledges to militia veterans, to children of veterans, to children of Loyalists, and to many retired soldiers and seamen (source: Historic Sites and Monuments Board of Canada).

- In 1830, the Chippewa of Lake Simcoe and Georgian Bay were gathered on a reserve along a newly opened road connecting Orillia and Coldwater.
- In 1838–39, land-hungry settlers influenced the government to move Chief William Yellowhead's band from Orillia across Lake Couchiching to Rama. The other bands were moved to Georgina and Beausoleil Islands (source: Archaeological and Historic Sites Board of Ontario).

Generation No. 3

Joseph Benson Nanigishking, born between 1813 and 1819 in Orillia (sources: 1851, 1861, 1871 1881, 1891 censuses). Died February 23, 1899, at age eighty-four. Cause of death: *la grippe* (death certificate 019299 99). Married unknown Bigcanoe. Married Sarah Young on July 17, 1837 (sources: 1851, 1861 1871, 1881 censuses). In the 1891 census, Joseph is listed as a widower.

Generation No. 4

James Benson Nanigishking, born in 1846 and died in 1918 (sources: 1851, 1861, 1871, 1881 1891, 1901, 1911 censuses). Married Charlotte Charles, born in 1850 and died in 1908 (registration of death 02176008).

Generation No. 5

Frederick William Benson Nanigishking, born in 1873 and died in 1936 (sources: 1881, 1891, 1901, 1911 censuses). First World War veteran. Died as a result of gas poisoning while fighting in the trenches. Married Phoebe Ann Snake of Georgina Island (1878–1918), daughter of Abraham Snake and Martha Goose.

Generation No. 6

Florence Edna Benson Nanigishking, born in 1900 and died in 1982 (sources: 1901, 1911 censuses). Married Edward Simcoe.

Generation No. 7

Maureen Benson Simcoe (1922–2013). Married Percy Scott Bartleman (1916–2003).

Notes

Globe and Mail, April 12, 2013

Lives Lived

Born in a tent during a fishing trip with her family at Lake Joseph in Muskoka, Maureen spent the springs and summers of her childhood at the Indian Camp in Port Carling, Ont., where her father trapped muskrat and beaver and worked as a casual labourer and her mother sold handicraft to summer visitors.

Each year after Labour Day, the family returned to their home on what was then called the Rama Indian Reserve, travelling by canoe to Muskoka Wharf in Gravenhurst and onward by train to their final destination....

Dirt poor, the object of prejudice by mainstream society and abused by her mother and grandmother, Maureen's early years were brutal. This changed when she met and married, at the age of 14, Percy Bartleman, a young, happy-go-lucky Orillia man who had spent the Depression years riding the rails across Canada.

Percy's wonderful parents, Maggie and Bill, and his brother and sisters, embraced Maureen as one of their own, and gave her the love she had been denied as a child.

Maureen and Percy, with their small children, Jim, Bob, Janet and Mary, moved in 1946 to Port Carling. Life was hard, as Percy was a poorly paid day labourer with a Grade 4 education....

After finding work as a cleaning lady, she pulled the family out of poverty, purchased a home and made many friends in the village, particularly at the Port Carling United Church.

Maureen was proud of the accomplishments of her children and grandchildren, who included in their number a marine mechanic, lumber saleswoman, tax inspector, social worker, high-school teacher, nurse, accountant, lawyer, physician and foreign service officer....

Maureen passed away at the Getsidjig Endaawaad extended-care facility at the Chippewas of Rama First Nation, surrounded by family and caregivers who spoke her native language. Percy had died in 2003. They were married for 66 years.

Generation No. 8

James Bartleman, born in Orillia on December 24, 1939. Married Marie-Jeanne Rosillon in Brussels, Belgium, on September 12, 1975. Marie-Jeanne, daughter of the medical director of Kasai province, was born in Luluabourg, Belgian Congo, October 15, 1948.

Generation No. 9

Anne-Pascale Bartleman, born November 3, 1976, in Brussels, Belgium.
Married to Brian Rauwerda.
Laurent Bartleman, born October 22, 1977, in Brussels, Belgium.
Married to Sara Hicks.
Alain Bartleman, born July 14, 1989, in Ottawa, Ontario.

Generation No. 10

Sebastien James Rauwerda, born December 13, 2007.
Nicholas Pascal Rauwerda, born June 11, 2009.
Marie-Anne Rauwerda, born June 20, 2014.
Henry Fraser Bartleman, born March 9, 2012.
Thomas James Bartleman, born January 7, 2015.

* * *

I then set out to trace the Simcoes, my maternal grandfather's side of the family, as far back as I could. Fortunately, my mother, who was alive at the time, was familiar with her family history. My mother remembered the funeral of Nancy Simcoe's father, Young John Simcoe, at the Rama Reserve when she was a little girl in the 1920s. She had also heard stories of Old John Simcoe, a family hero, who fought with the other men of the community under Chief Yellowhead in the War of 1812. They fought under Tecumseh at Detroit and later under Colonel Givens of the Indian Department at the bloody Battle of York in April 1813.

Yellowhead, known to the British as "The Yellowhead," was head chief. Muskoka was named after his son, William Yellowhead, also known as Musquakie, who succeeded him as head chief of the Chippewa of Lake Simcoe and Georgian Bay as well as of Obagawanung, the Indigenous village at the site of the future Port Carling. According to the 1871 census of Canada, Old John was born in 1787, John Junior in 1823, and Nancy in 1869.

Simcoe Family Tree

GENERATION NO. 1

Old John Simcoe, born 1787. Married unknown. Veteran of the War of 1812. Recorded in 1871 census as being eighty-four years old.

Notes

See the following extracts from documents from Library and Archives Canada attesting to Old John's participation in the War of 1812, sent to me by Professor Don Smith, author of *Sacred Feathers: The Reverend Peter Jones and the Mississauga Indians.*

> Sarnia, 17th July 1876
> Wm Plummer Esq. Indian Affairs
>
> Dear Sir,
> When I was visiting at Rama a fortnight ago, I called on Old

John Simcoe, and asked him if he had received his pension from the government. He told me he had not and was very desirous that I should present his case and claim to you. Old Simcoe is 95 years old and was present at several battles in 1812–1815 and fought nobly and bravely and at times barely escaped from being killed. Poor old man, never knew that the other veterans had been pensioned off. He was very glad when I told him that I would present his claim to you. Old Simcoe is now very feeble and it is most desirable that before he passes away that he should be remembered like his comrades. If you wish further information on Simcoe, address (yourself) to Reverend Woolsey, or to Chief James Benson Nanigishking.

Yours Truly, John Jacobs, Missionary

Rama, 22nd July 1876

I beg to inform you that John Simcoe served in the war and would like to get the amount the government agreed to give.

James Benson Nanigishking
Orillia, 26th August 1876

Orillia, 30th August 1876
Noted by D.L. Sauson, Justice of the Peace

William Bigwin, 81 years of age, Indian, appeared before me today and solemnly declared that he knows that John Simcoe Senior served as a soldier in the war of 1812.

William Bigwin X
J.B.Nanigishking, Chief Rama Band

Old John Simcoe would have been one of the unnamed warriors mentioned in the following article published in the 1954 annual report of the York Pioneer and Historical Society.

The Battle of York

The American invasion fleet had been spotted by lookouts east of the Don River on the evening of April 26, 1813. At dawn, April 27, the sixteen vessels carrying General Zebulon Pike and one thousand troops were in front of the fort, still moving westward. It became apparent that the landing would be made in the general vicinity of the mouth of the Humber. The Yellowheads, father and son, and their Ojibway and Mississauga warriors were lying in wait, hidden in the thick woods which lay back of the shoreline of Humber Bay. Soon the other members of the Sharpshooters, the volunteer militiamen and the Regulars, were making their way there too, to try and repulse the landing parties.

It is recorded that the brisk fire of the Sharpshooters did in fact repulse the first assault. But the odds were against the defenders: they could slow down the American drive to the fort, but their small numbers, the lack of adequate artillery, and the uncoordinated plans of defence could not stop the invaders. The details of the battle are known, but what is seldom if ever noted is the heroic and stubborn guerilla warfare of the Indian Sharpshooters, the persistent rear-guard action fighting which held up the taking of the Fort until the last possible moment. History records the efforts of the Regulars and the militia but overlooks the fact that tragedy overcame the Indians too: several were killed, others wounded, and the (senior) Yellowhead disfigured for life when his jaw was fractured by two musket balls.

Generation No. 2

Young John Simcoe, born 1823. Married Mary, surname unknown. Recorded in 1871 census as being forty-eight years old. Died of heart attack in late 1920s (source: Maureen Bartleman, who witnessed his death and attended the funeral).

Generation No. 3

Nancy Simcoe (April 1861–1941). Unmarried. Children: Edward, Howard, John, and Edward (source: Ancestry.ca).

Generation No. 4

Edward Simcoe (1900–1948). Married Edna Benson.

Generation No. 5

Maureen Benson Simcoe (August 28, 1922–March 28, 2013). Married Percy Bartleman (1916–2003).

> *Toronto Star,* November 4, 2003
>
> Percy Scott Bartleman knew a good story when he told one.
>
> With a glass of homemade raisin wine in hand and a tale on his lips, the master storyteller needed only to summon the script from his own life. It was the stuff of high adventure on the open railway, moving from one job to another, always with an eye on the next passing train.
>
> When Mr. Bartleman died last Wednesday in Gravenhurst after a brief illness, the rambling 87-year epic of his life found a peaceful final chapter.

Generation No. 6

James Bartleman, born in Orillia on December 24, 1939. Married Marie-Jeanne Rosillon in Brussels, Belgium, on September 12, 1975. Marie-Jeanne was born in Luluabourg, Belgian Congo, on October 15, 1948.

Generation No. 7

Anne-Pascale Bartleman, born November 3, 1976, in Brussels, Belgium.
Laurent Bartleman, born October 22, 1977, in Brussels, Belgium.
Alain Bartleman, born July 14, 1989, in Ottawa, Ontario.

Generation No. 8

Sebastien Rauwerda, born December 13, 2007.
Nicholas Rauwerda, born June 11, 2009.
Marie-Anne Rauwerda, born June 20, 2014.
Henry Fraser Bartleman, born March 9, 2012.
Thomas James Bartleman, born January 7, 2015.

9

Six Choir Boys

My mother told me that even in those days of open prejudice the villagers sometimes displayed compassion to Indian families in distress. For instance, in the late fall of 1927, my mother, then a little girl of four, her parents, and her brother of nine months, Dalton Lywood Simcoe, were living in their shack at the Indian Camp long after the others had returned to Rama for the winter. Dalton contracted pneumonia and died. Although my mother's family had no connection to the Port Carling Anglican Church, the priest there arranged a dignified funeral, with six little white boys serving as pallbearers. Dalton was then hurriedly buried in the Port Carling cemetery before the ground froze. His pauper's grave was among those of white pioneers, and his coffin was provided as a gift by carpenters at the village boat works. I can remember as a child my mother searching the cemetery for a marking that would indicate where her little brother was buried but never finding one.

Lloyd Cope, who lived in the village in those years, sent me a letter confirming my mother's account after he read my memoir *Out of Muskoka*. (The "grandma" mentioned in the letter was Nancy Simcoe, who lost her sight when she was hit in the face by the propeller of a boat

My parents in the front yard of their Port Carling home in 1950. *Courtesy Bartleman Family.*

that ran over her canoe on the bay in front of the Indian Camp.) She received $100 and a new canoe as compensation.

> A very poignant and memorable picture that I recall is of a small girl leading a blind Indian woman, who in turn was carrying small baskets, tiny birch-bark canoes and other trinkets. I saw her several times in down-town Port Carling as well as at the Indian Camp. I now know that the child was your mother,

short in stature, but so strong in spirit helping grandma make her way in the world after a terrible mishap, caused by a careless motor-boat operator. The little girl, like grandma as I recall it, was dressed in a long skirt, and both had the characteristic nice sweetgrass smell. One memory concerns your uncle Dalton who died as an infant. You mention six choir boys being pall-bearers at his funeral. I was one of those boys (about 10 years old) and this was the first time I was exposed to death, and the fact that other than the white race had feelings. I feel confident in saying that many of the residents of Port Carling similarly had a change of thought as a result of Mr. Smedley, the Anglican Minister, and his wife taking the initiative in providing burial procedures for the infant child.

10

A Story My Mother Told Me

My mother loved telling stories of her childhood at the Indian Camp. One of her favourites described a trip she took with her father one magical night in late April 1930, when she was a girl of eight, from the Rama Indian Reserve to the Indian Camp at Port Carling. A lot happened that night — a wake, a train ride, a canoe trip, hymn singing, the appearance of an apparition, an encounter with the Manido of the Lake, paddling by the ruins of Obagawanung, opening the family shack for the season, and her first day of school that year. The sights, sounds, smells, even her thoughts were as fresh eighty years later as they were when the events occurred. I drew on her account when I wrote the following story that I later revised to include in my novel, *The Redemption of Oscar Wolf*.

The Night Journey

Mary Waabooz, lovingly known as Old Mary to her friends and relatives, the oldest member of the Rama Indian Reserve, had died, and the people crowded into her one-room cabin late in the evening were singing the reassuring old gospel hymns in the language of their ancestors. The light of a solitary coal-oil lamp at the head of the open coffin threw a shadow down over her body, softening the gaunt features of her face, making her look decades younger and bringing a look of peace to someone who had spent the last weeks of her life in agony. It did the same for the other old people in the room, ironing out the creases on their foreheads, erasing the wrinkles on their dark brown, leathery cheeks, and concealing the slack flesh on their necks. There was a smell of decay mixed with sweetgrass in the stuffy room overheated by the presence of so many mourners. The mood was one of calm and acceptance. There was no weeping. Old Mary had outlived three husbands and two grown children and her time had come. And yet her death still hurt. It was like an ancient tree, a landmark in the history of the community, unexpectedly crashing to the ground, leaving a massive empty space in the lives of the people.

The mother, who had prepared the body for burial earlier in the day, stared at the flame of the lamp and did not sing. But the little girl, her hair pulled back and twisted into a thick black braid and with black watchful eyes set in her dark, high-cheek-boned face, sang along with the others. She was there mainly because she wanted to be close to the mother whom she loved but who did not love her. She was also there because she had been a friend of Old Mary and had often gone to her house on winter evenings to eat hot fried bannock, to drink tea with sugar and condensed milk, and listen to her talk about the old days.

At eleven-thirty, the father stood up and went around the room shaking hands and saying goodbye. Followed by the little girl, who could sense what he wanted her to do without being told, the father picked up his heavy packsack and started down the gravel road to the railway station. Suddenly, a half-dozen dogs burst out of the starlight and ran barking toward them but they ran whimpering back into the darkness when the father picked up a stone and threw it in their direction. His seasonal job at a tourist lodge started the next morning at eight o'clock and he had to catch the midnight train to Muskoka Wharf Station at Gravenhurst at the bottom of Lake Muskoka and paddle throughout the night to Port Carling if he was to report for work on time. Thirty minutes later, the father and the little girl smelled the creosote of railway ties and from off in the distance heard the shriek of a steam whistle. Quickening their pace, they reached the station just as the locomotive, shaking the rails and pulling two dozen passenger and freight cars, its headlight cutting a path through the night, came thundering around the curve of Lake Couchiching. It had left Toronto four hours earlier and was on time.

With a hiss of air brakes, a cloud of coal smoke, grease, and soot, the train came to a stop. The door at the rear of a coach opened and the conductor, a lantern in his hand, peered out into the night in search of passengers. He kicked down the stairs when he saw the little girl and the father standing on the platform.

"Tickets, please," he said, when they came aboard, and held out his hand to take and punch them. "It's dark in here," he whispered as he lighted the way with his lantern and led them into an overheated coach filled with sleeping passengers and reeking of sweat, stale food, and cigarette smoke. Coming to two empty places, he said, "These should suit you. Stow your gear on the racks above your heads. You'll be getting off at the next stop."

The little girl took the seat beside the window and sat silently in her separate world as the locomotive, panting with enormous gasps of steam like some primeval dragon preparing for combat, its driving rods pounding and its giant wheels straining as they turned, pulled out of the station. Scraping a peephole in the frost covering the inside of the window, she looked out at the starlit countryside as the train picked up speed and hastened forward at sixty miles an hour. She thought back to the wake, to the single mesmerizing coal-oil lamp casting its soft light over Old Mary's body and the elders in the room who had seen and done so much in their long lives.

What had the old people been thinking? Were they recalling the days when Old Mary was young and they were young? Remembering the days when the families had returned from their winter hunting and trapping grounds in the spring to spend the summer together at the Narrows where Lake Simcoe emptied into Lake Couchiching? The days when they would talk about births and deaths and finding the perfect person to marry? The days when the ancestors undertook spirit quests, when they gathered sweetgrass for ceremonies, and when they held community feasts? Or, as they looked at Old Mary in her plain pine coffin, were they mourning the loss of their youth and counting the days until the mother, who prepared the dead for burial on the reserve, appeared at *their* homes to wash *their* dead bodies and put *them* on display in plain pine coffins in *their* living rooms?

And what meaning did Old Mary's death have for her, still just a little girl with her head pressed against the window staring out through the opening in the frost as the train raced through railway crossings empty of traffic, its wheels clicking ever more rapidly on the rails, and its whistle wailing? She was sad because Old Mary had been her friend and was now no more. But at the same time, for some unexplainable reason, Old Mary's death made her feel more alive than ever and astonished at the wonder of existence.

The train slowed to a crawl, moved across the bridge spanning the gorge over the Severn River, which flowed northwesterly out of Lake Couchiching into Georgian Bay, and climbed laboriously up a steep grade to enter the District of Muskoka. Twenty minutes later, the little girl and the father were standing on the deserted platform at Muskoka Wharf Station as the sound of the train, with its load of passengers bound for Bracebridge and Huntsville and places farther north such as Timmins and the twin cities of Fort William and Port Arthur, faded away. Nearby, they could hear the groans of the steamers of the Muskoka Lakes Navigation Company rubbing their bumpers against the government docks as they waited for the beginning of the tourist season and the arrival of day trippers from Toronto.

The little girl followed the father down to the shore where the family canoe had spent the winter rolled over and covered with a piece of canvas. Although only eight, she was strong and was expected to do the work of someone twice her age. She helped turn the boat right side up, drag it to the shore, and slide it into the black water. They then took their positions, the little girl in the bow and the father in the stern, the packsack on the floor between them, and started paddling. There was no wind, but the ice had been off the lake for only a week, the nighttime April temperature was below freezing, and each breath of air chilled their lungs. If all went well, they would be at the shack at the Indian Camp in six hours.

As the little girl paddled, the words and melodies of the hymns sung around the coffin earlier that night played over and over in her head. At first she found them distracting, preventing her from concentrating on the things she wanted to think about on this special night. But she soon gave in and sang the words of her favourite hymn.

Shall we gather at the river?
Where bright angel-feet have trod,
With its crystal tide forever,
Flowing by the throne of God.
Yes, we'll gather at the river,
The beautiful, the beautiful river,
Gather with the saints at the river,
That flows by the throne of God.
On the margin of the river,
Washing up its silvery spray.
We will walk and worship ever,
All the happy, golden day.

As the little girl sang, she became conscious of a presence of someone, or something otherworldly. She looked up at the stars and saw the outline of a smiling face. *It's Old Mary,* the little girl thought. *Her shadow followed me here from the wake, and now her soul on its final journey is watching over me as I sing out here on the lake in the middle of the night.* Tears of happiness flooded her eyes and she shouted out the words of the hymn to the stars.

A fierce wind from the Canadian northwest plains that had crossed Lake Huron and Georgian Bay and swept up and over the leafless Muskoka highlands now came howling down onto the lake, whipping the water into rows upon rows of white-capped breakers that pushed the canoe off course. The little girl stopped singing and father and daughter fought their way to a protected passageway between a large island and the shore. For the next hour they paddled through a wide channel lined with oversized boathouses. Great steamer docks adorned with sixty-foot-high flagpoles, their ropes rattling in the wind, protruded aggressively a hundred feet out into the water. Behind the docks, scarcely visible in the starlight, were wide walkways leading up past tennis courts and wide lawns to huge summer houses with upper-floor balconies and wraparound verandas. This was Millionaires' Row, the preserve of the American and Canadian super-rich whose parents and grandparents had visited the district to hunt and fish in the late nineteenth century. It was still a land of poor bush farmers then and they were able to buy up the shorefront they needed at a cheap price to re-create the country-club life they enjoyed at home.

The waves were as high as ever when they left the shelter of the channel, but the wind was now at their backs and they began to make up for lost time. Sometime later, a splash of cold water coming over the gunnels struck the little girl, who had fallen asleep, in the face. She woke up to see, in the grainy light of the predawn, the head of a blind chief emerging from the rock on the north-facing outcrop of a deserted island alongside that of a smaller inert guardian companion. As ancient as Turtle Island itself, its face was covered in lichen, its cheekbones were fractured, and its nose was broken. Inscrutable, it exuded profound sadness and complete indifference to the waves crashing against its base and to the travellers who had come to pay it homage. The old people said it was, in fact, the Creator in another form.

Taking hold of her paddle, the little girl held the canoe as steady as she could in the seething waters, freeing the father to light his pipe, raise it into the air, and offer a prayer to the unsmiling deity.

"Oh, Great Manido, I beg you to protect two humble Chippewa canoeists from the wrath of the seven-headed water snake that dwells in the depths of this lake. I beseech you to allow us to travel in peace and safety to the Indian Camp. And bring us good luck, oh, Great Manido, as we try to catch a fish for our breakfast on this last leg of our journey."

He then blew an offering of smoke to the statue and told the little girl to fish while he paddled. The little girl pulled the gear from the pack — an eight-inch silver spoon armed with triple gang hooks at the end of three hundred feet of thirty-pound test copper trolling wire — and fed it slowly into the water until it was only a few feet from the bottom. She gave the line a jerk, making the spoon leap ahead in the deep, and a fish took the bait. The little girl hauled in the line, hand over hand, keeping tension on the wire to keep it from breaking free. The father turned the bow of the canoe into the wind and held the boat steady until the little girl pulled the fish, a two-pound lake trout, over the side. He murmured a prayer of thanks to the Manido for answering his appeal and, clenching his pipe in his teeth, paddled toward the mouth of the Indian River a mile away.

The final and emotionally wrenching part of his journey was about to begin, for they were nearing Obagawanung, a village that had been taken from his people by the Canadian government to make room for settlers a generation earlier. In the aftermath of the War of 1812, an Indigenous veteran had launched a search for a refuge from the white man's alcohol and religion. He had found such a place in the heart of the traditional hunting grounds of the Rama people at a site so isolated and with weather so harsh he thought white men would never want to settle there. A dozen other war veterans and their families joined him, and they erected their cabins immediately below the rapids at the headwaters of the Indian River, six miles upstream from where it fed into Lake Muskoka.

The father had grown up listening to his grandfather, who had been born at Obagawanung, talk about his early days in the community. "It was a holy place," he'd said, "where Mother Earth was most alive and where the Manidos were everywhere in the lakes and rivers and in the trees, the rocks, the animals, the fish, the clouds, the lightning, and the passing seasons. In winter we would go outside and stand at the shore listening to them whisper to one another in the mist that rose up from the current. In the spring, we would wait for the annual visit of the half-breed traders who came from their posts on Georgian Bay in birchbark canoes filled with guns, ammunition, and other supplies to exchange for beaver, muskrat, and wolf pelts. In the summers, we camped on islands in Lake Muskoka picking blueberries and fishing, and in the autumns the men hunted deer and bear. In the 1860s, however," the grandfather had said, "the government opened the Muskoka District for settlement. White men came and surveyed the lands, and the settlers followed in their wake. Not long afterward, the police told us we had to go, and we loaded whatever we could carry in our canoes and departed."

An hour later, although the sun was up, the ground was white with hoarfrost. As the father and the little girl rounded a bend in the river, the wind died down and paddlers could smell woodsmoke and hear roosters crowing and cows bellowing. Off in the distance was Port Carling, a cluster of clapboard houses on both sides of the river, their windows framed with white-lace curtains and their backyards filled with chicken coops, privies, and half-empty woodsheds. Twenty minutes later, they paddled past the village business section, a row of one- and two-storey frame buildings with high false fronts to make them appear bigger than they were. On the other side of the bay, cut off from the rest of the village by a ridge, was the Indian Camp where the little girl and the father would spent the next six months as they did every year.

A few minutes later they pulled their canoe up onto the shore and the father took out a key to unlock the door to the shack. But the door was already open. Someone had entered over the winter months, but nothing had been stolen. The beds and mattresses, the linoleum-covered table pushed up against the window facing the lake, the chairs, the old cookstove, the pots and pans hanging from nails on the bare studs, the axe and saw, the woodbox, and the cutlery and crockery in the orange crates scavenged at the village dump and used as cupboards remained as they had been left the preceding fall. The smell of stale ashes, woodsmoke, coal oil, and last year's fried fish meals hung in the air. Sunlight streamed through the windows devoid of curtains and blinds, but the room itself was cold and damp.

The little girl followed the father into the shack and pulled from the woodbox a yellowing copy of the *Toronto Star* dated August 1, 1929, its fading headlines still proclaiming, "Stock Market Crash, and Dozens Jump to Their Deaths on Wall Street." She stuffed it into the stove, added dry kindling, and lit a fire.

The father returned to the canoe, retrieved the lake trout, and cleaned and filleted it on the shore, tossing its guts to the seagulls that came swooping in, crying raucously to be fed. By the time he returned to the shack carrying the fillets, the little girl had unpacked the food supplies brought from the reserve and put the kettle on to boil. She picked up the heavy, fire-blackened cast-iron frying pan that had been in the family for generations, placed it on the stove, scooped a tablespoon of lard from its can, and spread it with her fingers over the cooking surface. While the little girl was busy doing these things, the father rolled the fillets in flour and eased them into the lard that had started to boil and spit. The little girl cut two boiled potatoes into slices and dropped them into the simmering mix. A short while later the father and the little girl, wearing their coats at the table against the cold, drank their tea and ate their breakfast in silence. The father glanced at his pocket watch and left for the tourist lodge, eager to meet friends he hadn't seen since the previous year.

The little girl finished her meal, washed the dishes, took a seat by the window, and stared out at the river. In a few minutes, she would trudge up through the snow on the north-facing ridge and go down the sunlit slope on other side to the four-room combined elementary and high school, each with its separate playground and entrance. The big boys from the high school would be standing just outside school property by the gate leading to their entrance, their shirt collars turned up against the cold. They would be shifting their weight from foot to foot, smoking roll-your-own cigarettes or chewing tobacco and spitting the wads on the ground as they waited for the bell to ring calling them to class. The big girls would already be inside their classrooms combing and brushing their hair and gossiping. In the playground of the elementary school, the boys would be playing marbles and the girls would be skipping rope. She would go inside to ask the teacher if she could attend class for the rest of the term. The teacher would smile when he saw her dressed like a little old Indian woman in a calico skirt that came down to her ankles, wearing a heavy sweater against the cold and smelling of woodsmoke and sweetgrass. He would then say yes, as he always did when she appeared at his door at this time of year. He seemed to like her but, with a mocking smile, never called her by her name, always addressing her as "little girl." The kids didn't call her "little girl." The nice ones laughed and called her "Pocahontas," and the mean ones held their noses, laughed, and called her "squaw."

11

Out of Poverty

As the 1950s started, my white grandparents stepped in to provide moral support, coming often by bus from Orillia to visit. Eventually, they built a small cabin next door and moved to Port Carling to spend their retirement years. I was close to both of them, especially my grandfather, William Bartleman, a Scottish immigrant who became a father figure to me. My grandmother, Maggie Shields Bartleman, a descendant of Northern Irish Protestant settlers who came to Canada in the 1820s, treated my mother like a daughter. They spent an enormous amount of time with their grandchildren and in the process passed on values for us to take into the wider world. The following is a summary of their family trees.

- My father, Percy Scott Bartleman (1916–2003), married Maureen Benson Simcoe on June 11, 1938, at Barrie, Ontario.
- Percy's father, William (Bill) Bain Bartleman (1886–1969), my grandfather, was born at Banchory, Kincardineshire, Scotland, immigrated to Canada at the turn of the century, and married Maggie Oracy Shields (1889–1971) on August

4, 1911. His father, James Bartleman (1854–1930), owned a small grocery store in Ballater, Scotland, and was a supplier to the Royal Household at Balmoral Castle. William's grandfather, another James Bartleman, was born on January 17, 1829, at Dirleton, East Lothian. His great-grandfather, Alexander Bartleman, was born in 1788 likewise in East Lothian as were a succession of previous Bartleman ancestors.

My grandfather told me he was present when the tsar of Russia disembarked at Ballater en route to visit Queen Victoria in the dying days of the nineteenth century. He also delivered groceries to the back door of Balmoral Castle. I told these stories to Her Majesty, Queen Elizabeth II, when Marie-Jeanne and I called on her at Buckingham Palace, and she remembered hearing her family talk about the visit to Ballater of the tsar. I have also travelled to Ballater several times over the years, always visiting the war monument where the name of my Great-Uncle Scott Bartleman, killed in action at Lens during the Battle of Hill 70, is inscribed. Scott was a sergeant in the Scots Guards in Scotland. After he immigrated to Canada, he joined the Highland Light Infantry of Canada at the beginning of the First World War.

The following is an excerpt from the War Diary of the 18th Battalion of the Canadian Expeditionary Force: "He was killed in action August 15, 1917, by a gunshot wound in his stomach as he was leading his men over No Man's Land. He enlisted at Galt, November 18, 1915, with the Third Battalion." My grandmother told me that Scott had been ordered into action by his brother, David Bartleman, another sergeant from Galt, Ontario. I can just imagine how David must have felt. David was promoted to the rank of captain and promoted again to major, becoming deputy commandant of Camp Ipperwash during the Second World War.

Maggie was the daughter of John Shields (1859–1950) and Janet Ann Robson (1860–1923). I had the privilege of meeting my great-grandfather Shields when he visited Port Carling in 1948 to preach to the people at the Indian Camp. He predicted that I would follow in his footsteps.

- Janet Ann's father, Thomas Robson, was born in 1839 at Chinguacousy, Ontario. On May 29, 1859, he married Elizabeth White, born in 1841 at Caledon. Elizabeth was the daughter of John White, born in 1810 in what would become Northern Ireland, and Anne McKay, also born in 1810 in what would become Northern Ireland.
- When I was child, my grandmother used to regale me with stories of the role John White played supporting William Lyon Mackenzie in the Rebellion of 1837. She had no use for the Family Compact and the big shots of nineteenth-century Ontario history.

By this time, I was no longer called racist names. The people of the village began to treat me as one of their own. Eventually, when I came to know them better, I found that many of them, gruff and reserved on the surface, were actually warm-hearted and fair-minded. Several stopped me on the street, told me they had heard I was doing well at school, and encouraged me to persevere. A businessman who had no sons of his own invited me to a father-and-son banquet at the Lions Club. Another, knowing that I attended Sunday school but unaware I was an agnostic, asked me to become a United Church minister when I grew up. But Bob wasn't accepted to the same extent, and it hurt me deeply when others treated him badly.

In the meantime, my mother found work as a cleaning lady and part-time cook in the homes of wealthy cottagers. The pay was low, but she obtained a steady supply of good-quality hand-me-down clothing and used books for her children. The lockmaster, responsible for opening and closing the swing bridge over the Indian River, and operating the lock gates to allow steamships and power boats to pass from one lake to another, then retired and needed to be replaced. My mother was well aware in those bad old days of political patronage that local members of the provincial parliament (if members of the governing party) were

My grade seven school photo in 1952. I was dreaming of a better life outside the village. *Courtesy Bartleman Family.*

allowed to pick their own candidates for government jobs, such as lockmasters, in their ridings without competition. The pay wasn't much, not much more than minimum wage, but it was steady work with a small pension after thirty years of service. After enlisting me to draft a letter for my father's signature applying formally to the Ontario Ministry of Public Works for the position, she went to work lobbying her employers to write to the local MPP to support my father's candidacy. The parliamentarian, a fair-minded gentleman, was inundated with letters from her employers, and my father got the job.

To celebrate the change in family fortunes, my parents decided to install an indoor toilet, add a room on the back, and paint the house. We did the work ourselves and started by hauling a heavily rusted used septic tank home on the back of a truck from the village dump. We then cleaned it as well as we could and peppered it with shotgun and .22 rifle fire to allow it to leak as much of its contents as possible into the surrounding soil (there was no room for a proper weeping tile system) and installed it surreptitiously to avoid attracting the attention of the health inspector.

With Bob and my sister, Janet, in Port Carling in 1953 about to start high school. *Courtesy Bartleman Family.*

My mother set Bob and me to work preparing the ground for the addition, but the earth was still frozen and we made no progress digging holes for foundation pillars. Bob came up with the idea of using the dynamite that our father stored in the house to do the job. We set off explosion after explosion, but the force of the blasts went up into the air and made no impression on the frozen soil. We decided at that point to forgo foundations and build the addition on the frozen earth.

My father and I (by that time Bob had lost interest) under the watchful eye of my mother, who knew more about carpentry than we did, erected the new room, neglecting to insulate the floor, which heaved every spring when the frost left the ground. The job of painting the house was accomplished courtesy of the provincial government. Every night after work until the job was finished, my father would "borrow" a pail of the green stain used on the public docks and buildings, and we would happily apply it to the thirsty exterior of our home. He never worried, although he should have, that suspicions might have been aroused by the trail of green that led from the government storeroom, down the street, and up our walkway to our house.

The old house in winter in 1954. An eyesore, but I loved it. *Courtesy Bartleman Family.*

12

The SS *Sagamo*

In the postwar years of my youth, five steamships — the *Sagamo*, the *Segwun*, the *Cherokee*, the *Ahmic*, and the *Islander* — plied the lakes carrying mail, freight, and tourists from Gravenhurst to Port Carling, and the grand hotels that then dotted the lakes. In those summers the morning and evening arrivals of the steamboats at the public docks were highlights of the day in Port Carling. Each steamboat would emit sharp whistle blasts as it approached the locks to alert the lockmaster and his assistant to make ready. Dozens of cottagers would crowd the wharf, mixing with Indians from the Indian Camp and those villagers who could spare the time in the busy summer months to watch the docking of the behemoths. Hundreds of passengers would disembark to mingle with the locals while mail and luggage were transferred from one boat to another. My grandfather Bartleman went almost every day, as did my relatives from the Indian Camp.

* * *

In the summer of 1949, Bob and I saved our money, bought tickets, and joined the tourists on a cruise on the *Sagamo*, the 744-ton flagship of the Muskoka Lakes Navigation Company fleet. Departure was a time of great excitement. We hurried to the bow, and soon the vessel started to plough through the channel of the Indian River, heading for the entrance to Lake Rosseau. I can still feel the rush of fresh Muskoka air on my face, see the smoke pour from the stack, and hear the screeching of seagulls wheeling above as they waited for the galley staff to dump their garbage overboard, as was the practice in those ecologically unfriendly days. A venerable musician who had been entertaining passengers for decades started banging on a piano and passengers broke into song; the clatter of dishes being washed and coal being shovelled into the firebox rose from below decks; and the clanging of signal bells echoed from the bridge to the engine room and back.

After calling at a number of the hotels on Lake Rosseau, the captain threaded the narrow cut to Lake Joseph. We passed Redwood, where my mother had been born thirty years before, and Yoho Island, where she had spent her early summers with her parents, following a way of life the passengers on the *Sagamo* probably didn't imagine still existed in twentieth-century Southern Ontario. Two hours later we entered Little Lake Joseph, the wild extension of Lake Joseph, and arrived at Natural Park. We accompanied the crowd up a steep hill to admire the view until recalled to the *Sagamo* by sharp blasts from its whistle.

On the return trip those who had the means ate in style in the dining room from tables covered in white linen. Bob and I ate junk food, precipitating an attack of seasickness during which I thought I was going to die. My mood didn't improve when a seagull decided to bomb the ship and dumped a load of excrement on my head. Sunburned and sick to my stomach but having undergone a Muskoka rite of passage, I was glad to disembark at Port Carling and go home.

13

My Big Break

When I was sixteen, I got my big break. The caretaker for Robert Clause, an American summer resident who maintained a ninety-acre estate on Black Forest Island on Lake Joseph, offered me a summer job. I was familiar with that part of the lake: my mother had been born on a nearby shore, and my father had often taken Bob and me on fishing and blueberry-picking expeditions in the neighbourhood when we were kids. My Indian grandfather, Ed Simcoe, had often taken the owner, and his father before him, on fishing expeditions to lakes in Northern Ontario. My father had also worked there for a time, and I had spent a summer living with the family when I was thirteen as a babysitter for one of Mr. Clause's grandchildren. I worked on the grounds for seven summers, cutting grass, gardening, painting, chopping firewood, and preparing boats for storage. The Clauses arrived each spring in the Pittsburgh Plate Glass Company aircraft (Mr. Clause was chairman of the board), accompanied by an Irish cook and household help, the first black people I met.

In the spring of 1958, I finished grade twelve, the final year offered at the Port Carling Continuation School, and went to work as usual on Black Forest Island. One day Mr. Clause asked to see me on the front veranda of the family compound. The request was unusual, since my contacts with the head of the family had been confined to a respectful greeting each morning when I went into the living room to light the fire in the fireplace. Mr. Clause, sipping his ever-present glass of Scotch, told me in his kindly, rasping American voice that he had been giving some thought to my future. The caretaker had told him I was a reasonably good student. Would I be interested in getting a higher education? If so, he would pay the costs for me to attend the high school of my choice to obtain my senior matriculation (grade thirteen) and then go to university.

After stammering out my thanks, I stumbled off the porch, my mind numb. I could now become anything I wanted to be — historian, lawyer, or maybe even diplomat. I had no idea whether I had the aptitude or the intelligence for such professions, but I had the blind confidence of youth. No challenge was now too great. I remember walking back in a daze to where I'd been cutting wood, staring at huge white cumulus clouds in a deep blue Muskoka sky and listening to the lapping of Lake Joseph water on the shore of that deserted part of the island, wondering — why me? I was to have that same sensation some years afterward when I opened an envelope from the then Canadian Civil Service Commission offering me a job as a Foreign Service officer in the Department of External Affairs, years later when I was nominated for the first time to be a Canadian ambassador, and decades after that when Prime Minister Jean Chrétien called to offer me the job as lieutenant governor of Ontario.

With my mother's encouragement and her promise to supplement Mr. Clause's financial assistance with the money she earned cleaning houses, I accepted the offer and left for London, Ontario, where I rented an apartment for the coming year. My Bartleman grandparents, welcoming the opportunity to escape Port Carling for the winter, moved in with me. I attended London Central Collegiate, which had one of the best records in the province in turning out graduates. I did reasonably well academically and moved up the road the following year to attend the University of Western Ontario, enrolling in the four-year honours history program.

I hated the high school and loved the university, but each played its own role in permitting me to escape my self-constructed Muskoka prison. London, even though it was only a medium-sized Canadian city, was a giant metropolis to someone who had spent his life in a community so small that it didn't merit a traffic light. The usual Friday evening crowds of shoppers were menacing. Using the public transport system and finding my way around the city were intimidating. I had never imagined that I could be so homesick. I longed to return to the embrace of my family and to the familiar surroundings of my village. I might not have liked my place in the Port Carling hierarchy, but it was familiar and I had established my niche within it.

The students at Central Collegiate all seemed to know one another. Every twenty-eight minutes bells rang and a mass of humanity moved like automatons to different classrooms to meet different teachers. The contrast with the tiny Port Carling Continuation School, with its complement of thirty-five students for all four grades, two teachers, and two rooms, couldn't have been greater. It was hard to make friends. Many of my new classmates were the offspring of the North London establishment who had known one another from childhood. But eventually, after I found that I could keep up academically, my homesickness faded away and I made a few friends.

University was liberating. I had made the transition from village to city the previous year, and having successfully passed my grade thirteen examinations, I didn't fear the academic challenge. I hadn't felt so free of inhibitions since the summer of 1946 when our family had arrived to start our new life on the Dump Road in Port Carling and I'd discovered the enabling power of reading. Psychological defence mechanisms I had put in place to cope with life as an outsider in a small white community fell away. I threw myself into the search for a liberal education, in the process gaining a glimpse of the attitudes of some members of Canada's intellectual elite toward Indigenous people. My otherwise witty and charming professor of Canadian history claimed French Canadians were inherently backward because they had bred with Indians in the days of the fur trade. Canada's most famous historian of the day, Professor Donald Creighton, flatly stated in his book *Dominion of the North* that the Indians encountered by Europeans in the early history of Canada were inherently inferior drunken and superstitious savages. I paid careful attention to the philosophical musings of one of my professors on the first day of classes that the true function of a university was to facilitate learning through the encounter of a student with books. Formal courses or marks, he said, didn't matter.

I took his advice literally. While this meant neglecting my course work, I learned a great deal by slipping into the classes of professors lecturing on global, religious, and ethical issues. I became a member of the history, United Nations, and social service clubs, and fully profited from the opportunity to meet students from Africa, Asia, and Europe. I sat in on music appreciation classes and spent long periods in the library, immersing myself in literature and history. It was here that my lifelong esteem began for Tolstoy and other Russian novelists and short story writers, as well as for Albert Camus, the French Nobel Prize–winning author and philosopher.

14
Freedom

When I graduated in 1963, I wanted to travel and see the Europe I had read so much about. A career would have to wait until I knew what I wanted to do for the rest of my life. I took a temporary job as a teacher at the Petrolia high school in Southwestern Ontario, saved my money, and in the spring of 1964 bought a one-way ticket to Europe. I was to learn more in the coming year than at any other time before or since; it was the key formative period of my life.

My journey began with a two-month backpacking trip to northern Scandinavia. So many years later it is hard to describe just how excited I was. Everything was new. Everything was an adventure. I relished the train trip to the port of Newcastle from London. I found the thirty-hour ferry ride to Stavanger on Norway's western coast fascinating. In contrast to today when hitchhiking is uncommon, in those days it was an accepted way for young people short of money to get around. The youth hostels I lodged in as I thumbed my way to Hammerfest high above the Arctic Circle, down to Helsinki, and over to Sweden were filled with other young backpackers from Germany, the United Kingdom, Australia, Denmark, and France. Norwegians, Finns, and Swedes in those days had

Graduation from the University of Western Ontario in 1963. *Courtesy Bartleman Family.*

a standard of living lower than Canada's, but the people were generous and welcoming, and I was often invited to their homes for meals and long conversations over coffee about the big international and existential issues of the day. The following is an extract from a letter dated August 5, 1964, that I wrote to my parents from Hammerfest at the top of Norway.

> Dear folks,
>
> Greetings from Hammerfest on the top of the world. I've spent the last three weeks thumbing rides first from Stavanger to Oslo, from Oslo to Trondheim, from Trondheim to Narvik, by which time I was almost out of money. I asked around looking for a job to replenish my stake and was told to head north to Hammerfest where I was certain to be taken on at the fish processing plant. The pay, I was told, was good, and it wouldn't take long to make a lot of money. The only problem was there wasn't any road to Hammerfest. I would have to buy a passage on one of the ferries that made regular runs to

> the north. At the ticket office I discovered that after paying for a supply of bread, cheese, and ham to sustain me on the two-day trip, I had only enough money to pay my fare. No matter. I would soon have lots of money.
>
> The trip itself was great. Midnight sun, picturesque fishing villages, the Gulf Stream, strange mountains bare of vegetation that could have come from a Disney movie set, snowdrifts twenty feet thick in places, nice people. Everyone seems to have relatives in British Columbia. First impressions of Hammerfest were good. Herds of reindeer on the loose, Lapps in their traditional costumes, etc. But imagine my surprise when I discovered that the fish plant had just closed for the summer. I'm now going to thumb rides south to Helsinki where there is a Canadian embassy. I should make it in two weeks and will live on blueberries and sleep in barns until I get there. Could you wire 200 dollars to me care of the embassy? That will get me back to London where there's lots of work. Will pay you back when I get home next year.

Back in London a month later I accepted an offer to teach English, geography, and history at a high school. The British teachers welcomed me, but I never adapted to the British teaching culture. The school was coeducational but in name only; one section was reserved for girls and the other for boys, and no mixing was permitted. At lunch the sexes shared one large cafeteria but fraternizing wasn't allowed. Teachers ate at one long table, but men sat at one end and women at the other. I caused an uproar when I suggested to some of the male teachers that we take our plates and join the ladies. Unable to adapt to a system where the pay was terrible and caning for minor offences was part of the culture (I'd seen enough teacher brutality at Port Carling), I resigned and obtained a job as a hall porter at the British Council Overseas Student Centre at Portland Place in London.

While the British themselves were standoffish, I became friends with university students and au pair girls (students learning English and earning their keep by doing light housekeeping chores) from Europe and the Commonwealth. My pay was £12 a week, rent for a two-room flat close to the Barons Court Underground station was £2, and my pass on the Tube was another £2. I lived very well. Canada House became my real home away from home — the place where I picked up my mail, read outdated Canadian newspapers preoccupied with political scandals and the debate over the introduction of the new Canadian flag, and met other young Canadians doing their thing in London.

The other hall porters were Irish war veterans who took me along to local pubs after work, introduced me to Guinness, and told me their war stories. My responsibilities were confined largely to checking identities at the door and directing people to the toilets. Several years later I was able to use these responsibilities to good effect when I submitted a curriculum vitae to support my Foreign Service application, noting with just a touch of exaggeration that I had been an information official at the prestigious British Council in London, England, at one time in my brief career. The kindly librarian at the council gave me free tickets for concerts at Albert Hall and Festival Hall and for other major cultural events in the British capital. I would rush off almost every evening to listen to the best symphony orchestras and the most gifted pianists, and on weekends I would take in the art galleries. It would have been a heady time for anyone, let alone for someone from a small rural community in Central Ontario.

The Second World War had been over for nineteen years and change was in the air. Newspapers were lamenting the fact that Britain, the ostensible winner of the war, was falling farther and farther behind the countries on the continent, whose economies had been destroyed in the fighting. There was much soul-searching over the loss of empire, and Winston Churchill's death in January 1965 was the signal that an era had ended. I stood in line for five hours outside Westminster Hall to file by his coffin and pay my respects. The next day I joined hundreds of thousands of Londoners on the route of his funeral cortège.

I was to have a taste of the great ferment that was occurring in the United States, which would in short order bring about the desegregation of the American South. During the Christmas holidays, while still working as a teacher prior to leaving for Europe in June 1964, I had travelled with my father to visit a sister who was living with her American serviceman husband on an air force base in Montgomery, Alabama. The U.S. South of that period was truly an alien and sinister place. I felt deeply uncomfortable at the sight of segregated restaurants, barbershops, and restrooms in the racially divided towns and villages that we passed through. Going through Birmingham, I could still see in my mind's eye the television images of "Bull" Connor, the commissioner of public safety who some months earlier had ordered steel-helmeted police officers armed with batons, firehoses, and dogs to attack marching black children. In Montgomery I visited the state capital where the era of "black awakening" had started with Rosa Parks's refusal to give up her seat on a bus to a white passenger in 1955, and where Freedom Riders were beaten with lead pipes and baseball bats in 1961. Governor George Wallace was still an unreconstructed racist in that winter of 1963–64, and there was little indication, at least to me, that the region was on the verge of momentous change. If change was to come, however, it was generally accepted that it would be led by Dr. Martin Luther King.

I was thus privileged to be present at a sermon by the leader of the U.S. civil-rights movement himself at St. Paul's Cathedral. I had come in to listen to an organ recital in the unheated and damp cathedral when the dean introduced Reverend King, who was on his way to receive the Nobel Peace Prize in Oslo. Dr. King's eyes were fixed on the back of the cathedral rather than on the congregation, and I had the impression that he was addressing history rather than us. After Dr. King described his efforts in the civil-rights campaign, he quoted John Donne, the seventeenth-century dean of St. Paul's: "No man is an island, entire of itself; every man is a piece of the continent, a part of the main … never send to know for whom the bell tolls; it tolls for thee." Assassinated by James Earl Ray on April 4, 1968, Dr. King could have been referring to himself.

When I finished teaching at the American School of The Hague for a term, I set out to explore General Franco's Spain. After standing at the side of the road on the Spanish side of the border for a few days without getting a ride (few people owned cars in those days), I bought a ticket, valid for almost 750 miles, at a railway station and headed for Gibraltar. The following is an extract from a letter I wrote to my parents on my trip.

April 4, 1965

Dear folks,

Excuse my jerky handwriting, but I am writing from a bumpy train carriage somewhere between Tarragona and Valencia in Spain on the way to Gibraltar. Since I'll be working for most of my remaining time in Europe, I decided to take the cash I had earned teaching at the American School of The Hague and hitch through Belgium, France, and into Spain. I left The Hague one sunny day about ten days ago and visited Namur (where I took in the fortifications), Reims (where I toured the Mumm champagne cellars sampling their vintages), Avignon (the palace of the popes), and Perpignan (a French border town). Three Canadian girls on holiday in Spain gave me a ride to the nearest town with a train station after I gave up trying to hitch a ride.

Third-class train travel is cheap — costing about one cent per kilometre. There are about eight of us in each compartment. The people are friendly enough but are suspicious, unsurprising since Franco's Spain is a police state and there are apparently informers everywhere. The floor is littered with garbage. A little girl sitting beside me vomited, but no one cared. Her grandmother just wiped it up with a rag and tossed rag and vomit out the window. As far as you can see are orange groves, olive trees, and vineyards. There are no tractors, just mules and farm labourers working the fields. The train travels about twenty kilometres an hour, stopping at every hamlet along the way to let off and take on new passengers and give dozens of Gypsies the chance to sell tortillas, soft drinks, and cigarettes through the windows to those of us inside.

From time to time it pulls into a siding and we are herded off to sleep in cheap hotels near the railway station while the crew takes on coal and water for the locomotive. I fell into a deep sleep during one of these stops and dreamed I could hear the staccato opening beats of Beethoven's Fifth Symphony repeating themselves with frantic intensity. I woke up in the pitch-black bedroom to hear someone knocking with four insistent hammer blows on each door on the floor, the sound growing in ferocity as it approached my room, summoning the passengers to take their places on the train. Half asleep and clutching my pack, I staggered into the pale artificial light of the station platform to board the train and continue the snail-paced journey across the vast highland plateau.

The passengers immediately fell asleep on the wooden benches, some with their mouths open, some snoring. I was reminded of the scene from *Wind, Sand and Stars* in which the author, Antoine de Saint-Exupéry, travelling by train in northern France in the 1920s, watches the faces of sleeping immigrants returning to their homeland from France and wonders who from among that mass of apparent brute humanity could be the world's next Chopin or Mozart, if only he or she had the opportunity. "The third-class carriages," he writes, "were crowded with hundreds of Polish workmen sent home from France. I made my way, stepping over sprawling bodies and peering into the carriages. I sat down face to face with one couple. Between the man and the woman a child had hollowed himself out a place and fallen asleep. He turned in his slumber, and in the dim lamplight I saw his face. A golden fruit had been born of these two peasants. I bent over the smooth brow, over those mildly pouting lips, and I said to myself: This is the child Mozart. This little Mozart will love shoddy music in the stench of night dives. This little Mozart is condemned. This little Mozart is murdered."

I remained awake to catch the first light of the day and to watch the sun rise over the neighbouring mesas. Eventually, we descended to the hot Andalusian plain where I picked oranges from trees beside the track from the windows of the slow-moving train, reaching Algeciras, the Spanish city at the crossing point to Gibraltar. In those days, Spain's dispute with the

United Kingdom over the ownership of Gibraltar was in one of its periodic crises; on my return to Algeciras from Gibraltar, the Spanish border guards emptied my suitcase on the ground to punish me for consorting with their British enemy but let me re-enter Spain. I would remember the train trip and Saint-Exupéry's words when I travelled to Ontario's north a half century later to meet a generation of Indigenous kids condemned by lack of opportunity to a life of poverty, racism, and marginalization.

The following is another excerpt from one of my letters, describing a bullfight in Madrid on the trip back.

> Can't complain about the cost of living. Beer is eight cents a bottle, wine twenty cents a quart. Two good meals and a bed at a two-star hotel a dollar a day. I went out after breakfast and walked around people-watching and taking in the Prado and its collection of Goya and El Greco paintings. Afterward, I bought tickets to a bullfight. A mistake. It was the first fight of the season. Seven huge bulls were tormented and killed as the crowd yelled for blood. But the bulls gave as good as they got. One bull lifted a horse in the air with its horns, threw the picador (that's a horseman who gores the bulls with a long spear to weaken it before the matador comes to finish it off) onto the ground, and stomped on him. As a matador distracted the bull, paramedics rushed out and hauled away the fallen picador on a stretcher. In another fight, the bull outwitted the matador and tossed him high in the air and stomped on him as well. I don't think he survived. I was rooting for the bulls but had seen more than enough cruelty and left before the spectacle ended.

I wouldn't see Spain again until I travelled with my wife to the world's fair in Seville in 1993 as a member of a delegation of NATO ambassadors as guests of the Spanish government. I returned again with Prime Minister Chrétien as his foreign-policy adviser in July 1997 to attend a summit meeting of NATO leaders during which the Canadian and Spanish prime ministers made an effort to put the 1995 confrontation over fish in the North Atlantic behind them. Franco had been dead for a generation, and

Spain had become a prosperous, democratic member of NATO and the European Union, rivalling Canada in the size of its gross domestic product. Gone for good were the impoverished peasants, the outdated infrastructure, and the pervasive climate of fear and suspicion of a police state.

My gap year in Europe over, it was time to return to Canada. I said goodbye to my friends in The Hague and left for Prestwick, Scotland, to take a Trans-Canada Air Lines flight to Gander, Newfoundland. Aware that my time for travel and exploration was coming to an end, I decided to hitchhike to Montreal and take a train to Muskoka to complement my newly acquired knowledge of Europe with a glimpse of life as seen from the open road in Atlantic Canada and Quebec. The weather was glorious and the people welcoming that June 1965 as I made my way home. The new Canadian maple leaf flag was flying from houses along the way. The Trans-Canada Highway from St. John's to Port aux Basques on the southwest coast of Newfoundland, my immediate destination, had just been built, and there were few cars and trucks on the road. However, I had little trouble getting lifts. Even if they were going in the opposite direction, people would turn around to help me on my way or offer to take me home for a meal. At Corner Brook, where I spent the night trying to sleep in the railway station, good-natured local veterans waiting for a train insisted that I join them as they drank and sang their regimental songs.

After crossing by ferry to North Sydney, Cape Breton Island, I followed the Trans-Canada Highway into New Brunswick where I spent a day standing on the side of the road waiting for a ride, eventually becoming so thirsty that I stopped a passing farmer on a tractor to beg for a drink of water. That night I slept in the dense brush beside the highway, tormented all night by mosquitoes and blackflies. After I waited another day for a ride, a truck driver on his way to Montreal picked me up just as it was becoming dark. The driver thought I'd help him pass the time, but I was so tired that my head drooped and my body pitched forward as I fell asleep. I'd wake up with a start and jerk back into my seat, only to collapse again, restarting the cycle. In the seconds of sleep snatched when I lurched forward, strange visions came to me. I cried out as scenes from my travels flashed in colour before my eyes. Fact mixed with fiction as my brain sought to integrate the experiences of other cultures into the world view I had taken on leaving for Europe. The driver made no comment but looked relieved when he dropped me off in Montreal at dawn.

My parents and grandparents joined Bob and Mary, my one sister still at home, to give me a hero's welcome when I reached Port Carling. My mother and father took me to a pub at Milford Bay, a neighbouring "wet" community, to celebrate the return of the son to his family and village. I then left Port Carling for good and joined the Department of External Affairs as a Foreign Service officer. The young man about to embark on a diplomatic career wasn't the kid who had once lived in a tent near the village dump in Port Carling nineteen years before. I had changed and that change would continue as I accepted ever more challenging responsibilities, learned other languages, and immersed myself in other cultures. I would never forget that I owed a debt to Robert Clause for giving me my start. That debt would be discharged when I was appointed lieutenant governor in 2002, regretfully decades after he passed away.

A 1920s photograph of Robert Clause, who funded grade thirteen and my university studies. *Courtesy Bartleman Family.*

Part Two

The Foreign Service Officer, 1966–1981

I was a junior- and middle-ranking officer for my first fifteen years in the Department of External Affairs, spending the first two years in training assignments at headquarters and at Canada's New York United Nations mission. A two-year posting as third secretary working under the uncertain supervision of a senior ambassador at Canada's embassy at Bogotá learning nothing useful followed. I then came to the attention of senior management at headquarters for my work on international terrorism during the 1970 Front de libération du Québec (FLQ) October Crisis, was posted as acting high commissioner to Bangladesh, and left to manage the mission by myself. As a reward for my efforts in Dhaka, the department cross-posted me to Canada's delegation to NATO as a general-purpose first secretary. Before the posting ended, I was promoted to the executive rank and on return to Ottawa was made head of officer assignments followed by the directorship of the Caribbean and Central American division.

15

Ottawa: A Time of Optimism

The glory days of the Department of External Affairs, now celebrated by nostalgic editorial writers and academics, were over by the time I reported for work in early July 1966. Certainly, I detected no superhuman individuals wandering the halls of the East Block, the Langevin Block, or the five or six other buildings in downtown Ottawa that housed Canada's Foreign Service elite until the department moved in 1973 into the Lester B. Pearson Building, its new home. The three officers most cited for putting Canada on the postwar map, Hume Wrong, Lester Pearson, and Norman Robertson, were gone. Wrong had been dead for more than a decade. Lester Pearson was still around: he was our prime minister but seemed to be more respected abroad than in Canada where his foreign-policy triumphs were a decade old. Norman Robertson was still alive but deathly ill; I would occasionally see him in the Centre Block of Parliament as he carried out special advisory duties for his good friend and erstwhile rival, the prime minister.

Paul Martin, Sr., was foreign minister. Like all foreign ministers who followed Lester Pearson, he would labour in the shadow of Canada's only Nobel Peace Prize winner, whose accomplishments took on a mythic character with the passage of time. The middle and senior ranks were a talented lot. They received the new recruits in their cluttered offices, desks overflowing with neglected papers marked with tags appealing for urgent attention, security cabinets bulging with files, and every available space adorned with enough kitsch from faraway places to do any garage sale proud. Hitching up their suspenders, they would take one last puff on the pipe every self-respecting officer seemed to possess in those days, and provide the junior officers their views on Canadian foreign policy.

Each would describe Canada's place in the world as seen from the perspective of his or her division or bureau. The sum of these parts didn't, however, a whole make. Nobody was able to say if Canada had an overriding goal or goals in its foreign policy. I had the impression that no one worried too much about the matter, since the unspoken assumption was that the United States would do the worrying for us. Washington would defend us to protect itself and would ensure our economic well-being by providing a huge and stable market for our exports. In the beneficent American shadow, Canada enjoyed the luxury of choosing niche areas for foreign-policy attention, promoting good causes such as peacekeeping and environmental protection. Not much would change in the years to come.

With little prompting, the elders would tell stories of first postings, eccentric ambassadors, exotic capitals in areas off the beaten path, fascinating people, official visits gone wrong, executive assistants acting as tyrants on borrowed power, triumphs, occasional failures, how their families coped, and dangerous or funny events. Consciously or not, they were describing their transitions from junior officers in small posts having the time of their lives to senior diplomats in major missions putting into practice decades of apprenticeship. In those days that was how officers learned their trade. Formal training didn't exist as it does today, and new officers were expected to pick up the art of diplomacy largely through a process of osmosis. These sessions with experienced colleagues constituted the best training anyone could have for the profession of Foreign Service officer — and perhaps for life in general.

The class of 1966 was larger than those of the past, which probably allowed me to make the cut. For the first time a large contingent of Quebeckers and a high proportion of women had been hired. There was a sprinkling of Oxford and Harvard graduates, but the majority were Canadian-educated lawyers, economists, and historians. There were also, I think, more entrants than before who were able to speak both French and English, to do business in difficult foreign languages such as Russian and Chinese, and to conduct negotiations in specialized subjects such as trade and development policy. The class proved to be an exceptional one, with many moving to the highest ranks of the public service during their careers.

It was a time of optimism. The pay was poor, but we were young and the prospects for adventure and promotion were more promising than they had been for years — and better than they would be for generations to come. The government was just beginning its rapid expansion at home and abroad, and new embassies were being opened every year. External Affairs was still one of the two or three most influential government departments in town, and star performers were still being recruited to fill deputy minister positions elsewhere in the bureaucracy. Canada's place in the world, while not yet starting its downward slide, was still high in this era when Canada had a decent-sized military, when the Europeans were preoccupied building their new institutional structures, when colonies in the Third World were in the process of achieving independence, and when newly industrializing countries such as South Korea, Malaysia, Singapore, Mexico, and Brazil hadn't started their economic takeoffs.

There was no formal training. Entrants were rotated through six-month jobs in the first year or two in the department to learn the ropes. I became desk officer for Belgium, the Netherlands, Luxembourg, and Switzerland from July until October when the department sent me to Canada's mission to the United Nations in New York as a so-called adviser or dogsbody to a more senior officer. I learned a lot by just watching the decision-making process in action. Every morning the ambassador held a staff meeting in which members of the permanent mission, delegates named by the government for the session, visiting MPs, and lowly misnamed advisers assembled to plan the work of the day. Decolonization issues, such as coping with the unilateral declaration of independence by Ian Smith in Rhodesia and the struggle for independence of the people of Southwest Africa (the future Namibia), were high on the agenda.

The most contentious subject was Beijing's demand that it, rather than Taipei, should represent China at the United Nations. Pierre Trudeau, then parliamentary secretary to Prime Minister Pearson, argued strongly for moving Canada's position from a vote "against" to an "abstention," which would represent a major foreign-policy change for Canada in those Cold War days. Paul Martin disagreed, concerned at the reaction of Washington. I watched Trudeau lobby the Liberal MPs on the delegation one by one. He then contacted Pearson, and instructions came from Ottawa for Canada to change its position.

As it happened, Trudeau's room was next to mine at the hotel, and we often walked together to the offices of the Canadian mission. He was fascinated by foreign travel and told me some of his adventures as a backpacker. We once shared a taxi to a diplomatic reception hosted by a Canadian diplomat. On arrival we were greeted by a remarkable scene of revelry and debauchery. The host and several of the guests were so drunk that they were on their hands and knees on the floor, laughing hysterically for no particular reason.

"We always have the best parties here," gushed one of the first people we met. Trudeau was visibly ill-at-ease and left after a few minutes. I remained to continue my wide-eyed education on how to be a diplomat. I was to run into Trudeau from time to time in my Foreign Service career. The first several times, when he was minister of justice, he stopped to chat or crossed the street to catch up on the latest news. The last time I saw him was at a lunch hosted by Prime Minister Chrétien at 24 Sussex Drive in June 1994 for the visiting president of the European Commission.

Most advisers, myself included, had never been to New York, and we took advantage of the free tickets available from the U.N. hospitality section. In the evenings, if there was time after committee meetings, we hurried to take in Broadway shows or the opera. Whenever we could, we gathered to trade accounts of our daily adventures in a hospitality room set up for the use of our delegation in the hotel. Friendships were forged that lasted a lifetime.

Sundays I spent exploring the city, appalled by the huge disparities in living standards of New Yorkers: wealth in Manhattan and urban decay in large swathes of Harlem. I had known poverty as a child, growing up on the wrong side of the tracks in rural Ontario. But what I saw in New York was of a different order: an urban squalor of uncollected garbage, old mattresses and sofas thrown negligently into backyards, and streets filled with the loitering and unemployed. President Lyndon Johnson had launched his project for the Great Society to bring hope to this underclass. But the war in Vietnam was consuming the wealth of the country, and neglected American cities were rotting from the inside. Black-white relations never recovered.

16

Colombia: Cockroaches the Size of Lizards

The Canadian embassy in Bogotá in February 1968 was a small one, consisting of an unhappy ambassador, two trade officers, two secretary-typists, and a junior officer on his first posting — me. My formal responsibilities involved managing the consular section, issuing visas and passports, and writing the occasional economic and political report. My real job was to listen to the stories of the ambassador on his postings abroad and his headquarters assignments.

He entered my office early in the morning, clutching a newspaper with an article he didn't like or a message from headquarters that had riled him. As a respectful junior officer, I rose to my feet and pretended interest in what he was saying. Two or three hours of grumbling later, he glanced at his watch and headed off for lunch at his residence. Exhausted from standing and listening to his rants for such prolonged periods, I gratefully sat down and finished whatever work was on my desk, since he would be back early in the afternoon to repeat the morning routine.

There was never much to do. In theory consular assistance to Canadians was a major part of my work. But upon my arrival at the embassy the ambassador told me that under no circumstance was help to be given to any Canadian in distress. Such a person, he earnestly said, was obviously guilty of something or else he or she wouldn't be in distress. And if guilty of something, then the person in question didn't merit consular help. Fortunately, few Canadians visited Colombia in those days, and I didn't have to turn away many people. One Canadian languishing without consular aid in the local jail took matters into his own hands and managed to escape.

In this, my first posting, I was expected to help the ambassador make his guests feel welcome at his dinners and receptions. This suited me well, since I needed pointers on how to be a successful host. I started off on the right foot. I arrived ten minutes before events at the ambassador's residence for instructions on who was who, then introduced guests to one another and made small talk when required. Seeing how eager I was, the ambassador decided to pay particular attention to my diplomatic education. Complaining that his Colombian staff were doing a poor job preparing for luncheons, dinners, and receptions, he invited me — as part of my training, he said — to help out with the preparations for major events. I arrived dressed in my old clothes and struggled in the rarefied air of the High Andes to set up tables, erect marquees, and haul cases of soft drinks, beer, and wine from his locked storeroom. The household staff watched quietly, trying hard not to laugh as I sweated and strained doing their work. I then rushed home, changed, and returned in time to help greet the guests. The ambassador, a product of the age when Canadian heads of post considered their junior officers constituted a pool of cheap labour, was happy exploiting me, and I knew no better.

The ambassador then accepted a speaking engagement in a remote part of the country. I would be in charge for the two days he would be away. I was thrilled. What an honour! Here I was only a junior officer and already responsible for the management of a Canadian embassy!

I quickly rushed through the preparations for the ambassador's trip. First, I crafted what I considered to be an excellent speech: "The English Language as Spoken and Written in Canada and the United States: Some Nuances." The ambassador had given me no direction on what type of speech he wanted, so I simply pulled the topic out of thin air. Likewise, I didn't consult him when I made his hotel reservations. This was a mere administrative detail that I delegated to a recently hired local employee, who assured me she had booked the best room in the town's best hotel. She neglected to tell me the hotel was the best because it was the only one in town. And how was she to know that it was also the town's bordello?

On the fateful day I handed the ambassador his itinerary and speech and he departed. I couldn't have been happier. At last I was in charge of the mission! If I was lucky, the telephone would ring and the foreign minister of Colombia would be on the line seeking my advice on some important point of Canadian-Colombian relations. My answer would, I imagined, be so brilliant that the ambassador upon his return would recommend me to headquarters for immediate promotion.

The telephone rang. It was the ambassador's wife, and it wasn't a call of encouragement. Instead, she demanded an account of everything that had gone on at the mission since her husband's departure an hour before.

Respectfully, I told her that it was a normal day at the Canadian embassy: nothing had happened. One hour later the telephone rang again. It was the ambassador's conscientious wife asking what I had been doing since she last called. "Nothing," I said, allowing just a whisper of irritation to appear in my voice. Every hour on the hour for the rest of the day she called.

A slow burn started in my chest and spread to my head, clouding all thought. What right, I asked myself, had this woman to interfere in the operations of the embassy? She was just a busybody. I, on the other hand, was an elite Foreign Service officer able to manage any crisis that might arise in Colombia without her help! Suddenly, something snapped. Rushing out of the office, I jumped into my car and sped off to the residence of my tormentor. Storming into the living room, I told her that since she thought she could do a better job managing the mission, she should go to the office and take over. "Otherwise, leave me alone! And never ever call me again!"

I then returned with a great feeling of satisfaction, leaving a stunned lady in my wake. I didn't care about repercussions. I had done what I had to do.

The next day there were no telephone calls from the ambassador's wife. There were, however, no calls from anyone else. As the day progressed and my chance to prove myself faded, I began to think about what

I had said in the ambassador's living room the previous afternoon. Like a repentant drunk the day after, I was now deeply sorry for my actions — and worried. There would be no letter to headquarters commending my management of the post. More likely the ambassador would request my removal for *lèse-majesté.*

The following morning a thoroughly unhappy ambassador appeared at the entrance to my office, but this time not to share with me his stories about the villainous nature of headquarters management.

"Mr. Bartleman, whatever led you to prepare a speech for me on an issue in which no one in this country could take the slightest interest? And the hotel with its wild women and their customers! And the room where I had to sit on the toilet to take a shower! And the cockroaches the size of lizards!"

And on and on. But no mention of my altercation with his wife or of revenge, for he needed my help with a load of fine French wines ordered from a diplomatic supplier arriving at his residence that very morning. He wanted me to unload his treasures and transport them to the residence storeroom.

Of course, I would help. Perhaps, I thought, he'd let bygones be bygones. I returned home, changed into my work clothes, and reported to the residence. The wife greeted me frostily, but the ambassador was all smiles, happy with the prospect of free junior officer labour. Then it happened. Carrying too many boxes of wine on a wheelbarrow, I hit a bump. A case flew off and landed on the concrete walkway in a crash of broken glass. The ambassador's face was ashen as he contemplated the fine expensive French wine oozing out of the elegant wooden box stamped with the name of a famous French château. Insulting his wife and making him sit on a toilet to take a shower in a house of ill repute were nothing compared to this.

"Leave the premises," he said.

Never again would I be asked to provide free manual labour at his residence. I was henceforth to restrict my role at his hospitality events to that of a guest rather than as a member of his household staff.

17

Colombia: The Antiques Road Show

I then made a road trip to Peru, which almost proved to be my last. Guenter, a pompous ass from the German embassy who up to then had barely deigned to speak to me because I was a mere third secretary and he was second secretary, invited me to accompany him in his Volkswagen Beetle (to share the costs) on a trip over the mountains and across the desert to Lima. His goal was to collect as many antiques as possible; mine was to see more of Latin America. We left Bogotá in high spirits, descending through the clouds from the high plateau where the Colombian capital sits to enter the so-called hot country close to sea level near Cali, later to become infamous as a centre of international drug trafficking. From Cali we headed south to the colonial city of Popayán where an earthquake struck several years later, burying worshippers in the ruins of the cathedral just minutes after Canada's ambassador and his wife walked out the door.

We then moved on to Pasto, the isolated capital of the department of Nariño, where Guenter allowed me to go with him as he paid consular visits to members of the German community. He was welcomed enthusiastically, but I was treated with wariness. The German colonists, Guenter said, had left Germany in a hurry at the end of the war and didn't want the outside world to know where they were. For my part, uncertain whether they had been Nazis or victims of the Nazis, I was relieved when he finished his business and we were able to continue on our way.

The route from Pasto to Quito, high up in the Andes and Ecuador's capital, was terrible, often reduced to one cobblestone lane. Numerous crosses indicated the spots where speeding cars, trucks, and buses had plunged over the edge into deep mountain valleys, killing the passengers. In Quito colleagues at the tiny Canadian embassy took us in hand to show us the sights and extend hospitality, overjoyed to have some company to reduce their boredom in a place where there was even less to do than in Bogotá. We then pressed on to Guayaquil, the hot, unhealthy port city of Ecuador, where the road ended. Undeterred, we took the ferry to the southern bank of the Guayas River and followed back roads and trails to the border of Peru where we met up with the paved coastal highway running through the Atacama Desert. Two days later we were in Lima, capital of Peru, which still retained its charm as a small colonial city. In the coming decade, the massive movement of the rural poor seeking a better life was to change its personality forever.

So far, so good. Guenter had found antiques, in particular wooden carvings of saints apparently worth a fortune in Europe, and was satisfied with himself. At that point in our travels we were still getting along relatively well and looking forward to relaxing after our long drive in the quiet charm of Lima. The morning after our arrival, however, Guenter hammered on my hotel room door shouting that a coup d'état led by the military was in progress. We had to leave before roadblocks were set up around the city or we could find ourselves stranded with the antiques in the Peruvian capital indefinitely. As we scrambled to grab all of our belongings and get them to the car, Guenter pulled out a revolver and said that it was to be used for our protection. The rules of engagement, as he described them, were simple: whoever wasn't driving (we were taking turns at the wheel) would ride shotgun and kill anyone who tried to steal his antiquities.

We set off at what I thought was a panic-stricken race for the Ecuadorean border, the precious antiques under blankets in the back and the revolver in the glove compartment with our passports. Guenter didn't appreciate my skeptical attitude. His mood worsened when I took the wheel and forgot that sand drifts on the highway along Peru's coastal desert weren't as easy to plough through as snowdrifts in a Canadian winter. I hit one at sixty miles per hour, and Guenter's car bounced high in the air and nearly overturned. He became downright nasty, however, after we crossed the border back into Ecuador and came to a railway bridge over a deep gorge. About two hundred yards in length, it was for trains only, but some public-spirited person had laid two narrow planks along the tracks for anyone willing to take a chance driving across.

Distracted by Guenter's back-seat driving, and a terrible driver at the best of times, I didn't hesitate and drove onto the bridge and off the planks. The front end of the car was caught by a railway tie. As we hung suspended over the void, Guenter let loose a string of what I assumed were nasty comments in German on the quality of my driving. He shut up in a hurry when we heard the whistle of an oncoming train. Fortunately, a group of *campesinos* rushed onto the bridge and lifted the car back onto the planks, allowing me to steer to safety.

Our next adventure was several miles down the road. We were travelling on a dirt track almost blinded by dust and burning refuse from nearby banana plantations. My colleague had taken the wheel and was no longer talking to me. Suddenly, out of the haze, a scruffy band of men looking like actors from an old Pancho Villa movie, armed with shotguns, pistols, machetes, and bandoliers full of ammunition wrapped around their shoulders, came into view, blocking the road. Guenter had no choice but to stop. I was riding shotgun and knew I was now supposed to shoot our way free. But I simply reached into the glove compartment and pulled out our diplomatic passports. I didn't know where the safety catch was on his damn pistol, and even though I was only a third secretary from Muskoka, I knew better than to take on a dozen wild-eyed Ecuadoreans in a gunfight.

But our troubles worsened. The gang couldn't have cared less for our diplomatic passports and told us to get out of the car with our hands up. Guenter muttered something to himself in German, clearly torn between saving our lives and saving his antiques. The antiques won. He put his car into gear and drove straight through the crowd, pushing the gunmen aside with the bumper as they hammered on the roof with the butts of their guns. When we reported this encounter to the Ecuadorean police, they told us the area was infested by criminals. We were lucky not to have been killed.

I wouldn't see South America again for eleven years. When I returned, respectably married with two children and a dog, my days of wild adventure over, it was to be chargé d'affaires, or acting ambassador at the Canadian embassy in Lima. My job was to re-establish order in a badly demoralized mission where the outgoing ambassador had been spending his time cowering in his office afraid of terrorists, soothsayers, parasites, amoebas, tsunamis, traffic jams, sandstorms, and earthquakes. Our first official engagement was to attend the swearing-in at the National Assembly of Peru's first democratically elected leader since the coup d'état that had led Guenter and me to flee Lima in 1969.

18

Ottawa Under Siege

Upon my return from Colombia, I bought a small rudimentary cottage on the bank of the Gatineau River opposite Wakefield, Quebec, and spent my weekends converting it into a winterized home and place of refuge. Mesmerized by the sound of the rapids just a yard from my bedroom window, I would rise in the middle of the night to test myself, battling the current in the dark until I could go upstream no farther, my canoe crashing against logs in those days still being borne downstream to mills on the Ottawa River. I would lift my paddle and allow myself to be swept back through the heavy mist where cold air met warm water in company with groaning tangles of wood pungent with the smell of wet bark, cedar, hemlock, and spruce.

In the mornings I left for my office early to get to work on time. I loved my new job in the department's Intelligence Analysis Division as an international terrorism analyst, a subject that fascinated me. Not long after I reported for work, my director sent me to Quebec City to take a three-week French-immersion course. I made friends with students from the Laval School of Music, and they in turn introduced me to a cross-section of university students, public servants, and young professionals. All were nationalists committed to the independence of Quebec, but neither they nor I allowed our differences over the future of Canada to affect our relations.

Then, at the beginning of October, members of the Liberation Cell of the FLQ kidnapped James Cross, the British trade commissioner in Montreal, and sought to exchange him for FLQ prisoners in jail, bullion valued at $500,000, and other political demands. Less than a week later members of the Chénier Cell seized and eventually murdered Pierre Laporte, Quebec's deputy premier and labour minister. Prime Minister Trudeau adopted a tough line, obtaining the approval of a rattled Parliament to invoke the War Measures Act, suspending civil liberties in Quebec. Almost 500 suspected FLQ sympathizers were rounded up and thrown into prison. None was charged with a crime. Thousands of soldiers occupied Ottawa and the major cities of Quebec to head off an "apprehended insurrection."

Meanwhile, in the assessments I wrote for the government, I confirmed that the FLQ had few ties with counterpart organizations elsewhere in the world. I also saw information that crossed my desk that the FLQ was few in number, didn't have the support of the Quebec population, and in no way threatened the security of Quebec or Canada. My friends in Quebec City were in a state of shock. Many people they knew had been arrested and beaten in the nighttime police raids. They couldn't understand, and neither could I, how such a thing could happen in a country that prided itself on its human-rights record.

I trudged to work in the mornings in an Ottawa under siege followed by the watchful eyes of nervous nineteen-year-old soldiers standing in doorways holding automatic weapons at the ready. Returning home in the evenings, I looked up to see military helicopters ominously silhouetted against the purple sky, their clattering rotor blades drowning out the cries of the Canada geese heading south. The silence of the public was deafening. It was a scene more suited to Colombia than to Canada. In later years I thought of October 1970 when I saw Costa-Gavras movies such as *Z*, *State of Siege*, and *Missing*, describing the descent to military rule in Greece, Uruguay, and Chile, respectively. From that experience came my conviction that human rights and democracy were fragile things and needed constant nourishing even in Canada. For that reason, when I wrote a novel (*Exceptional Circumstances*) on Canada's security agency dealing in torture in the post-9/11 world, I set it against the events of October 1970.

19

Bangladesh: The Gates of Hell

I first saw Dhaka, Bangladesh, on a sweltering afternoon in June 1972. The two-hour flight from Bangkok over Burma and the Bay of Bengal gave me time to sit back in air-conditioned comfort and feel that everything was going my way. Here I was from small-town Ontario setting out at the age of thirty-two to open the first Canadian diplomatic mission in Bangladesh. Life was good. Around me graceful flight attendants served exotic foods and supplied ice-cold beer in the luxury of Thai Airways business class.

Approaching landfall, the aircraft descended through black monsoon clouds until we could see the lush green delta of the Meghna, Ganges, and Brahmaputra Rivers. From that far up there were no signs of the recent catastrophes that had hit the newly independent Bangladesh: the cyclone of 1970 that had killed half a million people; the just-ended civil war against West Pakistan in which hundreds of thousands had died; and the massive smallpox epidemic still ravaging the population.

The landing at Dhaka International Airport was rough — the tarmac was still pockmarked with crudely repaired craters left over from the heavy bombing by the Indian Air Force the previous December. Workers rolled the airport's only functional set of stairs up to the aircraft door, and the petite flight attendant smiled as she opened the door to another world. A stench of humid, sweet-and-sour air poured in, upsetting the sterile air-conditioned comfort of the cabin. A mob of half-clad beggars waited just outside, clamouring piteously for baksheesh, or charity, as I went down the rickety steps to the tarmac. Some with hands but no feet shuffled forward on their knees, grabbing at my clothes. Others with feet but no hands stuck the damp stumps of their festering limbs in my face. Their eyes were wild and their skin pitted with smallpox scars. Within seconds I was drenched in sweat.

There were no officials of any sort present to keep order as I fought my way through packs of mendicants to the immigration counter and then to the baggage reception area. Once again I was besieged, this time by porters fighting among themselves to carry my one bag. I grabbed it myself and joined a half-dozen other expatriates competing for transport into the city. A solitary taxi waited at the exit. Like Milo Minderbinder in *Catch-22* in wartime Italy, I pulled out a carton of American cigarettes from the supply I'd brought along for times like this and held it aloft as our safari-suited band of brothers bore down on the driver. I was the chosen one. The driver flashed me a smile, opened the back door, accepted my offering and, leaving the others behind, drove me to the only modern hotel in the city.

Afterward, curious to learn more about this city that was now my new home, I made my way, fascinated and appalled, through the crowds that choked the roads and sidewalks day and night in Bangladesh's capital. The streets were filled with bicycle rickshaws decorated with hand-painted scenes from the civil war, pushcarts manned by sweating labourers, buses with more passengers on the roofs than in their interiors, wandering cattle, and wagons and stagecoaches drawn by skeletal horses. Overhead, tangles of wire cluttered the telephone poles and the sky was black with crows and, yes, vultures that I later learned had grown fat eating the bodies of the victims of the war. Cloying smoke from the burning dried cow dung used for cooking hung in the air, mixing with the acrid smell of black exhaust fumes spewing from ill-maintained bus, truck, and car engines and the odour of tens of thousands of unwashed bodies.

Women modestly enveloped from head to foot in burkas, black garments with openings for the eyes and nose, now relatively common on the streets of Western cities with large Muslim immigrant populations, and men dressed in dhotis, a type of skirt, thronged the thoroughfares. The disabled, often naked and filthy, competed with stray dogs foraging for food among the garbage heaps. In the absence of public toilets, men and women, their mouths crimson from the juice of betel nuts, squatted in the gutters with as much dignity as they could muster. Others exposed the corpses of their relatives on the sidewalks, begging for money to give them decent burials. In this, my initial encounter with South Asia, the colour, vibrancy, and authenticity of local life, which I was later to discover, were overwhelmed by poverty and human misery.

Beggars surrounded me just as they had at the airport. About 500 yards from the hotel, I gave a coin to a half-blind wretch crawling along on the sidewalk. Another, bigger and stronger, snatched it from him and a crowd sprang up appealing to me to give them money, as well. I turned and headed back to the hotel with the damned of the earth following behind, howling. The wronged recipient of my bounty wobbled after me, crablike, wailing that he had been robbed and appealing for another handout. I didn't want to run, afraid I'd find myself leading a mob back to the hotel. I walked faster. Somehow the poor soul kept up. The crowd followed, hoping I'd weaken and offer another coin they could steal. I went faster, but my new companion kept coming.

The crowd stopped at the hotel property line, but the unfortunate continued through. The uniformed doorkeeper opened the heavy glass door to let me in and slammed it in the beggar's face — literally. I looked back. His face and body were squashed against the glass, his tongue hung from his open mouth, and his protruding eyes met mine. Unable to stand his accusing gaze, I went up to my comfortable room but didn't sleep well that night, nor for many more to come.

20

Bangladesh: *La Condition Humaine*

Five times a day the air was filled with the cries of the mullah summoning the faithful to prayer. During the monsoon, rain pounded down with a ferocity unknown in Canada, transforming dust, feces, and garbage into mud, bringing fresh outbreaks of cholera, and worsening the already miserable condition of the people. Despairing women and children congregated daily at the gate to my house, their hands thrust through the entrance bars mutely appealing for something to eat. I looked away, aware that if I gave food to even one person, a mob of thousands would materialize and a riot would ensue. Frantic to find some way to help other than through the mission's aid program, I took to driving through the worst slums and quickly handing used clothing or food to some desperate-looking person and then fleeing back to my car before a mob could form.

Every day brought encounters with unique personalities, each with a story to tell. There were Irish and Indian nurses seeking to alleviate the suffering of the flesh, priests and nuns anxious to minister to the spirit, the occasional CIA or KGB spy trying to recruit people of influence, Canadian University Service Overseas (CUSO) volunteers, oilmen with American

Diplomatic Foreign-Policy Adviser, 1972–1998

A happy bachelor in Thailand in the spring of 1972. The Canadian government nominated me acting high commissioner to open a diplomatic mission in the newly independent Republic of Bangladesh. Since conditions in the capital, Dhaka, were chaotic, External Affairs in its wisdom decreed that I should reside in Bangkok under diplomatic cover to the local government and commute every week to Bangladesh. No one it appears had looked at an atlas and noted that the distance between the two capitals was 1,200 miles. After travelling back and forth for six months, I moved permanently to Dhaka where I should have been sent in the first place. *Author's Collection.*

As acting high commissioner to Bangladesh (far right), with Prime Minister Mujibur Rahman and Ivan Head, foreign-policy adviser to Prime Minister Pierre Trudeau. Not long afterward, rebelling army soldiers murdered the prime minister, known as the Father of the Nation. Twenty-two years later, I became foreign-policy adviser to Prime Minister Jean Chrétien. *Author's Collection.*

Despair in a refugee camp in Bangladesh in 1973. The Bangladeshis suffered greatly during their war of liberation against Pakistan in 1971. After independence, they took their revenge against the Bihari minority, who had supported the Pakistanis, by herding them by the millions into refugee camps, where their descendants remain to this day. *Author's Collection.*

In September 1975, Arthur Menzies (back to the camera), Canadian ambassador to NATO, and my boss, organizes the wedding party prior to my marriage to Marie-Jeanne in Brussels, Belgium. *Author's Collection.*

Fidel Castro meets Canadian parliamentarians at my official residence in Havana in September 1981. I'm fourth from the right. *Author's Collection.*

Shaking hands with Israeli Foreign Minister Shimon Peres, as External Affairs Minister Joe Clark looks on in March 1986. *Canadian Embassy, Tel Aviv.*

As foreign-policy adviser to Prime Minister Jean Chrétien in 1994. *Courtesy Jean-Marc Carisse.*

Here I'm taking a break during an official visit to Hanoi in November 1994. *Courtesy Jean-Marc Carisse.*

Genocide in Rwanda in the spring of 1994. Canada's General Roméo Dallaire receives the thanks of the nation from Prime Minister Chrétien and Defence Minister David Collenette in July 1994. *Courtesy Jean-Marc Carisse.*

In Ottawa in 1995 running the gauntlet. I'm on the left, with Premier Li Peng, Mrs. Li Peng, and Prime Minister Chrétien. *Courtesy Jean-Marc Carisse.*

Official talks hosted by President Boris Yeltsin for Prime Minister Chrétien at the Kremlin in October 1997. I'm on the far left near the door. *Courtesy Jean-Marc Carisse.*

Presenting diplomatic credentials: South African President Nelson Mandela and me in 1998. *Courtesy Canadian High Commission.*

President Castro with Chief of Staff Jean Pelletier and me in April 1998. *Courtesy Jean-Marc Carisse.*

accents claiming to be Canadians and attempting to talk the new government into granting them concessions to drill for gas offshore, and Soviet helicopter pilots counting the days until their assignments were over.

I met André Malraux, one of the great French intellectual figures and author of *La Condition Humaine*, one of the classics of twentieth-century literature. He spoke in aphorisms when I met him at the Alliance Française. A long-standing supporter of independence for the Muslim people of East Bengal, Malraux wore himself out following an exhausting schedule and died shortly afterward. I accompanied Lotta Hitschmanova, the legendary founder of the Unitarian Service Committee, on some of her rounds by rowboat to isolated villages. Although always surrounded by an ensemble of saffron-robed Buddhist acolytes, she interacted with the poorest of the poor in a way that maintained the dignity of donor and recipient.

I began to enjoy my posting. The Marine Club bar was my hangout on Friday nights — the beer was cheap, the music and laughter loud, and the company good. It was a place to unwind and forget the misery outside the gate; to meet new arrivals; and to plan expeditions to tea plantations in the Sylhet Hills, to refugee camps in the interior, and to major cities along the coast. There, too, we planned trips to Calcutta — surreal, polluted, ugly, overpopulated, and throbbing with life — for we all wanted to escape every so often to the world outside Bangladesh, a place where time had stood still. In Chittagong my Canadian hosts, members of a Catholic religious order implanted in the region for the past century, kept referring to the "recent" visit of Pierre Trudeau as a backpacker. He had, it turned out, been their guest a quarter century earlier.

The posting coincided with the dying years of the Vietnam War. In my liaison trips to Bangkok, the bars were filled with thousands of American servicemen on leave from the action. The mood was one of *fin de régime.* They were losing the war and no one supported them, not even their own people. Then came the American bombing campaigns of North Vietnam in December 1972 — the infamous Linebacker II Christmas bombings that killed thousands of civilians in Hanoi and which constituted the last gasp of American involvement in the war.

A half century later I can still see smallpox victims and street children; fleets of magnificent square-rigged sailing boats; a blind beggar and his caregiver waiting patiently for me to relent and give them handouts; a grizzled patriarch's giggling burka-clad teenage wives; a fierce tongue-lashing from a visiting senior officer from Ottawa for daring to question a foolish edict from headquarters; being forced to pay bribes for the smallest service; handing back a bag of black pearls to representatives of the Ismaili minority who wanted to keep me in a sympathetic frame of mind if their community was forced to seek refuge in Canada; a KGB spy who sought to entrap me; water buffalos, wooden ploughs, and the calm of village life; a rat scuttling across the floor; men and boys, hands bound behind their backs, squatting on a lurching flatbed truck as they were driven off to be shot or imprisoned; rifle fire shattering the midnight silence outside my bedroom window; shouting and people running; and people, people, and more people.

By late 1973, I had established a functioning high commission and it was time to move on. My next posting was to the Canadian delegation to NATO in Brussels, Belgium, where I witnessed the madness of the Cold War division of Europe in which a million and a half men backed by thousands of battlefield nuclear weapons faced one another across the Central European plain.

21

NATO: Dr. Strangelove

The cultural shock on arriving in Brussels in the fall of 1973 was almost as great as it had been when I first saw Dhaka. Bangladesh's capital had been poor, hot, and dirty, but teeming with people full of the vitality of their struggle for survival. Brussels was the rich capital of Europe, cloaked that dark November in thick fog and undergoing the heaviest snowfall and coldest weather in decades. The discomfort of the populace huddled indoors was made worse by a shortage of fuel resulting from the oil embargo imposed by Middle Eastern countries in the wake of the just-ended Yom Kippur Israeli-Arab war. I will never forget driving to a hotel in downtown Brussels to take part in a briefing for a visiting External Affairs minister. All traffic other than emergency vehicles and cars with diplomatic licence plates had been banned from the streets. It could have been a scene from Nevil Shute's *On the Beach* in the aftermath of a nuclear attack.

In Dhaka I had been entrusted with responsibilities many ambassadors didn't have in terms of budgets, personnel, and post programs. In Brussels I was just one of five or six first secretaries buried well down in the pecking order. In Dhaka I had worked as part of an international effort that included close collaboration with the Soviets, Hungarians, and East Germans together with the Americans, British, and Dutch in a common humanitarian goal. A quarter century of Cold War had hardened attitudes in Brussels. Warsaw Pact countries were the enemy. A million and a half men faced one another fully mobilized and ready to fight the greatest tank battle in history across the Central European plain.

Thousands of battlefield nuclear weapons on both sides were kept in a high state of readiness. Edward Teller, the fanatically anti-communist father of the hydrogen bomb who could have been a character in Stanley Kubrick's *Dr. Strangelove*, once came and scared me with his declaration that NATO would be the winner in a nuclear war with the Warsaw Pact.

I was present as the note taker in the NATO Council chamber when President Richard Nixon visited in June 1974, just two months before he was driven from office. Little deference was shown to him by the European ambassadors who muttered privately that their time was being wasted. The president, they said, was using his Brussels stop as a photo opportunity to show the American people that their leader was still a respected statesman. They didn't want to be props for an American domestic public relations exercise. We all stood when the president entered to be greeted with curiosity rather than with respect. He was smaller than I had imagined. In what was almost a caricature of the images I'd seen of him on television, his smile was fixed on a doll-like face heavily covered with makeup for the television cameras. His analysis of East-West relations was cogent, but he exuded no special magnetism. Years later, travelling with Prime Minister Chrétien, I saw the mummified corpses of Lenin in Moscow and Ho Chi Minh in Hanoi and thought of Nixon at NATO.

Henry Kissinger made an altogether different impression. An intellectual heavyweight who sounded like a European with his measured, grating, and accented English, he was the dominant Western statesman of the 1970s. Born in Germany in 1923, he immigrated to the United States to escape Hitler in 1938, served in the U.S. Army, and was educated at City College in New York and at Harvard University. His books on strategy shaped the American and NATO approach to fighting war in Europe.

When I first saw him in action in the fall of 1973, Kissinger was at the height of his international renown. He and the North Vietnamese negotiator, Le Duc Tho, had just won the Nobel Peace Prize for the agreement that allowed the United States to pull its troops out of South Vietnam. Throughout the fall of 1973 and winter of 1974, he was heavily engaged in high-profile shuttle diplomacy to separate Israeli and Arab forces following the Yom Kippur War.

As time went on, the lustre of Kissinger's accomplishments started to fade. The North Vietnamese tore up the agreement he had signed with Le Duc Tho, invaded South Vietnam, and chased the remnants of American diplomatic and military power from the country. He was also a bully. I once watched him physically push aside Canada's foreign affairs minister, Don Jamieson, when the latter tried to discuss an East Coast fishing dispute with him.

"I have no time for your eternal fish concerns," he snarled at the red-faced Jamieson, humiliating him in front of his European colleagues. Another time, during a NATO foreign ministers meeting in Ottawa, I was taking a shortcut through the narrow tunnel between the Convention Centre in the old railway station and the Château Laurier hotel. There, in the middle of the tunnel, stood Kissinger, loudly chewing out one of his aides for providing him with a text that didn't meet his standards. I tried to turn back, but an unsmiling U.S. Secret Service agent refused to let me pass, even though I was a representative of the host government. I squeezed by the hectoring Kissinger only to be blocked on the other side by another American agent. The target of Kissinger's venom and I stood quietly waiting for the verbal storm to end. I didn't know who was the more embarrassed — the aide or the Canadian witness to his humiliation.

Then, in 1974, in the highlight of my posting and my life, I met my future wife, Marie-Jeanne Rosillon, a flight attendant for Sabena. She was a Belgian born in the former Belgian Congo where her father had been a doctor, medical director for the province of Kasai, and a member of the Allied military expedition during the Second World War that trekked into Ethiopia from the south to free it from Italian rule. Marie-Jeanne had returned with her family to Belgium before the chaos that engulfed the Congo following its independence. She was only twelve when her parents passed away. Odette de Wynter, Belgium's first female notary, then took a close interest in her and became, in effect, her adoptive mother.

We got married on September 12, 1975, and Odette welcomed me into the family, dramatically improving the quality of my life. Her home, with notarial offices on the ground floor, was an inviting house with large lawns and flower gardens. Like many members of the Belgian bourgeoisie, she was well served by a devoted household staff, had a well-stocked wine cellar, and was a superb cook. Her house became our home away from home in Europe, a haven of smells, light, sounds, and tastes: the musty odour of notarial files, the fragrance of masses of freshly cut flowers, the bouquet of old Burgundy wine, the rich smell of strong coffee, the scent of apple blossoms, the golden light flooding in through the huge windows, the distinctive cooing of doves that nested under the eaves, the savour of the French-Flemish dishes that emerged twice a day from her kitchen, and the creamy succulence of Belgian chocolate to celebrate every family gathering.

In November 1976, our first child, Anne-Pascale, was born at Saint-Pierre Hospital in Brussels after a wild ride to reach it in time, the car radio blaring out the American presidential election results that would bring Jimmy Carter to the White House. Laurent would follow eleven months later at the same hospital. And after a wait of twelve years, Alain was born in an ambulance on the Ottawa Queensway, unwilling to hold off his arrival until we could reach the hospital. All three grew up making frequent visits to their Belgian grandmother, who provided stability for them in a life of constant travel around the globe.

22

The First Time I Saw Jerusalem

In September 1974, one week before my marriage to Marie-Jeanne, I received an urgent telephone call in my office at the Canadian delegation to NATO in Brussels. En route to Israel as a flight attendant with Sabena, she had been knocked unconscious by a hit to the head by a loose bulkhead door, aggravating an existing hairline fracture to her skull sustained in a car accident six months before. She was at the brain-injury section of Tel HaShomer Hospital near Tel Aviv. Could I go to Israel and sort matters out?

I left at once, arriving at Lod (later known as Ben-Gurion) Airport late on a Friday evening. Barricaded behind sandbagged counters as protection after a series of suicide terrorist attacks, the customs and immigration officials were nervous and suspicious of all incoming passengers. Emerging from the terminal building into the searing evening air, I joined a throng of people jostling and pushing to get on the bus to Tel Aviv. It was a mix of the Middle East, Eastern Europe, and New York City that greeted me when I got off at the Central Bus Station. The salty, humid Mediterranean air smelled strongly of overripe fruits and vegetables. The trash littering the road and sidewalks and the dogs scavenging from the overflowing garbage cans added atmosphere and vitality to the Levantine setting. Young entrepreneurs dipped into cauldrons of boiling water to fish out corn on the cob to sell to people hurrying to catch buses. I bought a steaming ear of corn and smothered it in butter and salt and ate it standing on the street as young men and women in uniform carrying assault rifles and pale figures dressed in black who could have come from the movie *Fiddler on the Roof* hurried by.

A friend, first secretary to the Canadian embassy in Tel Aviv, and his wife, met me the next morning and drove me to the hospital. Marie-Jeanne was crammed into a cubbyhole used to store oxygen tanks. The ward was filled with soldiers wounded earlier in the Yom Kippur War, and there was much shouting and moaning. The nurses were busy, didn't understand French, and were ignoring Marie-Jeanne. A doctor had walked into her cubbyhole, pinched her hard on the foot to check the state of her central nervous system, and walked away with a satisfied air when she screamed. Although in pain, Marie-Jeanne was desperate to leave.

I tracked down the doctor at his home and persuaded him to release her into my care. It was a simple matter to arrange medical evacuation for her on a Sabena flight out the next day. I then turned into a tourist, and headed for Jerusalem to see whether the image I held of the City of David conformed to reality. The taxi driver, an immigrant from New York, regaled me on the two-hour trip with stories of his participation in four wars. He pointed out battlefield sites, such as the Trappist monastery at Latrun, and drew attention to the wrecks of vehicles destroyed in the efforts to relieve the siege of Jerusalem in 1948. We picked up two hitchhiking soldiers encumbered with rifles and kit bags. Forbidden under Israeli military regulations to talk to strangers, they remained silent throughout the trip.

Jerusalem made an impression on me rivalled only by my first encounters with the Taj Mahal and the Parthenon on my way home at the end of my posting in Bangladesh. It was dry and clear that September day, and the light shimmered on the sixteenth-century city walls constructed by Suleiman the Magnificent. Situated on the heights between the Judean Desert and Dead Sea to the east and the relatively well-watered Judean Hills sloping down to the Mediterranean to the west, Jerusalem's location and the special translucent, almost ethereal quality of its air, I was later told, had attracted mystics and hermits throughout the ages. I spent the afternoon wandering the Christian, Jewish, Muslim, and Armenian quarters. Most of the religious sites were as depicted in our old family Bible printed in Philadelphia in 1874 and proudly proclaiming, "The Whole Embellished with Nine Hundred Illustrations, on Steel, Wood, and in Colours."

Entering the Old City by the Jaffa Gate, I made my way on foot through narrow passageways past hot ovens baking honey, pistachio, pine-nut, and almond-paste delicacies; open-air fruit, vegetable, and butcher shops selling foodstuffs to Arab housewives; coffee and tea stands frequented by old men playing dominoes; restaurants wafting out a mix of garlic and spices from falafel, hummus, and other delicious local dishes; and souvenir stores with tacky wares side by side with elegant boutiques offering expensive glassware, Jerusalem pottery, and pots and oil lamps 2,000 years old. My first stop was the Church of the Holy Sepulchre, the traditional site of Jesus's tomb. Despite its state of disrepair and its cacophonic mix of competing religious caretakers, it was an ecclesiastical refuge of shadows and flickering candles; cool, humid air and incense; priests and nuns in traditional garb; Roman, Greek, and Coptic chapels, tombs, icons, and wall hangings; and tourists — the curious and the devout. Standing under the main cupola, I tried to imagine the scene on this spot in July 1099 when fervent conquering Crusader knights prayed in blood up to their ankles after slaughtering the 30,000 Muslim and Jewish occupants of Jerusalem. Christ's tomb — the Chapel of the Holy Sepulchre — I entered with awe. An Ethiopian monk, crouching in the gloom, extended his hand in a silent quest for alms.

I then walked through the Jewish quarter, largely destroyed in the fighting in 1948 and reconstructed in Jerusalem stone when the city was retaken in 1967. The boutiques and shops were upmarket, selling expensive glassware, clothing, menorahs, and antiquities. Jewish tourists from around the world mingled with Israelis at the entrances to museums and synagogues and on the exposed ruins of the Roman city of Aelia Capitolina, built on the site of the old Jewish Jerusalem. I descended steep steps to the Western Wall where Jews have worshipped since the destruction of the Second Temple by the Roman emperor Titus almost 2,000 years ago. Then it was up again to the Haram ash-Sharif, the compound enclosing the Dome of the Rock and al-Aqsa Mosque. I followed the instructions of the attendants and removed my shoes to pay respect before entering these shrines, the third most holy to Muslims after Mecca and Medina. Then I returned to my taxi via the Armenian and Muslim Quarters, passing the spot where, fourteen years later as ambassador to Israel, I would be struck by a stone hurled from a rooftop during the First Intifada, or Palestinian uprising, of the 1980s.

The next morning I signed the release papers and went with Marie-Jeanne to the airport, bouncing around in the back of a pickup truck converted into a makeshift ambulance. A security official pulled me aside at the entrance to the tarmac to subject me to a harsh, threatening grilling before I was allowed onto the plane, which had been configured to take a stretcher. My diplomatic passport counted for nothing and neither did the presence of the embassy's first secretary, who confirmed my identity. My clothes were dumped out of my suitcase, and the reasons for my visit were disputed. My Canadian colleague ensured me the rough way I'd been treated was in no way personal — the Israeli immigration officials treated everyone the same way. External Affairs would send me there as ambassador in January 1986.

23

He Then Dismissed Us

I returned to a sombre Ottawa in July 1977, with the population still in shock over the victory of the separatist Parti Québécois in the Quebec elections the previous fall. It had been five years since I'd last lived in Canada, and the changes in my personal circumstances were profound. Gone was my carefree bachelor life. I was now thoroughly domesticated with a wife, an eight-month-old baby girl, a new baby expected in October, and a dog and cat. The cottage I'd built on the Gatineau River at Wakefield in 1970 was no longer mine. I had been forced to sell it after it nearly floated off in a flood when I was away in Bangladesh. We bought a house in the woods near Chelsea, Quebec, from where I commuted daily to the Pearson Building.

After two undistinguished years as head of officer staffing, I was assigned to the Commonwealth Caribbean Division in the summer of 1979. In the ensuing year, I completed a policy review of Canada's relations with the countries of the region and took on responsibility for managing Canada's relations with the countries of Central America, Cuba, and Haiti. It was an area in turmoil. Vicious civil wars, marked by gross violations of human rights, were raging in El Salvador and Guatemala.

The Sandinistas had just overthrown the regime of the Nicaraguan dictator Anastasio Somoza, and with Cuba's help were seeking to export their model of revolution elsewhere in the region. Panama was stable under a left-leaning military dictator, but Honduras was being sucked into the maelstrom of violence on its borders.

On instructions from the foreign minister, I visited Nicaragua to deliver a political message to the new Sandinista government: Canada wanted to be generous in the provision of aid but expected the new regime to adhere to the publicly stated principles of its revolution, which included respect for democracy and private property. I was to add that Canada wouldn't deliver a promised shipload of wheat if this commitment wasn't given.

The Canadian ambassador resident in Costa Rica, accredited to Nicaragua, briefed the Ottawa team at the Canadian embassy in San José, and we departed by air for Managua. A Hieronymus Bosch landscape of the end of the world greeted us. Rubble from an earthquake years earlier still clogged the centre of the city, and beggars scrounged for food among the ruins of the cathedral. There was evidence of a just-ended civil war everywhere: disabled cars and trucks pockmarked with bullet holes littered the sides of the roads, and windows in shops and homes were shattered. Young slogan-shouting fighters with red Sandinista scarves around their necks, looking like Garibaldi's nineteenth-century Italian revolutionaries, stopped us to check our identifications every few miles at roadblocks adorned with banners and flags proclaiming the victory of the Sandinista revolution.

We called on President Arturo Cruz, a respected former senior World Bank official, who said I could assure the Canadian government that democracy and respect for private property would be fully guaranteed by the revolutionary government. The same message was given to us by a variety of young ministers, recent idealistic recruits from the expatriate Nicaraguan community attending Ivy League universities in the United States. All said, "Please send the wheat. People here are starving." However, we still hadn't met anyone who represented the real power in the country: the Sandinista *commandantes.*

At my insistence our hosts eventually arranged a meeting with Tomás Borge, the minister of the interior. We were driven to a heavily fortified building, conducted though corridors lined with murals depicting short, dark-haired guerrillas slitting the throats of blond-haired oppressors, and into the office of the minister himself. All went well until I delicately delivered my message, including our threat to stop delivery of the shipload of wheat.

Borge's reply was unambiguous. The Sandinistas were grateful for Canada's sympathy. They wanted our aid. There was a great shortage of food, and our wheat was needed. But if Canada insisted on linking aid to adherence to the stated principles of the revolution, he told me, his voice rising, we could keep our help. Sandinistas would never be dictated to by anyone! Aid had to be given without conditions! He then dismissed us.

As I left his office, fuming, I thought he was a pompous ass. Imagine, kicking a well-meaning Canadian envoy out of his office when he came offering gifts, with just a little gratuitous advice. I told myself that this man was merely an ignorant dandy. Why else would he sport a silver-handled revolver and dress in a khaki uniform that made him look like a miniature version of Fidel Castro?

When I calmed down, I grudgingly realized the Nicaraguans wouldn't have accepted our conditions. What would my reaction have been had I been in his shoes? He was, after all, one of the original founders of the Sandinista movement and had been captured and tortured. Should I have expected someone who had spent most of the past decade hooded and in solitary confinement in a tiny cell to be sympathetic to the case I had tried to make? Should he have understood what a Western liberal democratic government really was? He had never lived under one as I had all my life. And as for myself, I had an intellectual but not a visceral understanding of what he had endured in prison, and of what Nicaraguans had suffered under half a century of Somoza's dictatorship. Our dialogue had been one of the deaf — of mutual incomprehension — and the fault wasn't all his.

I returned to Ottawa to advise the minister that in my opinion it would only be a matter of time before Nicaragua would seek to follow Cuba in establishing a form of communist dictatorship. Canada should, however, provide aid, anyway, since the basic human needs of Nicaragua's populace after so many years of war were enormous. The minister agreed and authorized a large aid program, starting off with the shipload of wheat I'd offered to Tomás Borge, but with no strings attached.

24

It Felt Good

Late one afternoon in October 1980, about five months after I became responsible for managing relations with Cuba, the director of External Affairs' security division walked into my office seeking help. He said an East German Interflug aircraft flying from Berlin to Havana had made a routine landing to refuel at Gander, Newfoundland. But as the passengers were disembarking, two Cubans, a man and a woman, broke away from the others and ran toward the Royal Canadian Mounted Police (RCMP) constable on duty to seek asylum. This wasn't unusual: two or three Cubans obtained refugee status in Canada each week from aircraft stopping over in Canada en route to Cuba from Eastern Europe. This time, however, the other passengers, all Cuban, took up the chase. The man escaped, but the woman was captured. About eighty passengers surrounded her in the transit lounge. Thirty RCMP special constables were brought in to maintain order.

What was the government to do? The airport authorities didn't believe that Canadian law applied to transit-lounge passengers and didn't want a violent confrontation between the Mounties and the passengers of the Interflug flight. There were no rules to govern cases like this, and I was just a junior director. I quickly visited the office of the External Affairs legal adviser. Did Canadian law apply to aircraft from foreign countries landing at our airports and to foreign passengers in the transit zones of airports? The answer was an unequivocal yes.

I decided to obtain the freedom of the woman. After checking with my director general, who gave me carte blanche to manage the crisis, I asked the Cuban ambassador, who by coincidence was attending a reception at the Pearson Building, to tell the Cuban passengers they had no right to hold anyone prisoner on Canadian soil. He didn't want to help, pleading that he was too busy to become involved. At the same time I maintained contact with the RCMP Security Service, the predecessor of the Canadian Security Intelligence Service (CSIS), which in turn kept in close contact with its officers at the Gander airport. With the ambassador unwilling to co-operate, I sought to enlist the support of his deputy, but the Cuban embassy refused to give me his unlisted home telephone number. That was no problem. The Security Service knew where he was and put me on the telephone with him.

Initially reluctant to become involved, he eventually agreed to speak by telephone to the senior Cuban among the passengers and tell them to co-operate with the authorities in Gander. I stayed on the line to confirm that he would do as he had promised. Perhaps he thought that I couldn't understand Spanish, but he was mistaken. Far from making an effort to encourage the passengers to co-operate with the Canadian authorities in Gander, he agreed they should continue their efforts to force the asylum seeker back onto the aircraft. He then told me a blatant lie — that the woman, of her own free will, wanted to return to Cuba.

I spoke to the airport manager, saying that he should interview the woman alone. If she said she wanted to leave, then of course she could do so; otherwise, she should be allowed to remain. The manager eagerly agreed, and I heard no more for over an hour. The RCMP Security Service then called me from Gander to say that the airport manager had disregarded my instructions. There had been no interview and the other passengers had forced the woman to return to the aircraft. It had taxied to the end of the runway and was awaiting clearance for takeoff. What should be done?

I told them to block the runway with police cars and force the pilot to disembark the woman. I had no idea whether I had authority to issue such an order, but it felt good. The police obeyed with alacrity, sending two squad cars out with lights flashing to take up positions on the tarmac in front of the aircraft. The door opened, a truck with mobile stairs pulled up, the woman emerged, and was interviewed alone.

Of course, she wanted political asylum in Canada. In the evening news coverage, it was reported that the Canadian government had acted with dispatch to help a woman seeking freedom in Canada. The minister and senior management and my director general were happy. I was well aware, however, that if matters had turned out differently, there would have been the devil to pay. Jim Bartleman the hero would have been Jim Bartleman the goat.

My personnel officer told me I was to be offered an ambassadorial posting in the summer of 1981 either to Cuba or Peru. The choice was mine. My wife and I were delighted. I was forty-one and hadn't expected to receive the call for years to come. Peru and Cuba were both appealing, but we opted for Cuba because it provided Marie-Jeanne and me with more time to spend with our children. We hoped the Cubans would overlook the little incident at Gander and agree to my nomination. They did.

Part Three

Ambassadorial Postings, 1981–1994

From 1981 to 1990, I served abroad as ambassador to two hot spots: Cuba and Israel. From 1990 to 1994, I was ambassador and permanent representative to the North Atlantic Council of NATO, at that time dealing with some of the most volatile international issues of the period, including the implosion of the Soviet Union and Yugoslavia and the First Gulf War. From 1998 until my retirement in 2002, in a change of pace, I was high commissioner to South Africa, high commissioner to Australia, and ambassador to the European Union.

25

Cuba: The Dead Fly

At the Havana embassy we were used to receiving eminent Canadians from the government, the private sector, and the artistic world coming to Cuba to do business, promote trade, enjoy a holiday, shoot a movie, or perform in cultural events. Headquarters would advise us of the impending visit and work with us to arrange appropriate programs. The visits usually took place without a hitch. I was thus happy when headquarters sent me a cryptic message saying Canada's minister of agriculture was including Cuba in a business trip he was making to Latin America. True, it was no secret in the Foreign Service that this particular minister wasn't fond of Canadian diplomats. But I wasn't unduly worried. I had always established good relations with visiting dignitaries, relying on hard work and meticulous preparation to ensure the success of their missions.

But there is a first for everything and the visit got off to a poor start. The plane was late, the sky was overcast, the air heavy, and the heat oppressive. My shirt was glued to my body by the humidity, and salty perspiration flowed into my eyes and fogged up my glasses. My wife and I stood on the melting tarmac with the Cuban minister of agriculture making small talk and scanning the horizon as time dragged on. Eventually, the Canadian government plane circled the airport and came in for a landing. A scowling minister, his wife, and a glum group of aides clambered out, giving the impression they had been sent against their will to carry out some disagreeable task. There were no apologies to the welcoming minister for the late arrival, only a grunt for greetings and the party left for the official guest house put at their disposal as a courtesy by the Cuban government.

One hour after arrival the minister emerged from his suite screaming at me: "I have never been put in such a dump! There's no cold water! What sort of useless, idiotic ambassador are you, anyway!" The tirade went on and on with much unprintable language, swollen veins on his forehead, fist shaking, and threats. He had seen a dead fly in his bathroom and the cold water had run out when the other members of the delegation had taken showers. As he yelled at me, I stood, open-jawed, thinking how I could possibly have gone wrong. I distinctly remembered inspecting his quarters the day before to make sure it was clean and in order. Either through gross incompetence I had missed the dead fly, or the fly had thoughtlessly died after I left. Either way it was my fault.

To my shame I realized I hadn't turned on all the taps in the building before I'd checked the availability of cold water in his bathroom. More likely, however, the minister had gotten his faucets mixed up, turning on the one marked C, thinking it meant *cold* when, in fact, it meant *caliente*, or "hot" in English. It didn't matter; I was still to blame for not being in his bathroom to guide his hand to the right tap.

In the circumstances, I wanted to follow the golden rule adopted by all public servants who wished eventual promotion when confronted with enraged politicians: contritely accept the blame and hope the offended one will forgive and move on. Unfortunately, I didn't have time to apologize. The minister stormed out the door. He didn't even wait for the briefing in which I had intended to tell him not to drink the water from the taps, which could cause diarrhea, but to use the bottled water set aside for the purpose.

We then left to call on a senior representative of the Cuban government in his office. The conversation was frosty. The minister was still furious and in no mood to talk business. The Cuban minister hesitantly noted that Cuba had been importing $500 million in Canadian products each year and paying cash. Could the minister use his influence in Ottawa to persuade the Canadian government to extend a line of credit to facilitate this healthy trade?

The minister ignored the question. The only thing on his mind was the fly in his bathroom and the lack of cold water. He gave the hapless Cuban a severe dressing-down, and we exited to prepare for our next event — the welcoming dinner at the government convention centre. My wife and I left in our car and the minister and his spouse followed behind in another.

More disaster awaited. The Cuban Ministry of the Interior, in a fit of pique, had arrested my driver on a trumped-up charge just days before the visit and had sent a member of its own service to replace him. I had rejected the ministry's man, obviously a spy, but had been forced to find a replacement from among my existing staff. I was to discover in short order that my new driver, promoted from his job as a gardener, was actually blind in one eye. In retrospect, I don't think the sight in the other eye was very good, either. Approaching the convention centre with the minister following behind, the gardener/chauffeur misjudged the entrance to the driveway, rolled over the lawn, hit a low-lying concrete barrier, tore out the muffler, and impaled the radiator on an iron post. The minister glanced at us with disgust as he was driven past. My wife and I abandoned our car, steam pouring from its radiator, and slunk into the building wondering what would happen next.

The minister's mood improved as he drank rum drink after rum drink as the evening progressed. Then I learned from a sympathetic aide why he was making me suffer. Before flying to Havana, the minister and his delegation had made an official visit to Colombia. The embassy in Bogotá had rented two aircraft to fly the party to a remote part of the country. When the visit was over, the embassy officers boarded their aircraft and left for the Colombian capital. The minister and his party boarded their aircraft, which broke down. The Canadians with the minister spoke no Spanish and the Colombians spoke no English. It was some time before they could leave, and the minister was furious and determined to wreak his revenge on the first member of External Affairs he found. I was the sacrificial lamb.

This insight didn't comfort me. I was similarly made uneasy by the minister's insistence that I join him in drinking a large glass of fiery Cuban liqueur after the meal. I declined because I have little tolerance for alcohol and the Cuban brew was deadly rotgut. The minister lifted his glass, downed the concoction in one swallow, looked me in the eye, and said, "This will separate the men from the boys."

I barely slept that night and presented myself early the next morning at the guest house to prepare for the day ahead. When the minister staggered into the dining room, his face was green. *Now,* I thought, *we see who's the boy and who's the man.* Having drunk copious quantities of water from the tap in his room to deal with the tremendous thirst of his hangover and been sick all night, he asked whether the water was fit to drink. I dodged the question. He started to berate me, but his wife told him to calm down. A senior aide then took over, embarrassing my wife with a liberal use of four-letter words and ordering me to get my act together or else!

We departed in a convoy of ten vehicles for a tour of a giant showcase dairy farm deep in the countryside. Three of the cars provided by the Cubans, all in poor mechanical condition, broke down en route, stranding members of the delegation on the side of the road. I was, of course, blamed. We visited the cows, made the usual appreciative noises to indicate our admiration for this agricultural triumph of the revolution, and proceeded to Varadero where we were joined in a beachside guest house by the members of the party abandoned on the side of the road.

I had a talk with the aide, who apologized to my wife but not to me for using foul language. He continued to complain, however, refusing to accept the accommodation arrangements made by the Cubans and saying that his room was too small for a man of his status. To escape the poisonous atmosphere, my wife and I gave him our room and moved in with our Cuban escort officers in a nearby guest house. The next day, when we rejoined the ministerial delegation, a junior aide sidled up to me and said quietly, "There is a god."

The room we had given up to keep the peace had been infested with fleas. The senior aide who had taken our room had suffered all night, was covered in welts, and whimpered throughout breakfast. Fortunately, another aide was an expert bird-caller. He kept the minister distracted and amused with an impressive display of cooing, whistling, and chirping that drowned out the snivelling of his colleague. Returning to Havana, my wife and I hosted a reception for the Cubans, but Fidel Castro, obviously unhappy with all the complaining, didn't put in an appearance and everyone went home. Around eleven at night, however, Castro changed his mind and sent word that he would visit the minister at the Cuban guest house. Despite his unhappiness at having to receive the president so late in the evening, the minister couldn't say no. An unsmiling Castro greeted him on arrival and looked around to confirm that all was in order.

Cuba, he said, tried to do its best to treat its visitors well. A developing country, however, couldn't offer the same facilities to its guests as Canada could. The minister responded saying that if he had known how poorly maintained his accommodations would be, he would have brought his (expletives deleted) tools. Castro wasn't amused.

The luncheon around the pool at the official residence on the last day was a sullen, silent affair. The minister and his wife sat at one end of the terrace and everyone else — the disgraced — at the other. The minister and his party then boarded their aircraft with a visible sense of relief. They hadn't enjoyed their sojourn in Fidel's socialist paradise any more than I had enjoyed receiving them. With a bleak smile, the minister promised he would write a letter of complaint to External Affairs about my poor performance, adding thoughtfully that this was only to help me do a better job next time.

He was a man of his word, sending a letter to the external affairs minister about the lack of cold water and the dead fly in the washroom of the Cuban guest house, saying I was to blame for these great hardships that had ruined his visit. However, the matter wasn't mentioned to me when I returned to Ottawa.

26

Cuba: Poisoning Zaka

Despite the apparent favour shown to me by Fidel Castro during our posting in Cuba from 1981 to 1983, the Cuban ministry of interior subjected me to constant harassment. Shortly after I arrived in Cuba, a general in the Ministry of the Interior (MININT), whose cover was that of a senior official in the tourism department, asked me to override Ottawa's objections and issue him a visa to visit Canada as a favour. This I refused to do. He was furious, as was his boss. I introduced myself to the minister of the interior at an official function sometime later. "I know you," he said, turning his back on me.

The first attempt to compromise me was farcical. One evening the telephone rang. Still unused to ambassadorial conduct, I answered it, rather than wait for the butler to do so. A woman with a sultry voice was on the line. She had seen me at an official function and wanted to know me better. Could we arrange a discreet meeting? I wouldn't be disappointed. My wife need never know. The next evening the telephone rang again and I answered. The caller had a supply of gold. He had no means of getting it out of the country. I could become rich if only I would meet him quietly and take it off his hands for a modest price. The third call, the following evening, was from a man. He had seen me, and I was so handsome. He had fallen in love with me and we just had to meet. I gave up answering the telephone, though I often wondered what would have been on offer in a fourth call.

Things then became nasty. One morning at the beginning of our second year the Cuban cooks and cleaners employed by the ten other Canadian families at the embassy were either thrown into jail or resigned without warning. Someone nailed a dead rat to the door of the commercial officer's house. My colleagues at the embassy were besieged by telephone threats and insults. The first secretary called to say that his dog had been poisoned and was dead. I checked our dog, Zaka, a beloved member of our family who had been with us since she'd been a pup. She had been poisoned and was dying. We rushed her to a veterinarian, who pumped out her stomach and kept her alive for the time being. I then raced to the Foreign Ministry and demanded to see the director for North America, a former ambassador to Canada.

My message was blunt: "Call off your goons!" He was taken by surprise and grumbled that someone was trying to destroy Canada's relations with Cuba. Within minutes of my return home, a Cuban government veterinarian was at the door to provide follow-up care. The Cuban staff reported for work later the same day. The harassing calls to my staff stopped on cue. I shipped Zaka to my parents in Canada in the hope that Canadian veterinarians could restore her to health. My father, who met her at Toronto airport, was shocked and saddened by what he saw. Her hair had fallen off in large patches, her kidneys were damaged, and she could barely walk. Within six months she was dead, and the entire family was in tears. I never learned why the Ministry of the Interior acted that day as it did but was deeply disappointed that External Affairs refused to complain to the Cubans. My wife and I could hardly wait for our posting to end.

27

Israel: A Shot to the Head

On December 8, 1987, a year after I arrived in Tel Aviv as ambassador, an Israel Defense Forces tank transporter collided with a civilian car filled with Palestinian workers, killing four. In a spontaneous uprising, the children and youth of Gaza and the West Bank, ignoring pleas from their parents not to put themselves in harm's way, poured into the streets to confront Israeli soldiers and police. In response, the Israelis closed the borders to the occupied territories, placed the areas under curfew, and moved in reinforcements. Defence Minister Yitzhak Rabin, on a fundraising drive in the United States, thought it would soon be over and didn't return to take control of the armed forces until late in the month. By that time the fire was out of control. The world press congregated at flashpoints to watch the confrontations between children and soldiers. The New Year arrived and the unequal conflict continued unabated. Raw emotion became the stuff of everyday life.

My wife and I often went to Yad Vashem, the museum devoted to the Holocaust in Jerusalem — it was an essential stop for Canadian visitors to Israel. The piles of shoes and clothing from death chambers, the ashes of thousands under a slab of black stone, and the memorials to millions of slaughtered Jewish children expressed a message no words could convey about the roots of Israeli psychology. Many of our neighbours were Holocaust survivors. All had lived through a succession of wars with their Arab neighbours. Many had fought in these conflicts. Some had lost family members. Even those who recognized logically that the violence of the First Intifada was confined to stone-throwing in the occupied territories instinctively looked upon it as another existential threat to their survival.

This period marked the low point for me personally in an emotionally draining posting. I listened, fascinated by the fanaticism of Palestinians and Israelis alike as they insisted that God, history, and justice were on their side only. My efforts to host encounters to which I invited Israelis and Palestinians from their respective peace camps were complete fiascos, with supposedly moderate individuals shouting abuse at one another over the dinner table. In Hebron, Nablus, and a dozen other Palestinian communities, I saw Palestinians, some as young as five or six, dare Israeli soldiers to shoot them, and they often got their wish. The following is an excerpt from my diary of January 23, 1988.

> For the past six weeks, I have been waking up with a sick feeling. My worst moment so far was when I found out Israeli soldiers had beaten to death the mentally handicapped son of our former Palestinian gardener in Gaza who hadn't understood their order to bring to a halt his donkey cart. The toll to date is 36 Palestinians dead, hundreds injured, many seriously, a disproportionate number children, against on the Israeli side of one broken jaw and several superficial wounds. Defence Minister Rabin has directed the army with public fanfare to pick up protestors, to tie their hands behind their backs, break their bones with clubs, and let them go. What has this country come to if the systematic clubbing of men, women, and children is public policy? As always after encounters like these, I asked myself basic questions, none of which have good answers. Why have organized religions arising from the Judeo-Christian-Muslim tradition led to so much bloodshed and suffering? To hatred, torture, and killings down through the ages?

We were invited to a dinner the other night by an Israeli couple with whom we had become friends. We were the only non-Israelis present. The others were upwardly mobile Israelis — a cross-section of immigrants and the Israeli-born. A recent British immigrant, a man, asked me in anguish across the table: "How can I send my son to the army? We didn't come to Israel for this! Beating and clubbing people at the direction of the state?" The hostess, from her place at the head of the table, screamed at him: "What did you expect? They want to drive us into the sea." Someone else said: "Where would we go? The first speaker didn't give up. "Where are our Jewish values? His wife attempted to calm him. The other guests took him to task. Marie-Jeanne looked at me, clearly wanting to go home. An entirely unpleasant evening.

Can a state that does not, for whatever reason, accord equal rights to a minority, hostile or friendly, call itself democratic? Will not power corrupt in the classic sense and the institutions and instincts of the majority be degraded? Why don't citizen soldiers refuse orders to beat children with clubs? How can soldiers raised in a democratic society kill a stranger in a crowd of demonstrators with a shot to the head to deter others? What psychological effect will treating Palestinians as demonized Others have on idealistic young Israelis? What role should friendly outside countries like Canada adopt? Should we judge Israel on the standards of a Western democracy? On the standards of Third World autocracy? What criteria should we use? Canadian governments in their foreign-policy pronouncements have tried to hold other countries to account whenever they violated universal human rights and values. Should the Israelis be exempted because of their history and geopolitical circumstances? Because they are friends? The answers are self-evident.

My visits to the occupied territories became dangerous. The Palestinians vowed to punish anyone, diplomats included, who violated their self-imposed strikes. Israeli soldiers looked at us suspiciously, clubs in hand, as we drove through West Bank villages and witnessed long lineups of children and youth, squatting on the ground, blindfolded, their hands tied with plastic handcuffs, waiting for their collective punishment to begin. Young Palestinians hit me with a stone hurled by a slingshot in a refugee camp despite the presence by my side of Palestinian elders. I escaped with a sore arm thanks to my heavy winter coat. Another time someone hurled a boulder at me the size of a grapefruit from a rooftop when I was escorting members of Canada's National Defence College through Jerusalem. It would have killed me had it hit me in the head; it hit my leg at an angle, leaving me with a limp but no lasting damage.

I became used to Palestinians throwing stones at my car, but usually they just dented the body or missed altogether. My luck changed. One Sunday afternoon, entering East Jerusalem with Marie-Jeanne, a gang of masked youths ambushed us, hurling rocks the size of oranges and caving in the side of the vehicle with thunderous blows. By some miracle, they missed the windows and we were just shaken up. On the same weekend, the back windows of my military adviser's Jeep were smashed as he travelled in Gaza. Alarmed, headquarters shipped us an old armoured car from its storage site at the Canadian embassy in Ankara, Turkey. It came armed with a launcher for smoke grenades fixed to the rear, a case of grenades in the trunk, windows that wouldn't open, and glass so thick that the view outside was like peering through the bottom of an empty Coca-Cola bottle. It did, however, allow us to drive through riots with impunity. The sound of rocks bouncing off armour became no more worrying than gravel hitting the old car of my youth on Muskoka's dirt roads.

Controversy broke out in Canada on the Israeli handling of the intifada. There were demonstrations by supporters on both sides, editorial pronouncements in the major newspapers, and questions in the House of Commons. Prime Minister Brian Mulroney and Foreign Minister Joe Clark squared off, the former saying he believed the Israeli armed forces were acting with restraint and the latter condemning Israeli tactics. Every visitor from Canada — ministers of the Crown, journalists, tourists, business people, and religious leaders — had strong opinions on the confrontation that they expected me to share. Few Canadian ambassadors, I believe, have ever been exposed to such pressure to take sides on an issue that polarized Canadian public opinion. I coordinated the flow of information to Ottawa, providing my own views and those of my team. Israeli and Palestinian journalists, other diplomats, senior Israeli military officers, members of the Israeli Knesset, senior figures such as former foreign minister Abba Eban and Jerusalem mayor Teddy Kollek, provided us with their perspectives, complementing our visits to the conflict zone.

The International Committee of the Red Cross was a particularly valuable source of reliable information. Every two weeks or so the director would drop by my office and brief me on what his staff had learned during their regular visits to the prisons where Palestinians were being held. I wasn't sure Ottawa really wanted to hear what the Red Cross told me about widespread Israeli mistreatment and torture of its prisoners, but I was issued instructions to call on Rabin to complain about Israeli tactics. Although not a member of the centre-right party Likud, Rabin was a hard-liner with dirty hands, having taken part in the ethnic cleansing of Palestinians, in which hundreds of villagers were shot after the 1948 War of Independence, and in the expansion of settlements in the West Bank in the 1970s and 1980s. He glowered and asked me whether Ottawa would prefer Israel to kill demonstrators rather than beat them. He showed me the door, saying Canada's concerns were of no interest to him.

Delegations of Canadian parliamentarians arrived to assess the situation for themselves. The first, in February 1987, was a fact-finding mission from the House of Commons Standing Committee on Foreign Affairs, determined to come up with objective truth on a difficult, complex, and controversial matter. The Israelis co-operated in arranging a series of briefings in Israel, and the embassy arranged a tour of refugee camps in Gaza and the West Bank under the auspices of the United Nations. The final session with senior Israeli officials at the Foreign Ministry was a stormy affair. The Canadians returned from the camps filled with indignation and ready to criticize the tactics of the Israel Defense Forces and Shin Bet. The Foreign Ministry staff robustly defended their security institutions, and the debate degenerated into a shouting match.

Determined to witness Israeli-Palestinian confrontations first-hand, several parliamentarians seemed overly interested in the novelty of watching an actual violent conflict and seeing the resulting human suffering. I was ill-at-ease, acutely aware that a fine line could be drawn between visiting victims for the purpose of bearing witness and engaging in disaster tourism sightseeing to obtain thrills from observing for themselves what live ammunition and rubber bullets could do to human flesh. After all, they had officials from the Canadian embassy as guides and were in no physical danger from either Palestinians or Israelis.

Visiting refugee camps, they watched from a safe distance the daily deadly ritual of young boys throwing stones at soldiers who shot rubber bullets or live rounds at them in return. One parliamentarian even remained over in a camp hoping he would catch an Israeli patrol abusing Palestinians. In Gaza, visiting a clinic filled with the wounded, another parliamentarian publicly berated a young Palestinian doctor, who had taken a break from his duties to brief us, for smoking a cigarette. In a patronizing tone, she told the young man — who was working twenty-four hour shifts for little or no pay, caring for the injured — that he was a poor example for his people.

Several spent the entire visit drunk, consuming enormous quantities of beer and whiskey in a hospitality suite I'd unwisely set up for them in their hotel. I was breathing a sigh of relief as their bus pulled out of the driveway to return them to the Allenby Bridge to cross to Jordan when the vehicle lurched to a stop. Members of the delegation piled out and ran by me without a word, returning several minutes later with all the remaining booze from the hospitality suite. "It's a long drive to the border!" they cried as they boarded the bus.

* * *

In September 1990, the undersecretary telephoned to tell me I was being cross-posted to become ambassador to the North Atlantic Council of NATO. True to form, Israel was once again caught up in a crisis when we took our leave in November. It was three months after Iraq's invasion of Kuwait, allied preparations to push the Iraqis back were well advanced, and the Israeli government had already issued gas masks to the public.

No one doubted that when the fighting started, Iraq would hit Israel hard with its arsenal of missiles.

On the flight to Brussels, my memories were a collage of chaotic images: blood-red azaleas growing wild on Mount Carmel in the early spring; white blossoms on almond trees on the Judean Hills; Jerusalem in the early morning seen from the Mount of Olives; the Muslim call to prayer resounding throughout the Old City; empty highways and full synagogues on Yom Kippur; fierce, exhilarating Mediterranean winter storms lashing our cliffside home; fishing with the children at a kibbutz in northern Israel with the dull thud of artillery firing into Lebanon off in the distance; the smell of tear gas; traffic jams in Tel Aviv; an offer of camels for our daughter; Passover dinners; feasts of lamb; little old ladies barging into grocery store lineups ahead of me; oranges in Gaza; injured children from both sides in their hospital beds; and the eyes … the eyes of the fanatics, the eternally optimistic, the duplicitous, the fearful, the cynics, the saints, the resolute, and the dying.

A quarter century has passed since I last saw Israel. The First Intifada, which had started in December 1987, came to a conclusion in 1993 when secret negotiations in Norway resulted in a framework to end the Israeli-Palestinian conflict. A short-lived period of hope ensued. Yitzhak Rabin, who had set the army on the demonstrators in 1987, became a leader for peace. In November 1993, while serving as foreign-policy adviser to Prime Minister Jean Chrétien, I met Rabin at a small working dinner hosted by the prime minister at 24 Sussex Drive. In late October 1994, two weeks before Rabin's assassination in Tel Aviv by a right-wing fanatic, I accompanied the prime minister when he called on him at the Israeli mission to the United Nations in New York. The Israeli leader had aged perceptively and his raspy voice was unchanged, but he was smiling — something I had never seen him do in my five years in Israel — and confident that the Israeli people would support him as he moved to implement the Oslo Accords. His death would end the best chance for peace with the Palestinians since the establishment of the State of Israel.

28

Khirbet Khizeh and Obagawanung

Khirbet Khizeh and Obagawanung are villages that no longer exist — the people who used to live there have been ethnically cleansed. Khirbet Khizeh was a Palestinian village within the redrawn borders of Israel after the 1948 War of Independence. The village's name is the title of a novella written by Yizhar Smilansky, the godfather of modern Hebrew literature, who served as a soldier in the Israeli army in 1948. The novella describes a day in the life of a unit of the Israel Defense Forces clearing Khirbet Khizeh of its Palestinian population to make room for Jewish immigrants building the new Israel. It was published in 1949 and is still studied in Israeli schools.

Obagawanung was an Ojibwa community located within the village limits of what would become Port Carling where I spent my boyhood and youth. Chief Pegamegabow sent a petition dated January 1862 to Lord Monck, governor general of British North America, to let his people keep their homes rather than be removed to make way for settlers from overseas. The crown rejected the chief's appeal, and it is now just one of many similar documents forgotten in Library and Archives Canada.

Excerpt from *Khirbet Khizeh* by Yizhar Smilansky

True, it all happened a long time ago, but it has haunted me ever since. I sought to drown it out with the din of passing time, to diminish its value, to blunt its edge with the rush of daily life, and I even, occasionally, managed a sober shrug, managed to see that the whole thing had not been so bad after all, congratulating myself on my patience, which is, of course, the brother of true wisdom. But sometimes I would shake myself again, astonished at how easy it had been to be seduced, to be knowingly led astray and join the great general mass of liars — that mass compounded of crass ignorance, utilitarian indifference, and shameless self-interest — and exchange a single great truth for the cynical shrug of a hardened sinner. I saw that I could no longer hold back, and although I hadn't even made up my mind where it would end, it seemed to me that, in any case, instead of staying silent, I should, rather, start telling the story.

Obagawanung by Chief Pegamegabow

[Father], We the Indians known as the Muskoka band of the Ojibwa tribe living at our village of Obagawanung, being in the straits between Lakes Rosseau and Muskoka, desire to convey through you to our Great Mother, Queen Victoria, the renewal of our dutiful and affectionate loyalty. Father, we are in trouble and we come to you to help us out. Father, this place is beautiful in our eyes and we found we could not leave it. Father, many winters have passed since we settled here and began to cultivate our gardens. We have good houses and large gardens where we raise much corn and potatoes. We live by hunting and taking furs. We wish you could send someone to our Council to make Treaty with us … and our land here can be pointed out … and reserved to us. We hope you will grant the wish of your Red Children, and do it soon, because the whites are coming in close to us and we are afraid that their surveyors will soon lay out our lands here into lots.

When I read *Khirbet Khizeh*, I think of the people of Obagawanung. And when I read the petition of Chief Pegamegabow, the people who once lived in Khirbet Khizeh come to mind.

29

The Balkans: You Don't Understand

In February 1991, the Swedish ambassador and his wife invited Marie-Jeanne and me to dinner at their elegant Brussels residence. There were perhaps eighteen of us around the table, drawn largely from countries where our hosts had served in the past, including Yugoslavia. The conversation was animated and our hosts regaled us with funny stories of their diplomatic experiences in the capitals of their guests. When the ambassador turned to Yugoslavia, no amusing anecdote came readily to mind. Instead, he toasted the Yugoslav people and expressed a pious hope that the civil war that had just started in that country would soon end. Everyone, except the Yugoslav envoy and his wife, raised their glasses.

"You don't understand," the wife of the Yugoslav said. "You just don't understand — the first blood has been shed. No one can now stop the killing." After an embarrassing pause — no one wanted to talk about serious matters at such an elegant dinner — the cheery conversation resumed around the table. But I never forgot her stricken face. I would see it before me in the coming years each time I participated in ineffectual NATO debates on the crisis.

The burgeoning crisis in Yugoslavia in 1989 and 1990 had initially been overshadowed by events occurring elsewhere in Europe. Everyone assumed that Yugoslavia would follow the path of Poland, Hungary, and other communist-led countries and opt for liberal democracy. The renaming of the Serbian Communist Party as the Serbian Socialist Party by the Yugoslav leader Slobodan Milošević in 1989 was seen as a step in the right direction. Milošević's suppression of the rights of the two largest minority populations in Serbia, the Hungarians of Vojvodina and the Albanians of Kosovo, passed almost unnoticed. This was possibly because the Albanians, the larger of the two minorities, were Muslim and not regarded by many Western Europeans as authentically European.

By 1991 the nationalist forces tearing Yugoslavia apart had become uncontrollable. Slovenia, followed closely by Croatia, reacted strongly against Milošević's efforts to impose Serbian hegemony over the Yugoslav Federation. Slovenia acted first, declaring independence and driving the Yugoslav army from its territory in June. This wasn't a major setback for Milošević, since there were few ethnic Serbs resident in Slovenia. Croatia's declaration of independence, however, was another matter. Full-scale fighting immediately broke out between Croatians and the sizable Serbian minority, supported by the Yugoslav army now reduced to its Serbian rump. Seizing the heavy weapons stored at the various military garrisons in the area, the Serb side inflicted severe punishment on the Croats, reducing villages and towns to rubble and occupying all areas where the Serbs were a local majority. In a foretaste of what was to come, both sides engaged in massive human-rights violations, including the indiscriminate killing of civilians.

Meanwhile, at NATO headquarters, we exchanged views on the deteriorating situation in the Balkans at our weekly meetings of the North Atlantic Council but avoided engagement. Civil war in Yugoslavia constituted no direct threat to the security of member states. The issues were, moreover, simply too hot to touch, since they raised old animosities among the allies. France, in the early days of the crisis, was strongly sympathetic to the Serbs, recalling its special links to Serbia dating back to the First World War. Greece, sharing a common religion with the Serbs and having historically close ties to Belgrade, believed Serbia could do no wrong. Germany, remembering its bloody conflict with Tito's partisans during the Second World War, was hostile to Serbia; it also had a long memory, unable to forget its First World War alliance with the Austro-Hungarian Empire, and strongly supported the independence aspirations of Slovenia and Croatia, which had been part of that empire.

The United Kingdom, with many of its front-line troops tied down in Northern Ireland, was afraid of finding itself caught in an insoluble Balkan quagmire and didn't even want to discuss the matter. The United States, in the words of Secretary of State James Baker, "didn't have a dog in this fight." Washington, suffering from Gulf War fatigue, was of the view that the Europeans should shoulder the responsibility for managing and resolving the Yugoslav crisis. Italy, a long-standing rival of the former Yugoslavia for influence in the Mediterranean and still resentful over the outcome of its post–Second World War disputes with Tito over Trieste, was suspicious of all the warring parties in the former Yugoslavia.

With NATO unwilling to act, the problem of Yugoslavia, by default, came to rest on the shoulders of the European Community. The Europeans were initially hopeful that they could handle the crisis without NATO and the United States; some countries even regarded the challenge as a means of demonstrating to their publics and to the world that Europe had come of age. Negotiations were well advanced among its members in that summer of 1991 to transform the European Community, with its focus on economic integration and political co-operation, into the European Union, with a single currency, full economic and monetary union, and foreign- and defence-policy integration. It was expected that the text codifying these gains would be incorporated into a treaty to come into effect in November 1993.

President François Mitterrand of France and Chancellor Helmut Kohl of Germany provided the leadership to drive ahead the construction of the European Union. They and many European leaders assumed that, with the collapse of communism, the evolving European structures would be able to handle the crises afflicting their neighbourhood, including in the former Yugoslavia. It was their belief, for example, that if moral suasion didn't work, they could always mount a peacekeeping mission to keep order under the auspices of the European Community. They couldn't have been more mistaken.

On July 1 the Netherlands assumed the presidency of the European Council, the supreme political body of the new Europe, whose leadership rotated among member states every six months and was responsible, *inter alia*, for coordinating European foreign-policy initiatives. The Dutch foreign minister, Hans van den Broek, representing the presidency, visited Belgrade and Zagreb to urge the warring parties to negotiate a peaceful settlement to their dispute, telling them that their chances for closer association with the European Community would be compromised if they didn't behave in a civilized manner. He obtained agreement for a three-month ceasefire and for the deployment of a European Commission Monitoring Mission, composed of several hundred unarmed observers, to supervise the truce. The Dutch were soon disillusioned; nationalist passion outweighed any economic incentive to compromise, and fierce fighting resumed. Henry Wynaendts, a senior Dutch diplomat who had been entrusted by the European Community to supervise the ceasefire, came to brief us at NATO, still shaken from a close brush with death when Croatian gunners had opened fire on his aircraft, paying no attention to its markings. His mission was in ruins.

Lord Carrington, former British foreign secretary and secretary general of NATO, was brought out of retirement and thrown into the breach. He organized a meeting in Geneva with the leaders of the opposing sides, who agreed to a ceasefire; it was never implemented. The United Nations Security Council became involved for the first time, calling for an embargo on the delivery of weapons and military equipment, but it had no means of enforcing its decree. Finally, U.N. Secretary-General Javier Pérez de Cuéllar appointed Cyrus Vance, the former American secretary of state, as his personal envoy to work with Lord Carrington.

The European Community and the United Nations, backed up by the crisis-management facilities of the Conference on Security and Co-operation in Europe, were now involved, yet the situation continued to degenerate. NATO, for its part, stood aloof, taking no action other than to issue press releases, metaphorically wringing its hands, condemning the violence, and calling for a negotiated solution. I recall listening to the perfunctory debate on Yugoslavia at the November 1991 NATO summit in Rome. As we met, the Serbs were bombarding Dubrovnik, a UNESCO

Heritage Site less than two hours away by air, and couldn't have cared less for the toothless communiqués issued by Presidents George H.W. Bush and François Mitterrand and the other leaders of the most powerful alliance in world history.

The conflict then spread to Bosnia. German Foreign Minister Hans-Dietrich Genscher precipitated the descent into the abyss by threatening to take unilateral action and recognize Slovenia and Croatia by Christmas 1991 if the European Community didn't do so itself. Unwilling to upset Germany in the wake of the signature of the Maastricht Treaty, the countries of the European Community fell into line. Canada and the United States with sizable Croatian immigrant populations followed suit. President Alija Izetbegović of Bosnia had no choice but to declare his constituent republic independent following a referendum boycotted by the Serb minority. A civil war was then ignited among the Serbs, Croats, and Muslims of the new country that would lead to hundreds of thousands of people killed and millions driven into exile.

30

The Balkans: Dodging a Bullet

By the summer of 1993, the Muslims, Croats, and Serbs in the former Yugoslavia were butchering one another — men, women, and children — indiscriminately. Warlords and criminals on all sides preyed on the weak, even extorting protection money from members of their own sides. In the most outrageous case, a Muslim warlord in the Sarajevo area combined fighting Serbs with running a smuggling operation and charging exorbitant fees for the safe passage of aid supplies to his own people. Dirty tricks, such as the shelling of one's own civilians by the Muslim leadership in Sarajevo and blaming the Serbs before the world press, became commonplace. But by this time the Serbs were clearly branded in the public mind as the aggressors, and there was growing support for having the international community intervene in the war on the side of the Muslims. Within NATO, opinion had also shifted. France was no longer on the side of Belgrade and only Greece was prepared to defend unconditionally Serbia's actions.

The United States, unwilling to commit ground forces to a war in which humanitarian rather than national security interests were at stake, was prodded by its public to take action. Washington began advocating lifting the U.N. sanctions that prevented the parties to the conflict from arming themselves, argued for providing large-scale assistance to the Muslims, and promoted intervention using air power against the Serbs. Those countries in NATO — Canada, France, Britain, Spain, the Netherlands, Belgium, and Luxembourg — that were contributing troops to the United Nations Protection Force (UNPROFOR) had blocked an American effort to have the alliance adopt such an approach in April. There was little confidence that air power by itself could stop the Serbs from attacking the safe areas, and the lives of peacekeepers would be placed at risk. Canada took the leading role in these debates, putting me in the spotlight. The stage was thus set for a major clash between Canada and the United States when the tightening of the siege of Sarajevo by the Serbs in July 1993 led Washington to launch a major effort to get its way.

On July 30, I left Brussels with Marie-Jeanne and the three children to spend our summer vacation at my sister's home in Muskoka. Early in the morning on August 1 the telephone rang. The Foreign Affairs duty officer (the department's name changed in 1993 from External Affairs and International Trade to Foreign Affairs and International Trade) told me the Americans had called an emergency meeting of the North Atlantic Council for Monday afternoon, August 2, to seek approval for a plan to allow NATO aircraft to intervene decisively in the civil war with heavy bombing of Serb positions throughout Bosnia to relieve the siege of Sarajevo and ease the pressure on other safe areas. The Canadian prime minister, foreign minister, and defence minister had been consulted. They had decided to block the American action to prevent the Serbs from taking retaliation against the lightly armed UNPROFOR troops, including more than 1,000 Canadian peacekeepers stationed in vulnerable positions in Bosnia. The secretary to the Cabinet directed that I return immediately to Brussels to defend the Canadian position.

After a difficult journey back to Brussels, marred by a long delay in the departure of my flight from Toronto to Amsterdam and a high-speed road trip from Schiphol Airport to NATO headquarters, I arrived tired and dishevelled at my office one hour before the meeting. A three-star general from the Department of National Defence headquarters was there to greet me, having flown directly from Ottawa in the comfort of a Challenger jet and arriving in time to get a good rest before the critical meeting. It turned out that his mission was to keep an eye on me to ensure that I obeyed the instructions from Ottawa. Although I had good relations with the senior Canadian military, I was a mere civilian and thus, it seemed, not to be fully trusted to protect its interests.

After receiving a quick briefing from my staff, I called on Manfred Wörner, the NATO secretary general, to say that Canada wouldn't join any consensus in favour of the American proposal. Prime Minister Kim Campbell, who had visited the Canadian delegation to NATO some months earlier as defence minister and was thus familiar with the issues, would monitor the debate and had been given instructions that the safety of our peacekeepers wasn't to be endangered by its outcome. Wörner, who favoured the American initiative, wasn't happy but was prepared for what was to come.

At the council meeting U.S. ambassador-at-large Reginald Bartholomew led the American side. He sought to railroad the proposals through, asking for an early decision to put air power at the service of diplomacy. The NATO commander in the region, he said, should be empowered to act at times and places of his choosing without having to seek the approval of the United Nations. The air campaign shouldn't be limited to protecting UNPROFOR personnel but should be used to protect civilians and to attack Serb targets anywhere in Bosnia. The German, Turkish, and Dutch permanent representatives strongly supported the American position. The others, after expressing initial misgivings, fell silent, indicating they would probably be able to go along with Bartholomew's proposals.

It was left to me to say no. I pointed out that some 300 Canadian peacekeepers were located in Srebrenica, an enclave surrounded by Serb fighters. Another 700 were in Visoko, fifteen miles from Sarajevo and within reach of Serbian artillery located on the surrounding heights. Canada had no intention of putting its soldiers' lives at risk by acceding to the American plan. Moreover, we couldn't endorse any initiative that would lead NATO to intervene in the war on the side of one of the parties or to undermine the role of the United Nations. Finally, if the United States got its way, Canada would take steps to pull all of its forces immediately out of the former Yugoslavia and would work to have the entire UNPROFOR mission ended.

Bartholomew was furious. In the ensuing marathon meeting that lasted until early in the morning the next day, he tried to corner me and show that no other country shared Canada's approach. I responded that, with no troops at risk on the ground in Bosnia, the United States was in no position to question the credibility of a UNPROFOR participant like Canada. At critical moments the French permanent representative intervened to lend support. The other permanent representatives generally remained silent. By arguing over every comma, by inserting conditions that safeguarded Canada's position, and by simply sitting in my chair and outwaiting the opposition, I eventually got my way. The NATO secretary general then called a recess in the proceedings to permit me to telephone the Privy Council Office. Prime Minister Campbell, who was standing by, quickly gave her assent, and I returned to give the news to a relieved council. The text I accepted stipulated that the U.N. commander in Bosnia would be consulted in drawing up plans for the use of air power and would have a veto on the choice of targets and the commitment of aircraft to action.

I had known in advance, from a report by a senior Canadian military officer in Bosnia who was a personal friend, that the UNPROFOR commander would never authorize air strikes that would put the lives of peacekeepers in danger. In fact, all the senior officers of UNPROFOR in Bosnia were prepared to ask to be pulled out of the field in protest if the American initiative had succeeded. Hence the "compromise" that I had come up with meant that, in effect, NATO air power would only be used to defend the lives of peacekeepers through the provision of close air support and wouldn't be used to intervene in the war on the side of the Muslims. Canadian soldiers would thus not be killed in Bosnia as a result of the decisions taken by the North Atlantic Council that night. But neither was the war any closer to solution.

The Canada-U.S. confrontation at NATO left the Americans with a sour taste in their mouths. They made strong representations both from the National Security Council and the State Department to the Canadian embassy in Washington, complaining that I had been too unyielding. Washington was most unhappy that I had watered down the original NATO declaration. The U.S. government reminded the embassy that

President Bill Clinton had gone out of his way to help Prime Minister Campbell at her first G7 meeting in Tokyo on trade issues. The U.S. administration had expected Canada to be more accommodating to strongly held American national security positions, and it hoped that Canada wouldn't repeat such heroics when NATO next discussed the use of air power in Bosnia.

Sarajevo was given a temporary reprieve from bombardment in the wake of the August 2 decisions, and the Serbs abandoned their most forward artillery position on Mount Igman. However, the fighting flared up again in the fall of 1993 and winter of 1994. France and Britain increased the size of their contingents to 4,000 and 3,000 respectively. Canada maintained more than 2,000 troops in the field, half in Croatia and half in Bosnia. A large force was cut off in Srebrenica, with Serb forces preventing the Canadians from leaving. This would precipitate another confrontation between Canada and its allies — this time with France and Britain as well as with the United States.

* * *

In early January 1994, NATO leaders gathered in Brussels to discuss an American initiative to strengthen ties with the countries of Central and Eastern Europe. It was the first NATO summit that newly elected Canadian Prime Minister Jean Chrétien attended, and he was blindsided on Bosnia by the other leaders. The evening before the start of the summit the prime minister and I attended a dinner for NATO leaders hosted by Belgian Prime Minister Jean-Luc Dehaene. Prime Minister John Major of the United Kingdom, without consulting us, circulated the text of a draft declaration that he wanted to release the next day. It threatened air strikes against the Serbs if they didn't allow the Canadian troops in Srebrenica to depart and let a Dutch force come in to replace them. The proposal was warmly received, particularly by Presidents Clinton and Mitterrand, with whom Major had probably consulted beforehand. The dinner ended before Chrétien could register Canada's views. As the leaders filed into the drawing room for coffee and liqueurs, the prime minister grabbed me by the arm and approached Major and Clinton one after the other to say that Canada had reservations about the British proposals, which he intended to spell out at the summit discussions the next day. Major earnestly tried to explain and justify the initiative. Clinton turned on the charm, putting his arm around the prime minister's shoulders and saying, "Jean, this will really work. Don't worry."

Chrétien refused the soft soap, and we left for the residence of Canada's ambassador to Belgium to discuss how to proceed. I pointed out that the Canadian troops in Srebrenica were in no particular danger, though their rotation out was long overdue. They would, however, be put at great risk if they were to attempt to fight their way through the Serb lines, even if supported by fighter aircraft providing close support. Our peacekeepers had been in situations like this many times in the past; they would eventually negotiate their way out. The prime minister was satisfied with this approach and went to bed.

During the night, the British briefed the international press on their initiative to put pressure on Canada to agree. The next day the prime minister reminded his summit partners that UNPROFOR had been given the impossible task of serving as a "Red Cross with guns." Canada, he said, would be the judge of the best way to extricate its troops from Srebrenica; we wouldn't agree to language in a NATO communiqué that served public-relations purposes only and endangered our soldiers.

Canada had dodged a bullet in Brussels, but it wasn't long before its troops and those of its UNPROFOR partners were endangered by the ambition of the U.N. mandates. UNPROFOR, despite absorbing reinforcements raising its force levels to more than 44,000 personnel from twenty-three countries, was too lightly equipped even to defend itself. Its mandates were missions impossible: a peacekeeping role when, in fact, the Muslims, Croats, and Serbs all wanted to resolve their differences by warfare; a humanitarian relief assignment when all convoys were at the mercy of thuggish local warlords; and a protection responsibility for six safe areas or isolated Muslim enclaves within Serb-held territory (Sarajevo, Tuzla, Žepa, Goražde, Bihać, and Srebrenica) — without sufficient troops or equipment for the purpose.

In April 1994, the United Nations was forced to back down when the Serbs seized hostages, Canadians included, from among the peacekeeping forces, refusing to release them unless NATO stopped bombing its positions. We were left to mull over the consequences of this failed test of strength. It would only be a matter of time, it seemed, before peacekeepers would themselves start to suffer heavy casualties, as they had in Somalia shortly before. But any effort by governments to pull their forces out of the former Yugoslavia would expose retreating troops to punishing attacks from Muslim and Croatian forces who would feel resentful at being abandoned to the mercy of the Serbs. And withdrawal would lead to accusations of cowardly abdication of responsibility by a world public opinion exposed to daily CNN coverage of the horrors of war in the middle of Europe. A cynical pattern then developed: NATO periodically threatened the Serbs with air power and occasionally engaged in ineffectual bombing when UNPROFOR troops (but not endangered civilians) were directly threatened; the Serbs would back down, temporarily, and then resume their egregious behaviour after the international community calmed down.

By July 1995, no foreign-policy issue had taken up more of Prime Minister Chrétien's time. I briefed him regularly and arranged frequent telephone calls to key international players, in particular U.N. Secretary-General Boutros Boutros-Ghali, U.K. Prime Minister John Major, French President Jacques Chirac, and U.S. President Bill Clinton. The prime minister sought to maintain our influence by going to the leaders themselves. The stakes for Canada were high with so many troops in theatre and the risk always present that they could suffer large-scale casualties — for which he would be accountable to their families and to the nation.

The civil wars in the former Yugoslavia came to a climax in 1995. Former U.S. president Jimmy Carter had negotiated a ceasefire designed to last from December 1994 to April 1995. The Serbs, who by now held 72 percent of the land, would have been happy to see the war end at this stage. The Bosnian government, however, wanted time to prepare for an offensive in the spring of 1995. With a fresh supply of arms obtained clandestinely over the winter months, it launched attacks in May against Serbian positions around the Sarajevo and Bihać areas, but matters didn't turn out as expected. The heavily outnumbered Serbs broke the back of the Muslim offensive, but provoked pinpoint air attacks from NATO fighter bombers based in Italy and on American aircraft carriers in the Adriatic.

In an all too familiar response, the Serbs rounded up UNPROFOR peacekeepers from a dozen countries, including Canada, the United Kingdom, and France, and chained them to potential target sites. NATO halted its bombing efforts for the time being. The emboldened Serbs then cut off all land routes to Sarajevo, except the perilous Mount Igman route, and turned their attention to the safe areas. On July 12 they swept into Srebrenica, whose 35,000 refugees were ostensibly protected by the Third Dutch Air Mobile Battalion with 450 soldiers equipped with twenty-seven armoured personnel carriers. The Dutch peacekeepers, who had replaced the Canadians in February 1994, allowed themselves to be disarmed and then stood by as 8,000 men and boys were murdered. The Serbs then overran Žepa, a neighbouring safe area, but the men managed to escape through the surrounding hills.

The Srebrenica massacre and the Žepa fiasco marked the low point in the war. A new crisis and new humiliation for the international community appeared on the horizon as Serb forces turned their attention to Goražde. This time the UNPROFOR peacekeepers in the safe area were the Royal Welch Fusiliers who faced the choice of fighting and being mauled or stepping to one side and watching the slaughter of the civilians in their care. Either option would constitute a humiliating national setback to the United Kingdom, which prided itself with good reason on the fighting traditions of its armed forces. The British issued a call to members of the international community to attend a conference in London on July 21 to decide whether UNPROFOR should pull out of the Balkans or stay and fight — the status quo was no longer an option.

On the eve of the conference, most troop-contributing countries, including Britain and Canada, were seriously considering the first option. The fourth winter of the war was approaching and there was a risk that Canada's troops would get caught in the crossfire of escalating conflict. At NATO headquarters plans for the deployment of up to 60,000 NATO soldiers, including more than 20,000 American combat troops and armour, were ready to protect the retreating UNPROFOR troops from the armies of contending parties. But Jacques Chirac, elected president

The Queen's Representative in Ontario, 2002–2007

Welcoming His Holiness Pope John Paul II to Toronto in July 2002. *Office of the Lieutenant Governor.*

Welcoming Her Majesty Queen Elizabeth II to Toronto during the 2002 Golden Jubilee Year. Ontario Premier Ernie Eves is on Her Majesty's left. *Photo by Tom Sandler.*

Meeting Canadian veterans at Queen's Park in March 2002. *Office of the Lieutenant Governor.*

My official coat of arms as lieutenant governor of Ontario, with the caribou totem of my mother's family; chief's headdress; Order of Ontario; canoes for children Anne-Pascale, Laurent, and Alain; scales of justice; and coq de Wallonie. Note: The governor general and all lieutenant governors are given coats of arms upon taking office. *Office of the Lieutenant Governor.*

My wife, Marie-Jeanne, and me in 2002 with aides-de-camp who volunteer their time helping lieutenant governors with their official duties. *Office of the Lieutenant Governor.*

Giving condolences in September 2003 to elders during Nibinamik First Nation Day of Mourning after a plane crash killed eight residents. *Office of the Lieutenant Governor.*

Nishnawbe Aski Nation (NAN) Chiefs Winter Meeting in Timmins in February 2004. Grand Chief Stan Beardy is on my right. *Office of the Lieutenant Governor.*

Visiting CFB Petawawa in 2004 to address troops being deployed to Bosnia and Afghanistan. *Press Office of the Canadian Forces.*

It was a delight to hold this baby in its *tikinagan* or cradleboard at Kasabonika First Nation in the summer of 2005. *Office of the Lieutenant Governor.*

Helping the Salvation Army deliver soup to the homeless in downtown Toronto in February 2005. *Photo by Peter Bregg.*

In northern Ontario, the Canadian Rangers perform ceremonial duties and carry out search and rescue missions. Here, they are accompanying the platform party attending 2005's one hundredth anniversary celebrations of Treaty 5, which ceded vast terrorities to the Crown. From right to left: Connie Gray-McKay, chief of Mishkeegogamang Ojibway Nation; Phil Fontaine, national chief of the Assembly of First Nations; Stan Beardy, grand chief of the Nishnawbe Aski Nation; and me. *Office of the Lieutenant Governor.*

Celebrating the life of local hero Bobby Orr at Parry Sound's Bobby Orr Hall of Fame in 2006. *Office of the Lieutenant Governor.*

With the Dalai Lama at the Fairmount Royal York in Toronto, 2004. He answered an existential question that I had wondered about for years. *Office of the Lieutenant Governor.*

Greeting Mikhail Gorbachev, former general secretary of the Communist Party and president of the Soviet Union, during his visit to Toronto in 2006. *Office of the Lieutenant Governor.*

To meet Wiarton Willy on Groundhog Day, 2006. Apparently Willy insisted on a strict dress code: all members of the platform party had to dress outrageously or he wouldn't predict the weather. *Office of the Lieutenant Governor.*

Governor General Michaëlle Jean arriving for an informal lunch at my suite at Queen's Park in 2006. Canada's vice regal representatives are autonomous in their own jurisdictions, the lieutenant governors for the provinces and the governor general for the country as a whole. But lieutenant governors usually maintain close informal contacts with the governor general. *Office of the Lieutenant Governor.*

Welcoming Princess Anne to Queen's Park in 2006. *Office of the Lieutenant Governor.*

With Lincoln Alexander, my mentor as lieutenant governor, in 2006. *Office of the Lieutenant Governor.*

I met with every group of incoming parliamentary pages (grades seven and eight) to brief them on the constitutional role of Canada's vice regal representatives. The subject is a dry one, so I always brought along the family dogs — Ado, Ida, and Stella — to help the new pages feel more at home. December 2006. *Office of the Lieutenant Governor.*

Marie-Jeanne and me with our three dogs, Stella, Ado, and Ida, in Toronto in 2006. *Author's Collection.*

Ontario

2015 James Bartleman Aboriginal Youth Creative Writing Award Recipient

"When I opened a book I was able to travel wherever I wanted to go."

Established to commemorate the Honourable James K. Bartleman's term as Lieutenant Governor of Ontario (2002 – 2007).

Her Honour the Honourable Elizabeth Dowdeswell	**The Honourable Kathleen Wynne**
Lieutenant Governor of Ontario	Premier of Ontario

In 2007, at my request, the Ontario government established the James Bartleman Aboriginal Youth Creative Writing Awards program administered by the Ministry of Citizenship. Each year a panel of judges picks six winners from hundreds of submissions. To date, 60 awards with prizes of $2,500 each have been made. The recipients are role models in their communities. *Ministry of Citizenship.*

Marie-Jeanne and me at Christmas dinner in 2006 with Ontario Provincial Police bodyguards. From left to right: Mike Gayos, Jim Withers, John Riggs, and Norm Penny. *Office of the Lieutenant Governor.*

In July 2007, as a legacy gift from the people of Muskoka, Island Park in Port Carling was renamed James Bartleman Island Park. It's the place where my ancestors camped during the summer months. *Office of the Lieutenant Governor.*

My mother and me in 2009 at the unveiling of my official portrait, which now hangs along with those of my predecessors in the lieutenant governor's suite at Queen's Park. *Office of the Lieutenant Governor.*

Shaking hands in May 2012 with His Excellency Governor General David Johnston at the official ceremony marking my appointment as an Officer of the Order of Canada. *Photo by Master Corporal Dany Veillette reproduced with permission of the Office of the Secretary of the Governor General.*

of France in May 1995, wanted to stay and fight, even if that meant joining the war on the side of the Bosnian government.

Chirac was enraged that twenty French soldiers had been killed, several deliberately shot by the Serbs, while carrying out peacekeeping duties over the years, and his sense of national honour as the president of France was offended by the continuing seizure of French troops as hostages. The president had already forcefully expressed his views to his peers, disrupting the Halifax summit in June by insisting that the participants focus on the carnage in the former Yugoslavia rather than devote all their time to the reform of the Bretton Woods institutions. He had called the head of the French armed forces a coward to his face and castigated the Dutch prime minister for the pitiful showing of his forces in Srebrenica. He now urged UNPROFOR to take on the Serbs with a new Rapid Reaction Force, currently deploying into the area and equipped with armoured fighting vehicles, anti-tank missiles, heavy mortars, and artillery.

The Americans, while still unwilling to put their ground forces in harm's way, welcomed the French president's pugnacity, so unlike the hand-wringing passivity that European leaders had displayed since the crisis had begun. Over the past year Washington had also become more engaged. In addition to winking at the provision of arms from Muslim countries to the Bosnian government in violation of U.N. Security Council resolutions, it had helped Croatia retrain and re-equip its armed forces using a private security company headed by retired American generals and other guns for hire. And it had become more active diplomatically, assuming de facto leadership of the Contact Group. The U.S. Congress stepped in at this stage, preparing legislation to force the administration to provide arms directly to the Bosnian government. The problem was that should it succeed, Russia would likely retaliate by opening up an arms pipeline to the Serbs, their Slav cousins, almost literally pouring oil on the fire of conflict. Prime Minister Chrétien raised the matter with President Clinton, who assured him that he would veto the bill. And he eventually did so.

The Canadian team in London included the defence and foreign affairs ministers and me. The ministers were divided: the defence minister favoured keeping Canada's troops in Bosnia and Croatia and fighting it out in company with our allies; the foreign affairs minister wanted to redeploy Canada's forces from Bosnia to Croatia to consolidate our military presence and establish shorter lines of communication in the area should the warring parties turn on the peacekeepers and make Canadian troops fight their way out. Chrétien was clear in his instructions to me: don't enter into any new commitments but don't oppose a consensus for a more muscular approach against the Serbs should one develop. He asked me to keep him informed by telephone as the meeting proceeded, emphasizing that he wanted to keep Canada's options open for later discussion and decision by the Cabinet.

We arrived by Challenger jet on the evening of July 20 and retired early to prepare for the discussions at Lancaster House the next day. Unknown to us, the British met overnight with the Americans and French and then with other members of the Contact Group. They decided to draw a line in the sand around the remaining sanctuaries of Sarajevo, Goražde, and Bihać. The Rapid Reaction Force, they decided, backed up by massive NATO bombing of Serb military and strategic targets, would enter into action on the side of the Bosnian government if the Serbs didn't back down. The next morning the British team met separately with delegations from countries not in the inner circle, including ours, to seek our support. I consulted the prime minister to obtain his blessing, and he authorized us to join the consensus. Unsurprisingly, when Britain's prime minister, John Major, circulated his draft agreement, it was quickly approved by the conference participants; whether intended or not, the international community had taken sides.

The period of greatest risk for the peacekeepers was now at hand. The Serbs eased their military pressure temporarily on the remaining safe areas, but the Bosnian government continued its offensives. It would only be a matter of time before the Serbs used their heavy weapons against civilians once again, precipitating intervention by the Rapid Reaction Force and NATO air power. UNPROFOR commanders urgently moved garrisons and military observers from vulnerable locations. In a diplomatic coup, the British persuaded the Belgrade government to allow them to evacuate their troops from Goražde across the international border into Serbia proper and out of harm's way. Britain, France, and the Netherlands, the three nations providing the Rapid Reaction Force, redoubled their efforts to move their units into position, taking up stations on Mount Igman, ready to take on the Serbian heavy guns when the shelling of Sarajevo resumed.

In the meantime, at NATO headquarters in Brussels, at the headquarters of Supreme Allied Commander General George Joulwan in Mons, and at Southern Command in Naples, the blueprint to evacuate UNPROFOR was shelved in favour of frantic efforts to dust off and revise long-standing plans, dating back to the days when I was in Brussels in 1993, to punish the Serbs from the air. New rules made it easier for the United Nations and NATO to authorize air strikes; now, the decision to attack would be made by the military commanders in the field. The U.N. secretary-general, considered too vulnerable to political pressure from nervous governments in the post-London world, was dropped from the decision-making process. No longer would air power be used only to protect endangered UNPROFOR troops; it would henceforth also be applied to defend the civil populations. Planners also took to heart the harsh lessons learned in applying air power in Bosnia over the past year when pinpoint attacks on selected targets were ineffective. Although this option remained on the table, the new military thinking was that only an all-out air campaign against a broad range of strategic and military targets would get the attention of the Serbs.

A new worry emerged. On July 25, troops of the Republic of Croatia punched through the Serbian lines, cutting off communications between Serb Krajina and the territory controlled by the Bosnian Serbs. The Croatian government, most members of the international community (including Canada) then discovered, was in the final stages of preparations to rid its territory of its Serb minority. I called my opposite numbers in Washington, London, Paris, and Bonn. The prime minister called Clinton, Major, Chirac, and Kohl. Our efforts complemented the soundings being made by diplomats from Foreign Affairs and military officers from the Department of National Defence, since we all knew that in modern-day crises, we all must work together. We asked whether the Croatian drive would lead to generalized war in the Balkans. No one knew. There was a general agreement, however, that Croatia was emerging as a major military power, able to stand up and perform creditably if

Serbia were to challenge it on the battlefield. And what would happen to the 14,000 peacekeepers of the United Nations Confidence Restoration Operation (UNCRO) in Croatia, including more than 800 Canadians scattered in isolated observation posts between the Croatian and Serbian lines? Our friends told us they should be safe if they kept their heads down when the fighting started.

Matters rapidly came to a head. Anthony Lake, national security adviser to President Clinton, called me late in the afternoon of August 3, 1995, to provide a warning: a full-scale offensive by the armed forces of Croatia against the breakaway Republic of Krajina would begin at midnight; the two other Serb-held areas of Croatia, East and West Slavonia, he said, would be attacked later. The region, seized by Croatia's small Serbian minority in the fighting of 1992, made up almost one-third of Croatia, and the government in Zagreb wanted it back. Lake told me the Pentagon believed the Croatians would take their objectives in a matter of days, then push northward into the Livno Valley in Bosnia and join up with forces of the Bosnian government in a drive to relieve the safe area of Bihać. The U.S. State Department and the CIA, Lake said, differed with the Pentagon on the time it would take for the Croatian army to capture Krajina, but all agreed that the days of the self-proclaimed Serb republic in Croatia were numbered. Lake asked me to ensure that the word was passed to the Canadian military to alert our peacekeepers manning observation posts in the line of advance.

I didn't waste time asking Lake how the Americans knew all of this, but immediately alerted National Defence Headquarters, telling them to treat the information as genuine. Colonel Andrew Leslie, later promoted and made head of Canada's land forces and then the senior Canadian officer at battalion headquarters at Knin in the area of the projected attack, told me later that he received the urgent message from his headquarters within minutes of my warning. It was one in the morning local time on August 4, and he issued urgent orders to the Canadian troops to take cover. They in turn passed on the word to the Kenyans and other peacekeepers in the danger zone. Soon, all were hunkered down in their bunkers, waiting for the first artillery barrages to begin. The batteries opened up at 3:10 a.m., the shells passing over the heads of the peacekeepers and into the civilian-populated areas. Using tactics perfected by the German Wehrmacht in the Second World War, the Croatian high command was just as interested in terrorizing the Serb civilian population and forcing them to flee as in destroying military targets. Newly equipped and freshly trained assault troops, 100,000 strong, cleared out the military opposition. Special police units then moved in to loot, rape, and kill civilians, driving them out of the area and burning their houses to ensure they would never return. Some 180,000 civilians fled into exile in Serbia within a matter of days in the largest ethnic-cleansing operation in Europe since the days just after the Second World War.

As they passed through the Canadian lines, the Croatian forces rousted the Canadians from their bunkers and moved them out of the area to try to keep the number of witnesses to their looting and mayhem to a minimum. But when they tried to do the same at the U.N. headquarters building, Colonel Leslie refused to be bullied and ordered his troops to fight. They fought back so well that with thirty of their men dead, the attacking Croatians finally withdrew. Leslie and his forces, however, were confined to their base in company with 1,400 civilian Serbs who had sought refuge in their compound from the Croatian Special Police. The standoff went on for five days while the ethnic cleansing in the city continued.

Leslie had no idea how he could take the civilians to safety through the Croatian army lines but got his chance after the Croats had cleared the town of the bodies of hundreds of massacred civilians. That was when Croatian President Franjo Tuđman arrived with a group of journalists to celebrate the capture of the region; Leslie gambled that the Croatian Special Police wouldn't intervene as long as the media were present. Under the noses of the unhappy Croatians, Canada's senior officer in Knin then moved the refugees by convoy to the no man's land separating Croatian and Serbian fighters and out of harm's way.

The offensive changed the military balance. Within three weeks the Croatian army had driven Croatia's Serb minority from its national territory. After pulverizing the military opposition in Serb-held Krajina and ethnically cleansing the population, the Croatian army swept into Bosnia and rolled up the Bosnian Serb forces. The stage thus set for the massive use of NATO air power, the Serbs duly provided the excuse for NATO intervention. On August 28, they fired five mortar rounds into Sarajevo, one of which ricocheted off a building into a crowd, killing twenty-eight and wounding eighty civilians. The Muslims had shelled a Serb funeral the previous day and the attack on Sarajevo might have been a retaliatory strike, but no matter. NATO fighter bombers started large-scale air attacks on Serb targets. French, British, and Dutch artillery and the heavy mortars of the Rapid Reaction Force went into action, systematically destroying the Serb heavy guns around Sarajevo. The decisions taken at London on July 21 were now being translated into sustained military intervention on the side of the Bosnian government. It was only a matter of time before the Serb forces in Bosnia were defeated. Prolonged bombing, plus the sustained land offensive led by the Croatian army, forced the Serbs to their knees. By September 20 the land and air routes to Sarajevo were open and the Serb forces elsewhere were defeated.

Anthony Lake spent much of August in Europe, calling on Contact Group governments with an American-designed "Endgame Strategy" and obtaining approval for an imposed political settlement once the dust settled militarily. Under the American proposal, Bosnia would retain its territorial integrity as the Bosnian government of Bosnia-Herzegovina, divided into two entities — the Federation (for the Muslims and Croats) and the Republika Srpska (for the Serbs). Final arrangements on the sharing of power, the return of refugees, and other details were then worked out in talks in Dayton, Ohio, in November with the leaders of Serbia, Croatia, Bosnia, and the key warring factions. A new 60,000-strong force, including divisions of American combat forces under NATO command, replaced the discredited UNPROFOR. Canada provided a combat task force of more than 1,000 men and women to the Implementation Force (IFOR) that took over on December 20.

Bosnia then disappeared from public view. And what were the consequences of the wars in Croatia and Bosnia? All sides lost: 250,000 dead, 50,000 tortured, 20,000 women raped, 15,000 children killed, and three million refugees. Ethnic cleansing had returned to Europe for the first time since the Second World War.

31

Russia: The Hard-Liners Were Taking Over

"President Gorbachev is ill at his dacha in Crimea and has been replaced by a state committee." It was early morning on August 19, 1991, and I was watching CNN at home in Brussels. The announcer added that the head of the KGB, the prime minister, and the defence minister had taken over in Moscow and the country was calm. Despite the reassuring words, it was obvious that a coup was being mounted that might push the· Soviet Union back to hardline communism and return the world to the Cold War. NATO was facing its most serious crisis in years. I needed guidance from the Canadian government on what to do.

NATO's relationship with the Soviet Union in the aftermath of the collapse of its empire in Central Europe had been the most important issue facing the alliance since the fall of the Berlin Wall in 1989. Whether to take at face value Mikhail Gorbachev's protestations that the Soviet Union would never again threaten the West was the question we ambassadors debated in our weekly meetings. Representing Canada, I had been arguing that NATO should focus on capabilities and not on intentions. While the Soviet Union would remain a powerful nation, the withdrawal of Soviet forces from Central Europe, then under way, had changed the military balance irrevocably and for the better.

Old habits die hard, and other permanent representatives didn't accept the Canadian view. The Europeans couldn't imagine a European security landscape devoid of a Soviet threat. Moscow had acquiesced without a whimper in the freeing of the satellite states; it had meekly accepted the reunification of Germany, reversing its single most important foreign-policy goal since the time of Stalin; its economy was collapsing; and its constituent republics were restive. Common sense, they maintained, dictated that the tide would eventually turn and sooner or later there would be a reassertion of Soviet power in Europe.

Now the hard-liners were taking over — or so it seemed. I telephoned Ottawa for instructions. Those colleagues at headquarters in Ottawa not on vacation had no more information than I had on what was going on and were in no position to help. NATO Secretary General Manfred Wörner then called an emergency meeting of the North Atlantic Council. I went to NATO headquarters to take my place in the council chamber to find out that I wasn't alone in having no guidance. But even without instructions, we had to do what we could to prevent a return to the Cold War. We thus issued a press release warning the coup leaders of "serious consequences" if the Soviet Union abandoned reform. Our communiqué was a bluff, since we had no authority from our governments to make such a threat and it would have been inconceivable for NATO to take military measures against even a weakened Soviet Union that retained such an awesome nuclear capacity. The most we could have done would have been to cut off our diplomatic contacts with Soviet liaison officers at NATO headquarters. The coup leaders, we gambled, wouldn't know this.

Foreign ministers from across the alliance scurried to Brussels to take over the management of the crisis from their ambassadors. Shortly after the ministerial meeting began, Wörner was summoned from the room to speak on the telephone with Boris Yeltsin, calling from his command post in Moscow. The Russian leader, the secretary general said on his return, was encouraged by our communiqué, considered it helpful, and appealed to NATO to stand firm. Later, while the meeting of ministers was still in session, Wörner announced that Soviet President Gorbachev had been released and the coup attempt was over. Gorbachev was free, but Yeltsin was the hero and the new leader of the country. Russia then emerged from the ruins of the former Soviet Union and declared its intention to embrace liberal democracy — an intention it was to abandon under President Vladimir Putin.

32

Russia's Slavonic Soul

In my high school years haunting the local library in Port Carling and later in university, Leo Tolstoy, Fyodor Dostoevsky, and Boris Pasternak had been my introduction to the wider world — rich in aesthetic genius, social commentary, religious and philosophical insight, and the art of storytelling. And who couldn't feel admiration for the heroism of the Russian soldiers in the Second World War? One of my family's closest Aboriginal friends came back from the war to tell us of meeting and drinking with cheerful but poorly clothed Russian soldiers. The Russian people had more than their fair share of oppressors, including Napoleon, Hitler, and Stalin. Their tribulations didn't come to an end with the collapse of communism.

I visited Moscow for the first time in February 1994 when I was still ambassador to NATO, ostensibly to make the acquaintance of a future colleague — President Boris Yeltsin's diplomatic adviser — before I reported for duty with Prime Minister Chrétien. We held talks. As expected, he expressed concern about any enlargement of NATO and I departed — never to see him again. This didn't matter since the real purpose of my journey had been to catch a glimpse of a nation whose military and ideological challenge to the West had dominated global politics since the end of the Second World War, for I was a product of my times — raised in the atmosphere of a life-and-death struggle between East and West. With two postings to NATO, assignments in the security and intelligence world, and two years in communist Cuba, I had lived through many confrontations with the former Soviet Union and was present as ambassador and permanent representative of Canada in the North Atlantic Council when it collapsed in December 1991.

Moscow was a city of surprises. The Cold War might have been over, but suspicious, cheerless grey apparatchiks dressed in Soviet-era uniforms still manned the immigration and customs counters at the city's airport and behaved as if the war was still on. Meanwhile, a savage type of dog-eat-dog capitalism, not seen in Western Europe since the nineteenth century, had taken over. On the road in from the airport, billboards advertising luxury products and casinos lined the boulevards. At the luxurious Metropol Hotel where the embassy had booked me a room, CNN, BBC, other international channels, plus the latest movies and porn channels, were available at the click of a switch, just as they were in similar hotels around the world. Within seconds of my arrival, a hotel employee knocked on the door of my room to deliver pink Crimean champagne and the best of Caspian Sea caviar, compliments of the management. Yet outside on the square in front of the Bolshoi Theatre, old babushkas stood in the cold trying to sell their miserable possessions to buy food, and dirty snow was piled high on Red Square and the grounds of the Kremlin.

My first objective was to visit Canada's embassy on Starokonyushenny Street in the old Arbat or Turkish trading area of the city to call on the ambassador. As a former director general of security and intelligence in Foreign Affairs just a decade earlier and as someone who had been targeted in the past by both the KGB and its ally the Cuban Intelligence Service, I looked over the building with professional interest. The KGB had been dissolved in the fall of 1991 after its chief, Colonel-General Vladimir Kryuchkov, participated in the failed coup attempt. But its successor organization was suspected of being just as active as its predecessor. Perhaps it was just a touch of paranoia, but I imagined that the Russians were listening to our conversations through microphones in the walls.

During the Cold War, our security officers had regularly discovered hidden microphones and had even uncovered evidence that the Soviets had drilled from a neighbouring building to implant listening devices in the basement of the mission. Soviet agents would enter the apartments of our staff members when the occupants were out, rifle through personal papers and books, and deliberately leave everything in disorder. Occasionally, staff attempting to use their telephones would hear the contents of previous conversations played back to them. The KGB wanted to ensure that Canada's diplomats were aware that Big Brother was watching.

The KGB had also used more traditional means of blackmail to intimidate staff and obtain information. The Russian local employees at the embassy, it was assumed, reported to the sinister Soviet security and intelligence organization. The cleaning ladies at the embassy were sometimes prepared to offer sexual services to lonely Canadians. From time to time, supposedly unilingual Russian-speaking employees, especially the drivers, displayed an unsuspected fluency in English. On occasion, gullible Canadians would be caught in KGB entrapments, surreptitiously photographed selling goods illegally on the black market or having sex with prostitutes. Usually, the transgressors would rush to confess their sins to the mission security officer and be immediately recalled to Ottawa to remove them from the clutches of the KGB. Their files ended up on my desk in the years I was in charge. Following the practice of my predecessors, I usually recommended that such employees be treated leniently. After all, it was in Canada's security interest to have employees admit their indiscretions to allow us to limit the damage. Their spouses, I assumed, would be less understanding, but there was nothing anyone could do about that.

Canadians probably behaved no worse and no better than our allies in Moscow in these years. In one high-profile case, a British ambassador confessed that he had crawled into bed with a particularly attractive Russian maid but swore on a Bible that he had betrayed no secrets. I think he was likewise forgiven by his authorities. Of course, no one has any idea how many Canadians were recruited by the KGB to labour for the Soviets, undetected by Western intelligence services. And no one will ever know for sure how much secret information was obtained by the Soviets by these methods. Although we didn't publicize the matter, the allied security and intelligence services, including the Canadian one, targeted with equal zeal Soviet and other Warsaw Pact diplomats and military staff in our capitals.

And we did win the Cold War.

On this cold winter day, I walked up the stairs to the official residence, located in an apartment above the chancery offices, to greet Ambassador Jeremy Kinsman, Canada's man in the new capitalist Russia. Jeremy was one of Canada's top diplomats, destined to serve in later years as ambassador to Rome, high commissioner to London, and ambassador to the European Union in Brussels, where he would replace me in 2002 when I was called back to be Ontario's lieutenant governor. I looked around the elegant nineteenth-century drawing rooms and the plasterwork on the ceilings painted gold, green, and blue. The dining room was large enough to host twenty-four guests at a sitting and had an unimpeded view of the distant Russian foreign ministry constructed years before in the grim concrete-block Soviet realist style. Many of Canada's most distinguished diplomats had sat around this table, including Arnold Smith, John Watkins, Robert Ford, Vern Turner, Geoffrey Pearson, and Peter Roberts. Each had left his mark on Canada's relations with the former Soviet Union. Watkins was a victim of the Cold War, dying while being interrogated by members of the former RCMP Security Service in an isolated Montreal motel, his reputation sullied by unproven accusations of treachery.

The evening before I returned to Brussels, Jeremy invited me to join him and two or three of his English-speaking Muscovite friends for a quiet meal in a local restaurant. The Russians were bitter. While paying lip service to the new capitalist age, they lamented the decline of their country from its superpower status to one that was poor, corrupt, criminal-ridden, and violent. As the evening progressed, the conversation turned to literature and the mood changed. One was an author. The others, well versed in the arts, wanted to discuss a book he was just completing. He at first modestly resisted but then opened the floodgates, describing setting, plot, and character development with great enthusiasm. He didn't care, he said, whether any copies of his book would be sold but desperately wanted it to be respected by his peers and to influence the ongoing debate on the future of his country. The others eagerly jumped in, offering opinions on his creation, especially on the extent to which it reflected Russia's Slavonic soul. The discussion could have been taken from a nineteenth-century novel in which passionate members of the intelligentsia debated Russia's mission in the world. I returned to Brussels the next day, happy that in the wasteland of post–Cold War Russia, at least the spirit of artistic expression and creativity had survived the many decades of communism.

33

Ukraine: The Late-Autumn Sun

In 1992, as it is today, Canada's policy toward Ukraine was driven by domestic politics, especially the need not to offend the large number of Canadians of Ukrainian origin. In a dramatic step, we blocked other NATO members from delaying recognition of Kiev, after Ukraine declared independence in December 1991, until it undertook to destroy its nuclear arms inherited from the former Soviet Union. This caused deep unhappiness in other delegations that thought we were taking our support for Ukraine too far.

They were appalled when I began hosting working dinners at my residence in Brussels at which speakers provided in-depth briefings to senior visiting Ukrainian military officers and civilian officials. My colleagues were even more upset when we opened our doors to diplomatic interns from Ukraine and exposed them to the day-to-day workings of a NATO delegation. Proper security procedures were in effect to protect confidential documents but, without exception, the other ambassadors objected, saying that only nationals of the member states should have access to the offices of the NATO delegations. One ambassador even said that becoming a member of NATO was akin to taking holy orders and that my actions were equivalent to heresy. But once we challenged the old ways of thinking, the other delegations began following our lead. Within two months the American and German delegations were welcoming interns from other former Warsaw Pact countries into their offices.

I then successfully lobbied to be sent as a representative of the NATO Council to brief key figures in Kiev and Odessa on the advantages of drawing closer to the alliance. Accompanied by a Danish admiral and a senior official from the international staff, I arrived in Kiev on a cold late October day after a direct flight from Brussels. The immigration and police officials still wore their Soviet-era uniforms and were brusque and unsmiling. We were met by representatives of the Foreign Ministry, who expedited entry procedures and whisked us to the largest and most modern hotel in the city. The avenues were broad and lined with trees in the final phases of fall colours. The late-autumn sun glistened off gilt-ornamented churches and monasteries.

The beauty of the city masked private hardship and despair. Ukraine's leadership was weak and corruption was widespread. Relations with Russia, with which it was disputing the ownership of the Black Sea fleet, were at a crisis point. The standard of living had declined drastically after the collapse of communism and had fallen even more following Ukraine's declaration of independence. Inflation was at astronomical levels and the value of the local currency was derisory. The most expensive seat at the opera was less than five cents in Canadian money. Food was expensive and difficult to obtain, and it was a struggle for the people to pay their heating bills. Old women stood at street corners selling their meagre possessions in an attempt to make ends meet.

We weren't spared at the hotel. Although the outside temperature fell below freezing at night, the heat hadn't been turned on and I shivered in my room. When I complained, the hotel manager told me to go to bed. Since it was only five in the afternoon, I visited a dollar shop. Ubiquitous in all communist or former communist countries, the store sold imported luxury goods for foreign currency; I bought a gigantic hair dryer. Taking it to my room, I set the controls to maximum but found that as much heat was escaping the poorly fitted windows as the dryer was generating. I tried directing the flow of air at a fixed spot on the bed and lying carefully in its path. Finally, I gave up and crawled under the covers when it became apparent that while part of my body was being roasted the rest was becoming glacially cold.

The warmth of the welcome from ministers, senior officials, leaders of the military, the press, and even the Ukrainian KGB, several of whom I had hosted during their visits to Brussels, more than made up for freezing in my room. They greeted us enthusiastically, eager for our support to establish closer ties with NATO. We were then supposed to be taken by plane to Odessa on the Black Sea to meet the political and military leadership in this militarily sensitive area. However, the Russians cut off gas supplies and all internal flights were cancelled for lack of aviation fuel, so it was decided that we would take the night train. It was a return to the past, a journey that would have been familiar to Boris Pasternak, the Nobel Prize–winning author whose accounts of rail traffic in First World War Russia were among the most poignant in his novel *Doctor Zhivago.*

With electricity supplies low, the streetlights weren't operating as the liaison officers drove us to the railway station, itself plunged in darkness. Thousands of shabbily attired people with shawls or blankets over their shoulders waited in the obscurity, clutching cheap suitcases and waiting impassively for trains to take them to destinations around the country. Our guides led us by flashlight through a maze of corridors to the train for Odessa in which two compartments, one for the NATO team and one for our escorts ("minders" from the Ukrainian version of the KGB), had been reserved. A female attendant lit a fire, stuffing newspaper and wood into a stove at one end of the railway car to heat a boiler that would warm radiators in our compartments.

As the train crawled out of the city, we ate sausages, herring, and black bread washed down with vodka as we looked out at the dreary, desolate, and phantasmagorical scene. Derelict factories and rusty machinery were faintly visible in a desert landscape, testifying to the disintegration of Ukraine's industrial base, which had collapsed with the communist dream. As dawn approached, collective farms, the pride of the old Soviet Union, came into view, but all I could see was abandoned farm equipment lying amid high grass and weeds. We arrived, however, in another world. Odessa, with its wide esplanades and rich store of pre-revolutionary architecture, including one of the world's finest opera houses, proved to be a jewel on the Black Sea. I took in a performance of Giuseppe Verdi's *Il trovatore*, obtaining a front-row seat.

The same messages conveyed to us by the elites of Kiev were repeated. The commander of the Odessa military district said that he and his men were prepared to fight to the death to defend their new country against Russia. I noticed, however, that he and his fellow generals were more comfortable speaking Russian than Ukrainian and spent much time describing in proud detail the heroic struggle of the Red Army against the Nazis in Crimea during the Second World War. They were uncomfortable receiving a delegation from NATO, their sworn enemy throughout the Cold War. The officer-training establishment where they received us reeked of the urine of 6,000 cadets and gave the impression of being in terminal decline, with windows broken and paint peeling from the walls. Two decades later, as Ukrainian troops clashed with Russian-supported rebels in Eastern Ukraine, I would think of my visit to Odessa and lost opportunities.

Seeking to obtain a sense of what life was like in the days before the 1917 revolution, I visited a local monastery. Long-bearded monks, rubber boots deep in the oozing manure and cassocks brown around the bottoms where cloth met dirt, were shovelling the ripe fertilizer onto the fields from horse-drawn wagons. The chapel was crowded with the faithful — old ladies dressed in black were in the majority amid a sprinkling of younger people. The air was filled with smoke from burning tapers, and the devotions were interspersed with frequent signs of the cross. It was as if I had stepped into a scene of rural life in old Russia described by Tolstoy himself. I sensed the spiritual resurrection of a people who had survived seventy-five years of communist persecution and who now had no idea what to do with their new freedom.

Part Four

Foreign-Policy Adviser to the Prime Minister, 1994–1998

In March 1994, I transferred from the Department of Foreign Affairs to the Privy Council Office to become assistant secretary to the Cabinet and foreign-policy adviser to the prime minister. In June 1998, I left his side with my memories of an extraordinary four years close to the centre of foreign- and defence-policy decision-making — the dying French President François Mitterrand, the scowling Israeli Prime Minister Yitzhak Rabin, the happy Princess Diana, the resolute Pope John Paul II, the raging Cuban President Fidel Castro, the drunken Russian President Boris Yeltsin, the evil Chinese Premier Li Peng, the smooth-talking Italian President Silvio Berlusconi, the bad-tempered Canadian fisheries minister Brian Tobin, and the traumatically wounded Canadian General Roméo Dallaire. And the places — Paris, Rome, New York, London, Birmingham, Edinburgh, Brussels, Bonn, Lisbon, Madrid, Budapest, Moscow, St. Petersburg, Bucharest, Canberra, Auckland, Hanoi, Shanghai, Manila, Kuala Lumpur, Seoul, Tokyo, Osaka, Bangkok, Calcutta, Buenos Aires, Rio de Janeiro, Santiago, Cotonou, shell-shattered Sarajevo, polluted Beijing, overcrowded Mumbai, traffic-clogged New Delhi, austere Islamabad, artificial Brasilia, and baking Sharm el-Sheikh.

Not to mention the bedlam in Mexico City following the assassination of a presidential candidate, the dignified funeral of Mother Teresa, the anti–land mines crusade, the boring state dinners, the adrenaline rushes, the motorcades, and the friends I made to last a lifetime.

34

A Testing Time

I made my first trip abroad — to Mexico — as foreign-policy adviser in March 1994. It didn't go well. The flight from Ottawa to Mexico City was endless. The Challenger droned on hour after hour until at last it landed at Dallas to refuel. Everyone deplaned to catch a breath of Texas spring air and then we squeezed back on for the final leg of the journey. The atmosphere on board the twelve-passenger jet was chummy — for everyone except me. Prime Minister Chrétien smiled at me benignly, but the others didn't. They were all strong-willed, talented people who formed the heart of the political team that had led the prime minister to victory the preceding fall. In their world, everyone had to earn respect, and I hadn't paid my dues.

Staff officers were waiting in the dark to hustle us to waiting passenger vans when we arrived at Mexico City's airport. Then, with much shouting and waving of flashlights, the motorcade, escorted by motorcycle outriders, snaked toward the city centre. Sirens wailed into the polluted night air, vehicles on the roads were pushed to one side, and orders barked into a microphone by an operations officer in a police car somewhere up ahead poured forth from radio sets installed in each vehicle. As we approached the target, a gigantic luxury hotel, his disembodied voice provided a countdown to arrival worthy of a space launch.

"Three minutes out! Two minutes out! One minute out!"

The tension and excitement in his voice reached a fever pitch.

"Thirty seconds out! Twenty seconds out! Ten seconds out!"

We roared, tires screaming into the entranceway.

Waiting staff officers jerked open the doors to the cars and vans. The official photographer sprinted forward as if his life depended upon it — to catch a shot of the prime minister shaking hands with the hotel manager. Staff officers yelled for everyone to hurry. Members of the team stumbled along encumbered with briefcases filled with secret documents and overcoats that would be of no use until we returned to the winter blasts of Ottawa. There was then a scramble to share the elevator with the prime minister. The fortunate few rode up, basking in reflected glory beside Canada's leader and his wife who just wanted to go to bed. The rest of us waited anxiously for another elevator, certain that decisions were being made by those who had managed to accompany the prime minister to his suite and worried that they hadn't been there to offer their indispensable advice.

At last we arrived at the delegation office, the operations centre for the duration of the visit. That was when I found out there hadn't been any particular need to rush in from the airport and up the stairs. But rushing was apparently how the programs of world leaders were organized, and I had better get used to it. At the briefing session the next morning I drew on notes prepared for me back in Ottawa to go over the day's program, but no one, including the prime minister, paid much attention. When I stopped to take a drink of water, the others jumped in, giving their unsought advice on how to deal with major bilateral issues likely to come in talks with the Mexicans, press lines, points of protocol, and anything to impress the prime minister. And before I could regain control, the prime minister got up and went to the waiting motorcade, with the rest of us straggling along behind.

The major event of the day was a state banquet offered by the Mexican president, but before it started a government spokesperson announced that the person chosen by the ruling party to become its next candidate for president of the country in the forthcoming elections had just been assassinated. All official functions were accordingly cancelled. With time on his hands, the prime minister decided to pay his respects to the murdered candidate who was lying in state at the headquarters of the ruling party. Everyone on the team naturally wanted to go along. And so off we went, sirens wailing as we forced our way through crowds of weeping mourners until the motorcade could go no farther. At this point the prime minister opened his car door and plunged into the multitude, accompanied only by his RCMP bodyguard following in his wake.

I hesitated. Still nursing my wounds from messing up my first briefing that morning, I didn't know what to do. Was it the job of the foreign-policy adviser to risk his life by accompanying the prime minister into a sea of grief-stricken followers of an assassinated leader? I decided that it wasn't. About thirty minutes later the prime minister reappeared, fighting his way through the mob, followed by his RCMP bodyguard who as before let his boss open the way for him.

Before we left Mexico, an unhappy chief of staff gave me some less than fatherly advice. The adviser and no one else, not even the local ambassador, was responsible for ensuring that the prime minister was properly briefed each morning. The adviser and no one else was responsible for remaining close to him throughout the day. The adviser and no one else was responsible for providing the substance of press releases on foreign-policy issues. Everyone on the team, and that included Jim Bartleman, had to produce or get out!

I returned to my house in Ottawa, my confidence shaken, regretting that this wisdom hadn't been given to me at the beginning and not the end of the trip — maybe I would have stayed at home.

35

Anti-Personnel Land Mines

Prime Minister Chrétien received the president of the International Committee of the Red Cross (ICRC), Cornelio Sommaruga, the bespectacled, heavily built former foreign minister of Switzerland, in his Centre Block office early in his first term in May 1994. Sommaruga raised the issue of anti-personnel land mines and said something had to be done to ban their use. Having worked with the ICRC in Bangladesh, where it ran refugee camps housing millions, and in Israel, where it monitored the treatment of Palestinian prisoners, I knew the organization and a number of its senior officers. One of its top officials, Frédéric Maurice, with whom I'd developed particularly close ties, had just been killed by Serb artillery fire as he led a convoy of trucks laden with humanitarian aid into Sarajevo. When I expressed by heartfelt condolences, Sommaruga's eyes filled with tears.

Sommaruga told the prime minister that ICRC's mandate included reunifying families divided by war and bringing help to prisoners of war. It was also, he said, to press governments to eliminate weapons of war that caused indiscriminate or unnecessary suffering. Thousands of people were being killed and maimed each year and huge areas of fertile farming land rendered useless for cultivation by one particular blind instrument: anti-personnel land mines scattered by rampaging armies during the proliferating conflicts of the Third World. Civil society in the form of more than 1,000 non-governmental organizations from countries around the world and loosely grouped under a steering committee of the International Campaign to Ban Mines, headed by an American, Jody Williams, was mobilizing international public opinion. Governments were starting to move; growing numbers were banning the export of any type of mine. Toothless provisions governing their use were already on the books — in the form of the 1980 Convention on Certain Conventional Weapons. An international treaty banning their use, however, was needed.

After his meeting with Sommaruga, the prime minister made the ban on the production and use of anti-personnel mines a Canadian foreign-policy priority. His initial move was to raise the issue at the June 1994 Naples summit, the first leader of the G7 to adopt the cause. His colleagues heard him out but weren't interested: the mines issue was an idea whose time hadn't come yet. The prime minister carried on with his missionary work, lobbying presidents and prime ministers and encouraging Foreign Minister André Ouellet to commit Foreign Affairs to the struggle. Throughout 1995 and early 1996, world leaders gradually began to show interest, stimulated by the growing support among their publics for a ban. But even those who were personally sympathetic found themselves faced with reluctant military establishments that argued removing anti-personnel mines from their arsenals would endanger their troops and put them at a disadvantage in fighting wars.

In January 1996, Lloyd Axworthy replaced Ouellet as foreign minister and enthusiastically adopted the cause, making it the centrepiece of his human-security agenda. The prime minister continued his efforts with world leaders. In summit meetings in May and June, he persuaded the leaders of the Commonwealth Caribbean and European Union to issue political declarations favouring a ban. In September he dealt once and for all with foot-dragging from Canada's own defence establishment by ordering Canada's military to destroy immediately one-third of Canada's anti-personnel mine stocks. The other two-thirds would be disposed of "in the context of successful negotiations." And in what would be the turning point in the campaign, he accepted Axworthy's recommendation that Canada issue a challenge to delegates at an international meeting in Ottawa to return to Canada's capital to sign a final treaty before the end of 1997.

Nobody and no country, Canada and the United States included, anticipated the wave of popular support that followed. More than 1,000 non-governmental organizations in the Mine Action Group swung into action to pressure governments in a massive public-relations campaign. Chrétien and Axworthy lobbied relentlessly. The prime minister alone would eventually raise the matter in private meetings with more than 100 world leaders at various G7, G8, Asia-Pacific Economic Cooperation (APEC), Commonwealth, and Francophonie summits, with official visitors to Canada, and during his official travels abroad. One after another the recalcitrant countries, including France and the United Kingdom, fell into line. The big holdout was the United States. Ostensibly, the Americans were on side. In May 1996, Clinton announced American support for an international agreement to ban anti-personnel mines. At the same time, however, he said that American negotiators had red lines they wouldn't cross. The first and most important was that the treaty wouldn't apply to Korea where American and North Korean troops had been confronting one another for more than 40 years across a heavily mined so-called demilitarized zone. The second was that anti-personnel mines used in conjunction with anti-tank mines would be exempt from the ban. And the third was that a nine-year period would be allowed to phase in the treaty.

The negotiations to finalize the draft treaty opened on September 1 in Oslo, Norway. The Americans arrived with a senior delegation and worked hard but achieved nothing. By September 15, President Clinton was very unhappy. The conference was scheduled to wind up on September 16, but none of the American conditions had been accepted. Princess Diana, a great champion of the cause, had been killed just the day before the conference opened, imbuing the movement with a saintly aura and attracting massive interest from the world press, which played up the isolation of the United States in company with the likes of Iran, Iraq, China, Cuba, and Russia. Making matters worse, the president personally supported a treaty and even kept an inert mine on his desk as a symbol of his commitment. In an act of desperation, therefore, he intervened personally with world leaders to see if language could be found that would meet the concerns of his military without undermining the substance of the treaty. His interlocutor of choice was Jean Chrétien.

During the evening of September 15, the telephone rang at home. It was the Prime Minister's Office switchboard: President Clinton wanted to speak to the prime minister urgently. Assuming the president wanted to discuss anti-personnel land mines, I called Foreign Affairs Undersecretary Don Campbell for a quick update on the Oslo negotiations. Campbell told me that he and Axworthy had been responding to appeals all evening from their opposite numbers in Washington to help them bridge their differences with the rest of the international community. The call from the president, he told me, was an indication that the situation was desperate for the Americans. The call I then put through would be the first of four or five that would take place throughout the night as the two leaders sought a formula that would allow the Americans to join the consensus. The prime minister, while unwilling to compromise the substance of the treaty, did his best to be helpful, waking up Canada's negotiator in Oslo to try out ideas, discussing options with French President Chirac, and calling South African President Nelson Mandela to enlist his support to give the Americans more time to solve their internal problems. In the end, Clinton couldn't persuade the Joint Chiefs of Staff to agree and was forced to tell the prime minister that he had failed.

Chrétien, however, wouldn't take no for an answer, telling Clinton he couldn't understand why the leader of the most powerful nation on earth couldn't overrule his generals. And surely the country that had put a man on the moon could overcome the technical obstacles to accepting the draft treaty? The failure of the U.S. administration to come on side, he added, would isolate Washington on an issue of critical importance to humanity at the end of the twentieth century. The prime minister, of course, adopted a high moral tone. After all, we Canadians have always felt that it was our duty — even our birthright — to point out to our American cousins how they could better organize their affairs and those of humanity. And he was following in the noble tradition of Canadian leaders such as Prime Ministers John Diefenbaker, Lester Pearson, and Pierre Trudeau, who consistently gave excellent, if unsolicited, advice on the big foreign-policy issues of their day to their presidential contemporaries, even if their wise counsel merely infuriated their good American friends, leading one famous former U.S. secretary of state in the 1960s to call Canada the "Stern Daughter of the Voice of God."

In this instance, however, it was the American president who had sought the help of his Canadian counterpart. Nevertheless, faced with a persistent Canadian leader who continued to press him not to give up the fight when he had already done so, the president fought back. No one, he said, had the right to question the goodwill of the United States! And his country wouldn't, he said, be the skunk at the garden party when the treaty was signed! That, unfortunately, was the way things played out.

In December 1997, U.S. delegates were forced to look on as representatives 2,400 strong from 122 signatory and thirty-five observer countries plus a roomful of non-governmental organizations celebrated the signature of the convention in the Conference Centre at the old Ottawa Union Station.

36

The Awful State of His Health

I accompanied the prime minister when he travelled to Europe to participate in the fiftieth anniversary commemorations of the Normandy landings in early June 1994. The first event was a ceremony in London at Green Park to mark the inauguration of a memorial to Canadian war dead. I watched from my place two rows back as a happy Princess Diana, separated but not yet divorced from Prince Charles, took her seat beside Prince Andrew. They had been friends since childhood when she lived with her parents on the royal estate at Sandringham and their spectacular marital problems with their spouses had been splashed across the newspapers for years. But if there was any pain, it wasn't evident on that sunny, cool day in London as we waited for the arrival of Her Majesty and Prince Philip to start the official ceremonies. They launched into a playful conversation with much joking and laughing, but I tried not to listen — it was their business.

What a contrast to the cold, almost sullen Princess Diana whom my wife and I had met some years earlier at a diplomatic reception in Brussels. I didn't blame her at the time; the event was just another dull gathering to promote British exports that, to tell the truth, we attended only to meet the famous spouse of Prince Charles. I was to think of that day in London when I heard the news reports of her death on Labour Day weekend in 1997. And again in May 2003, when as lieutenant governor of Ontario, I hosted Prince Andrew at an official luncheon at Queen's Park in Toronto.

We spent the weekend at Gosport on the south coast of England, attending ceremonies to mark the embarkation of the more than 15,000 Canadian troops who stormed ashore at Juno Beach on June 6, 1944. The chill pouring rain didn't bother our British hosts in the slightest. Cold and damp, I sought shelter under the platform holding the official party but was soaked, anyway, from water dripping through the cracks. The next day Prime Minister and Mrs. Chrétien were scheduled to make the ceremonial crossing of the English Channel on the Royal Yacht HMS *Britannia*. The prime minister was allowed to take one bodyguard and one flunky with him. I was the designated flunky. We went on board in good class-conscious British style. Flunkies and bodyguards negotiated the service gangway, leading into a lower deck close to the kitchen, to be greeted by cheerful ordinary seamen. The leaders and their spouses strolled aboard on a magnificent walkway to the upper deck to be met with formal whistles and salutes by the captain and his officers in full-braid uniform.

After I had been confined to cabin with an RCMP officer long enough to make sure that I knew my station in life, an equerry of the Queen came to get me, saying that Her Majesty had decided to allow diplomatic advisers to mix with the others. I abandoned my newfound RCMP friend to her lonely existence in the cabin and headed for the action. In the main stateroom, Her Majesty was issuing last-minute instructions to the serving staff on how to receive her distinguished guests. Her conscientious attention to detail and concern for the well-being of her invitees aroused my admiration, a feeling reinforced when my wife and I called on her at Buckingham Palace shortly after I assumed my duties as her representative in Ontario in 2002.

The fifty-two guests included assorted kings, queens, presidents, prime ministers, and foreign ministers representing the coalition that defeated Germany in the Second World War. The Germans and Austrians had pointedly not been invited. Soon a gaggle of the great of the world congregated for morning tea. The British Royal Family was out in force and threw themselves energetically into playing the role of good hosts. I drank my tea with the other advisers, all of us casting furtive glances in the direction of our particular leaders in case he or she had need of our wisdom.

The guests then moved outside to watch as HMS *Britannia* took the salute from one of the greatest arrays of warships assembled for review in British waters since the Second World War — fifty-five destroyers, frigates, aircraft carriers, and landing craft plus ten merchant ships. Finally, fast modern military jets from eighteen nations, followed by thirteen different types of Second World War aircraft, including Swordfish, Lancasters, Hurricanes, and Spitfires, flew by in a show of air power and nostalgia. In mid-channel, President Clinton departed to board the American aircraft carrier *George Washington* — it would not do, it seemed, for the president of the United States to arrive in France to commemorate D-Day on a British ship when it was the Americans and not the British who had sustained the greatest losses fifty years earlier coming ashore on the beaches.

The host at my table for lunch was Princess Margaret, Countess of Snowdon, the Queen's sister, who showed no sign of the illness that would end her life a few years later. Lech Wałęsa, president of Poland, and Douglas Hurd, British foreign secretary, both of whom I had met at NATO when I was ambassador there, and neither of whom remembered me, were among the eight lucky guests at my table who feasted on what my souvenir menu tells me was *Couronne de tomates à l'homard*, *Suprême de volaille Edouard VII*, and *Framboises St. Georges* washed down by Gewürztraminer Grand Cru Altenberg 1989 and Pauillac Château Latour 1990. The Duke of Edinburgh presided over a dinner of similar quality later that evening when our table for eight included Prime Minister Paul Keating of Australia and President Václav Havel of the Czech Republic. In all of this, I shouldn't have been surprised when I discovered that Royals enjoy talking about everyday matters just like the rest of us, but of course I was. And just when I was beginning to believe it was my natural lot in life to consort with the great and famous, the Queen's equerry came to remind me and the other diplomatic advisers that we shouldn't forget to use the servant gangway when exiting the ship.

In Normandy I took my place in the crowd at Omaha Beach to watch the victors of the Second World War, led by Presidents Mitterrand and Clinton, solemnly commemorate the landings that spelled the beginning of the end for Adolf Hitler in 1944. It was raining and cold, but the assembled veterans, now old men, didn't mind; they knew this would be the last pilgrimage to France for most of them. Charles Lynch, a Southam news columnist and a former war correspondent whose work I had admired for years, ignored the weather in his medal-bedecked blazer and stood laughing with another old veteran, Michel Gauvin, winner of the Distinguished Service Order and a retired Canadian ambassador. Both would pass away shortly afterward.

The Canadian delegation headed for Courseulles-sur-Mer where the Canadian soldiers had come ashore, making greater gains than either the Americans or the British before being bogged down in the fighting further inland. I thought of my mother's cousin from the Rama First Nation, wounded as he parachuted in the dark behind enemy lines fifty years before with his mates. I thought of a boyhood friend of my mother, Sanford Stinson, also from Rama, who had been killed in the fighting at Caen several weeks after D-Day. I took the prime minister aside to speak to him about the sacrifice Indigenous soldiers had made for Canada in the wars of the twentieth century. My own Indian great-grandfather had been wounded in the First World War and returned to die on the reserve, his lungs ravaged my mustard gas. I told him that Indigenous soldiers were wounded or died for a Canada that, in those days, treated them as second-class citizens and didn't accord them the same benefits as white veterans when they returned from overseas. The prime minister included a reference to Sanford Stinson in his speech broadcast direct to Canada.

The next morning commemorative ceremonies led by Prime Minister Chrétien and French President Mitterrand were held at the Bény-sur-Mer Commonwealth War Cemetery where Canadian soldiers killed in the Battle of Normandy were buried. Before they began I joined the veterans as they walked between the rows of tombstones looking for fallen comrades. Sanford Stinson's tombstone, I saw, was adorned with flowers among the freshly cut grass and chairs set up for the Canadian war veterans coming later to honour their fallen comrades. The son, I noted, was now twice the age his father had been when he had died. The father, I also thought, would have been proud to have known that his son had grown up to be a leader of his people. His son, a long-time and progressive chief of his First Nation and a friend, had never seen his father's grave, and I took a picture of it for him.

I would think of this day at Bény-sur-Mer six months later as I accompanied Prime Minister Chrétien when he called on President Mitterrand at the Élysée Palace. One of the giants of postwar French political life and a man of contradictions, the president had been a right-wing supporter of Vichy France in the early days of the war, eventually joining the Resistance and emerging at the liberation of France as a leading socialist. After his second election as president, he moved his party to the right economically and shed his early reliance on the Communist Party to gain a second seven-year term. He was a strong supporter of Israel over the years and confidant of Israeli leaders as different politically as Golda Meir, Menachem Begin, Moshe Dayan, and Yigal Allon. Yet he quietly protected former Vichy officials guilty of sending French Jews to death camps during the war. René Bousquet, Maurice Papon, and Paul Touvier, who were compressed into one character played by Michael Caine in the movie *The Statement*, are three of the notorious anti-Semitic Vichy-era officials associated, fairly or not, with the French president. And defying conventional morality, Mitterrand fathered two children with his mistresses at no cost to his relations with the media or with the French public.

Mitterrand treated the prime minister with genuine affection, making a determined effort to be a good host despite the awful state of his health, greeting him at the entrance to his office and leading him inside where the fragrance of roses was overwhelmed by the smell of a hospital room. Ravaged by prostate cancer, his condition had deteriorated markedly since Normandy. His face now had the pallor of death, there were dark splotches under his washed-out brown eyes, his lips were purple, the skin on his sallow face hung loosely, and his neatly combed black-and white hair was thinner than I remembered. Obviously in pain, he shuffled his legs and shifted his position in his chair in an attempt to be more comfortable. He would, I was certain, have willingly traded his elegant office with its Louis XVI furniture, ancient tapestries on the walls, giant crystal chandeliers, and gilt over everything for a moment of good health.

When I was Canada's ambassador to NATO in the early 1990s, I had seen Mitterrand in action at summit meetings in Rome and Brussels where I had the impression that his peers listened to his pronouncements with superficial respect, hiding a sense that they were in the presence of a lame-duck leader who was over the hill. It was only later, when I sat in on his discussion with Canada's prime minister in Paris and read his *Memoir in Two Voices*, written jointly with Elie Wiesel, Auschwitz survivor and Nobel Peace Prize winner, that I saw the depth of his wisdom and the warm and caring side of his nature. But by the time of our December 1994 visit, everyone, himself included, knew he was dying. The newspapers and weekly magazines were filled with retrospective examinations of his life that were premature quasi-obituaries in another guise. Far from being offended, the president was making his own farewells on French television, seeking to justify his protection of Vichy-era war criminals and formally presenting Mazarine Pingeot, his daughter, to the French people.

I would think of François Mitterrand when I called on Fidel Castro in 1996 and again in 1998 as a secret envoy from the prime minister seeking to persuade the Cuban leader to introduce democratic reforms in his country. The same medicinal odour was pervasive in Castro's private office, and he, like Mitterrand, looked like a shadow of his former self at the time. Mitterrand died in January 1996, but Castro fought his way back to health.

37

The Scorching Heat of the Italian Summer

We flew into Rome in the scorching heat of the Italian summer in July 1994 to make official calls at the Vatican. The Holy City of the Roman Catholic faithful is also a sovereign European state with a national territory, a superb diplomatic corps, a foreign policy, and excellent bilateral relations with Canada. And the Holy Father, in addition to being the spiritual head of the church, is also a head of state. Ambassador Leonard Legault told us that while frail, Pope John Paul II was maintaining a full work schedule. He was, however, tired and would depart for a summer of rest at his retreat at Castel Gandolfo following his meeting with our party.

The next day the prime minister's team — Catholics, Protestants, and Jews — accompanied the Chrétiens to the Vatican. Everyone was dressed soberly. We were received with full protocol honours by members of the Papal Guard in sixteenth-century Swiss military uniforms and lay members of the papal court in striped pants, white ties, and swallow-tailed jackets with elaborately decorated silver chains holding papal medals of high distinction hanging from their necks. They escorted us up wide marble staircases and along long gilt-painted corridors adorned with statues and

Renaissance frescoes to an antechamber outside the private quarters of the pontiff. We waited while the Chrétiens were received in private audience. Time dragged on. An RCMP bodyguard stumbled against a priceless Ming vase that rocked back and forth, almost causing heart attacks among our elegantly dressed escort officers, but it didn't fall over. I filled the time admiring the rooftops of Rome and staring down on Saint Peter's Square, seeing in my mind's eye the multitudes of pilgrims who gathered there on great religious occasions to receive the blessing of the pope.

I was excited at the prospect of meeting the Holy Father, a person of deep and fervent religious faith whose spiritual strength had touched the lives of millions. And although not a Roman Catholic, I recognized the enormous role played by the church in the lives of individuals and societies throughout the ages and in the world of the twentieth century. During my first posting as a junior foreign-service officer to Canada's embassy in Bogotá, Colombia, in the late 1960s, I had watched with admiration the rise of liberation theology in the Latin American Catholic Church of the period. Exposed to the brutality of the rigid and unjust social and economic conditions imposed on the average Colombian of the period, I had hailed the emergence within the Catholic Church of theologians who took the side of the poor and agitated for social and economic change. A highlight of my time was climbing to the roof of my apartment building to join a crowd of pious maids, who had emerged via the servants' stairs from the luxury apartments where they quietly toiled for starvation wages, to watch Pope Paul VI go by in an open car en route to the 1968 Latin American Conference of Bishops at Bogotá's cathedral. They hoped that the church would be a force for social and economic change. And Paul VI didn't disappoint them, openly denouncing the lack of justice in their society.

John Paul II was no fan of Liberation theology, perhaps judging it too heavily influenced by Marxist doctrines of the type he had fought against for many years in his native country. He was, however, a fierce defender of social, political, and economic justice in Poland, supporting materially and spiritually Father Jerzy Popiełuszko and other church leaders who had resisted communism. I was sure that the 264th Roman pontiff, born Karol Wojtyła and the first non-Italian elected pope since 1523, would go down in the history books with Ronald Reagan and Mikhail Gorbachev for helping tear down the Iron Curtain by supporting Poland's Solidarity Movement. His influence extended beyond Europe. When the pope visited Cuba in January 1998, he praised the socialist ideals of the people while calling for greater religious freedom. Fidel Castro was still under the force of the pope's personality and message when I called on him to make arrangements for Prime Minister Chrétien to visit Cuba shortly after the Sovereign Pontiff left Havana. In the course of a night-long conversation, Castro returned time and again to the subject of John Paul II, speaking of him with great reverence. What irony, I thought, one charismatic leader devoted to a credo of dialectical materialism overwhelmed by another whose life was dedicated to the spiritual.

Then it was time to file in to meet the pope. The ladies anxiously pulled their veils into place and the men adjusted their ties. Everyone was solemn as the prime minister introduced his entourage. There were no speeches: the pope looked older than I expected, his shoulders were stooped, and his hands trembled as he handed over small gifts of rosaries and medallions. Aware that we all wanted souvenir photographs, he twisted his body to be able to make direct contact with us from his one good eye, kindly taking care that the Vatican photographer captured the moment for our scrapbooks. In this, and in three subsequent brief encounters in the coming years, I found him as impressive in person as he was in reputation despite his failing health.

The audience over, the prime minister, the chief of staff, the ambassador, and I went on to call on Cardinal Angelo Sodano, secretary of state and prime minister of the Vatican in its temporal capacity. The others returned to the hotel. The cardinal, accompanied by Archbishop Jean-Louis Tauran, officially known as the Vatican secretary for relations with states but in reality the Vatican foreign minister, pressed the prime minister to have Canada adopt a conservative position on family planning at a U.N. conference in Cairo. The discussion was animated, but the tone was subdued and my mind wandered. The black cassocks, wide red sashes, purple silk trimmings, and skullcaps, together with the heavy gold pectoral crosses and chains of the two clerics, matched in elegance the decor of the office with its pink marble floors, white marble tables, plush carpets, antique furniture, and paintings and tapestries on religious themes.

The room was hot and airless. A faint smell of roses hung in the air, though there were no flowers to be seen, leading me to imagine a busy nun hurriedly removing a vase filled with dead blossoms just before we arrived. I listened to the quiet ticking of a grandfather clock and examined an El Greco picture of Christ, seeing but neither feeling the passion nor understanding the genius of the Spanish artist. Except for the telephone on the table in front of the cardinal, incongruously coloured green, white, and red, the decor of the room could have been taken from a 16th-century Renaissance painting.

38

The Law of Unintended Consequences

On April 7, 1994, the news agencies began reporting that the aircraft carrying the presidents of Rwanda and Burundi had been shot down on its final approach to Kigali's airport. The next day a slaughter of Tutsis started in Rwanda. A Hutu militia, called the Interahamwe or "those who attack together," set up secretly in 1993 for the specific purpose of killing Tutsis, murdered the Rwandan prime minister, the president of the Supreme Court, and cabinet ministers. A mass murder of Tutsis began, fully covered in the international press, until three interminable months later, from 800,000 to one million people, largely Tutsis but including moderate Hutus, had been slaughtered.

In June 1994 in Naples, the leaders of the most powerful economic nations in the world, the G7, held their annual summit meeting. I sat in as the prime minister met privately with the host, the corrupt Prime Minister Silvio Berlusconi of Italy, before the beginning of the official meetings. Everything about the Italian leader was smarmy. He was one of Italy's wealthiest people and had made good use of his ownership of a television and newspaper empire to win the recent elections. Berlusconi lamented the fate of the Tutsis in Rwanda, musing aloud about the need for the world "to do something" to stop the genocide. Chrétien suggested that an international military force be sent, saying Canada already had two aircraft flying into Kigali and a distinguished general on the ground with the United Nations. Berlusconi quickly changed the subject. The leaders of the seven most powerful economic countries on the planet all studiously avoided the issue during their summit.

In the early summer of 1994, a well-trained Tutsi army swept out of its strongholds in northern Rwanda to save the surviving remnants of the Tutsi civilian population. France then dispatched a large military force to seize the western part of Rwanda. Its ostensible goal was to put an end to the genocide, but its real aim was to save its traditional allies and long-standing customers for arms purchases, the Hutu militants and their families, from the revenge of the Tutsi. Hundreds of thousands of Hutus, including the main body of Interahamwe militia and Rwandan army units involved in the genocide, then escaped the country to seek refuge on the western side of Lake Kivu in eastern Zaire.

Throughout this period the world followed the attempts of Canadian General Roméo Dallaire to bring an end to the massacres; but neither I nor anyone I knew had any knowledge of his desperate efforts before the beginning of the genocide to obtain authority from the United Nations to conduct searches for weapons to head off the planned killings. Nor were we aware how dangerous and isolated his position was. Canadians regarded him as a genuine hero then, and even more so later when the facts surrounding his role came out. I remember meeting him outside the prime minister's office in the Centre Block in Ottawa and escorting him in to receive the prime minister's and the nation's thanks after he had completed his mission. A true soldier, he made no complaint regarding the disgraceful way the United Nations had behaved, and successfully hid the inner trauma consuming him. I remember thinking that it wasn't only the United Nations that had let him down. The international community and his own country could have done more.

* * *

The next crisis was not long in coming. In March 1996, the Rwandan army of battle-hardened, well-trained, and competently led Tutsi war veterans, claiming self-defence, attacked the Hutus in their refugee camps in eastern Zaire. The armed forces of Zaire had totally collapsed by this time. The U.N. secretary-general issued an erroneous statement claiming that 1.2 million refugees had been displaced in heavy fighting and that tens of thousands of people were dying of hunger and cholera. He then withdrew all humanitarian personnel from eastern Zaire "for their own safety," indirectly creating a blackout on reliable information on developments. World leaders developed a sense of impending tragedy, heightened by their guilty knowledge that the international community had stood by just two years earlier during one of the worst genocides since the Second World War.

On Thursday, November 7, 1996, in surprising back-channel calls to me from President Bill Clinton's national security adviser, Anthony Lake, the Americans offered to place their military forces under Canadian command if we would lead an international mission to save the Hutus in their eastern Zairian refugee camps. When I briefed the prime minister, his instant reaction was it would be irresponsible of Canada not to say yes. Before providing a definitive answer, however, he wanted to consult the U.N. secretary-general, potential troop-contributing countries, his Cabinet colleagues, and the Leader of the Opposition.

My team in the Privy Council Office then went to work throughout Friday, November 8, setting up telephone calls to some twenty world leaders. I then called Lake to brief him on the prime minister's response. On Saturday, November 9, the prearranged telephone calls began to come in. The leaders of the United Kingdom, Belgium, Senegal, and Ivory Coast told the prime minister they would support a force led by Canada. The United Kingdom and Senegal pledged troops. The British added that they would consider putting a brigade group of 5,000 in the field. Belgium said that it would provide transport aircraft and other assistance to help Senegal field a battalion, but wouldn't put troops into the area. The U.N. secretary-general publicly endorsed the prime minister's initiative, saying there was no other way forward.

On Sunday, November 10, the presidents of France and Kenya pledged sizable contingents, as did the prime ministers of the Netherlands and Italy. In the coming days, the presidents of Tanzania, Cameroon, Argentina, Brazil, Chile, and the prime ministers of Japan, Spain, and Ireland, promised their support. Those who couldn't provide troops said that they would finance African contingents. All urged Canada to persevere since we held the key to American participation and were acceptable to all parties in the conflict. We were eventually to have offers of between 12,000 and 16,000 troops, pledges for more than $100 million, and the moral backing of Canada's closest friends internationally. And this didn't even include American military support, which the Pentagon assured us via military channels would be provided.

The Cabinet met on Monday, Remembrance Day, and formally took the decision that Canada would lead the mission provided certain caveats were met, including a commitment by the United States to follow through with its undertaking to back us up and put forces on the ground in eastern Zaire under our command. I then called Anthony Lake, who initially expressed appreciation but then called back with bad news. He said that he'd just chaired a meeting of the "principals" (the secretary of state, the secretary of defense, the chairman of the Joint Chiefs of Staff, the director of the CIA, and the national security adviser) who served as the top crisis managers in the American system. There had been last-minute problems, he said, in particular with the proposed command structure. Lake wouldn't be able to get the president to sign off on our understanding until he managed to forge a consensus. He was prepared to come to Ottawa with a team to discuss matters, but that could take a day or two.

I was suspicious. Expectations, I told him, had been raised that a force led by Canada backed by the United States would shortly be en route to eastern Zaire. We couldn't waste time while he put together a team to come to Ottawa. I would depart immediately for Washington with the members of the task force to sort matters out. I then called the prime minister with the news. The Americans seemed to be having second thoughts. I was leaving with a team of senior civilian and military officials for Washington immediately to try to put the train back on the tracks. An unhappy prime minister told me not to hesitate to seek guidance from him even if the negotiations proceeded into the night.

The Canadian chargé d'affaires met our private flight at Dulles Airport in Washington and accompanied us to the back entrance of the White House. After a lengthy wait at the guard post, a visibly uneasy Anthony Lake came out to meet us and escort us to the underground Situation Room of the National Security Council where the big crises affecting the security of the United States were managed. From the furtive looks on the faces of our American colleagues, we guessed they had left us to cool our heels outside while they frantically worked out a strategy to present to their betrayed friends. After a round of hand-shaking, Lake gave the floor to Peter Tarnoff of the State Department. Tarnoff stopped smiling, screwed his face into a tough, uncompromising scowl, and began lecturing us with a high-pitched, bad-cop, northeastern American accent that matched the buttoned-down, Ivy League attitude he'd adopted for the occasion.

"You Canadians," he said patronizingly, "have done a good job in assembling a coalition. The principals, however, have come to the conclusion that the job is too big for you to handle. We have, accordingly, reconsidered our proposal. The United States rather than Canada will now lead the mission. Canada, however, will have its chance 'to play leader.' Exactly thirty days after the beginning of the operation, American troops will be withdrawn, leaving the command to Canada. And please understand that our troops will pull out, no matter what the conditions on the ground are at that time. It will be up to you guys to decide on the nature of the follow-on force, should you decide to have one." He smirked and stopped talking.

Then it was Lake's turn, and his role was the good cop. Looking pained and solicitous, he sadly noted that "things have not turned out exactly as foreseen. The United States, however, really appreciates the efforts the Canadian prime minister has made. You Canadians shouldn't worry since his efforts to put together a force won't be in vain. We will now command it and ensure that it carries out its proper role for thirty days. As Peter said, Canada will have its turn at the controls when we pull out."

I decided to stop the meeting before any of the stunned and enraged Canadian party could comment. I headed for the door followed by Lake, who earnestly told me as I hurried up the steps out of the bunker that we all should be relieved that a formula had been found for the United States to participate. I said that I needed to consult Prime Minister Chrétien immediately, and Lake ushered me into his private office. As I dialled the PMO switchboard in Ottawa, I glanced down at Lake's desk. There in black and white was a memorandum to the American national security adviser from a member of his staff outlining the strategy the Americans intended to use that evening to deal with their earnest Canadian cousins. I looked away, not quite ready to read a friend's mail, even if we were being double-crossed in a neighbouring room. A cheerless prime minister then came on the line. The operator had summoned him from the table at the residence of the Japanese ambassador where he was the guest of honour; he knew that whenever I called him it was usually with bad news. The prime minister didn't take my message well, shouting into the receiver so loudly that I had to hold the telephone a foot away from my ear. I undertook to do what I could to put matters right and said I would call him back.

I repeated to Lake the exact words of the prime minister, and I swear that he blushed. I added that my advice to the prime minister had been to call the president if the officials involved couldn't come to an arrangement. We Canadians were as disturbed as any member of the international community at developments in eastern Zaire and had been prepared to participate under the leadership of the United States or any other credible big power in a mission. We had, moreover, acted responsibly in responding favourably to the American request that we take the lead, backed by American military might. We would now look ridiculous in the eyes of the nations the prime minister had contacted if we went along with the change in scenario. Canada would also be reluctant to help the United States out of jams in the future if the matter weren't resolved to our satisfaction.

Lake, a decent person, seemed embarrassed at the antics in the Situation Room, and didn't want the prime minister to telephone the president, who wouldn't be happy with the way his officials had been handling the file. "Give me time to find a solution," he asked. He then led our somewhat overwhelmed band of Canadians to a large office and told us to wait. Two long hours later a smiling Lake came to fetch us. Everyone in the bunker was now a good cop. Of course, Canada could take the lead. Of course, American military forces would be placed under the operational control of a Canadian general. Why not send out for pizza? The pizza delivery boy, I admiringly noted, made it through White House security much faster than we Canadians had some hours earlier!

The Americans then told us that, by the way, in return for giving us the command, there would be a few changes in the plan. The United States would cut back on its commitment of military forces to reduce the risk to its personnel. Instead of sending 4,000 or 5,000 ground troops to the theatre, the number would be limited to 1,500 personnel, plus airlift and other support elements outside eastern Zaire. Instead of taking control of the airports and deploying troops to help form a protective corridor from the Rwandan border to the refugee camps, American forces would protect only the several hundred yards of road from the Rwandan border town of Gisenyi to the airport at Goma. Moreover, the United States opposed allowing the troops to use force to accomplish their mission. Were fighting to break out between any of the rival forces in the area or a slaughter of civilians to start, the force commander wouldn't be authorized to use his soldiers to intervene.

If Lake had said that the Americans intended to keep their forces out of harm's way when he had telephoned me on November 7 to seek our help, I doubt the prime minister would have seriously considered his proposal. At this stage, however, with thousands apparently dying in eastern Zaire and with Canada already committed to leading the mission, we had no choice but to carry on. We reasoned that even if the American forces cowered at the airport at Goma, their presence would guarantee the participation of the coalition the prime minister had put together. The presence of even one American soldier on the ground in the danger zone would provide a guarantee to coalition members that the U.S. cavalry would ride to our rescue if we had to leave in a hurry.

In the ensuing discussions, we gritted our teeth and worked on the American texts to reach agreement on the basic issues. Lake proposed that he and I meet in New York on Thursday, November 14, to draft a resolution for U.N. Security Council approval incorporating these principles. I telephoned the prime minister around midnight to get approval; Anthony Lake disappeared into the private quarters of the White House to obtain the blessing of the president. Our team then departed for the airport to board our waiting Canadian Forces aircraft for home.

* * *

The deal we struck with the Americans remained intact for just three glorious days. On Wednesday, November 13, President Clinton appeared on national television to say: "Following consultations with Canadian officials last night, we reached general agreement with Canada on the mission definition, command, and control arrangements, duration of the mission, and other key issues. We will work through the details in the next day or two." He added that the United States welcomed Canada's offer to lead the mission but that the final decision on U.S. participation would depend on the findings of an American military assessment team sent to the region on November 12. The Canadian media went wild. For once it seemed that the United States was following Canada's lead on a major international event rather than the other way around. Story after story appeared, focusing on the so-called conversion of the prime minister, like St. Paul on the road to Damascus, on a rainy Remembrance Day weekend in November to the cause of rescuing civilians caught in the war in eastern Zaire. The media raised the prime minister so high up on a pedestal that the fall from grace, when it inevitably came, was all the harder.

On Thursday, November 14, Anthony Lake met me at our New York delegation and we quickly hammered out a draft text acceptable to both Canada and the United States based on our discussions in Washington two days earlier. But as I watched the debate in the U.N. Security Council on November 15 move ponderously to approve the resolution establishing the mission on one television channel, another channel began showing a tidal wave, twenty-five miles long, of refugees moving toward the Rwandan border. More than 750,000 crossed peacefully in the next several weeks, soon to be joined by large numbers from camps in Tanzania. I called the prime minister to say that the problem was being solved without the need to deploy the mission. Canada's initiative to mobilize an international rescue mission had forced the Rwandans to intervene decisively and solve a humanitarian problem that affected their own nationals. The initiative then died the death of a thousand cuts with Canada eventually telling its increasingly fractious allies at a meeting in New York on December 13 that there was no longer any need for a mission. I supported ending the operation. The purpose of the Security Council resolution had been fulfilled, however messily: those refugees who so desired had returned home. The prime minister made the final call, reluctantly giving instructions for the windup of the mission.

The law of unintended consequences then came into play. When the rescue force didn't deploy, the Tutsi army was free to occupy eastern Zaire, to assemble a motley collection of anti-Mobutu Zairean fighters, and to march on Kinshasa, Zaire's capital. The Tutsis then installed Laurent Kabila, an obscure Zairean rebel, as president of Zaire, replacing Mobutu Sese Seko, who went into exile. Kabila, whose chief claim to fame up to then had been an unsatisfactory collaboration with the famous Che Guevara in a failed rebellion decades earlier, renamed the country the Democratic Republic of the Congo and turned against his Tutsi friends. In the ensuing turmoil, "the widest interstate war in modern African history," in the words of Amnesty International, broke out. The armed forces of Rwanda, Namibia, Chad, Angola, Zimbabwe, and Uganda allied themselves with competing Congolese factions and joined the bloody fight for diamonds, precious metals, and spheres of influence.

More than a million would die, towns and cities would be destroyed, entire regions would be depopulated, the vestiges of civilization would disappear in vast areas, children and youth would be turned into hired killers, and even cannibalism would reappear in the eastern part of the country. The Western press would largely ignore the story, even though the number killed would exceed by far those massacred in the Rwandan genocide of 1994.

39

Killing the White Whale: A Drama in Three Acts

Act One

Spanish ambassador Enrique Costa José Luis Pardos didn't take the news well. He had arrived at my Blackburn Building office on Sparks Street in Ottawa on short notice on Friday, March 3, 1995, to warn the Canadian government not to apply the provisions of the Coastal Fisheries Protection Act to Spanish fishing boats operating beyond the 200-mile limit on the continental shelf on the Grand Banks of Newfoundland. I couldn't provide the assurances he sought. In fact, I knew that as we were meeting, an official was walking from one minister's office to another seeking the requisite four signatures on an order-in-council document to amend the act. Before the end of the day, Spanish (and Portuguese) fishing vessels would be barred from what until then had been international waters off Canada's East Coast. I therefore reiterated Canada's well-known position: Spanish fishermen were destroying the last commercially available ground fish off the Grand Banks of Newfoundland. Canada had negotiated an international agreement to conserve the stock, which Spain and the European Union were ignoring. We intended to arrest offending fishing vessels if need be.

Pardos stared at me for a long, silent minute. He then carefully put down his cup of coffee, rose to his feet, hitched up his trousers, clenched his hands into fists, and approached. Fierce and distraught, he towered over me. I was sure he was trying to decide whether to throttle or to smack me and braced myself and held tightly to my mug to keep the coffee from splattering over my suit. He chose a different option. Dropping to one knee, he thrust out his jaw, pounded his chest with his right fist, and told me "as a Spaniard" that his country would never accept the jurisdiction of Canada on the high seas. If Canada's "gunboats" tried to arrest Spain's fishing vessels, "Canada would bear the consequences." He then rose to his feet and stalked out the door, muttering that I harboured a personal anti-Spanish bias and was doing everything possible to punish his country for innocently fishing off Canada's East Coast.

Act Two

On the morning of March 9, after one last effort to achieve a deal with the European Union through telephone talks had failed, the Canadian government gave the order to arrest a Spanish fishing boat. Forty-two Fisheries protection officers and an RCMP team were embarked on two protection patrol vessels: the *Cape Roger* and the *Leonard J. Cowley* as well as on the Coast Guard vessel *Sir Wilfred Grenfell*. The *Cape Roger* was designated the lead vessel. Crew members trained by the Canadian Forces manned .50-calibre machine guns on the vessels that had been on station waiting for a call to action since March 4. The personnel were highly experienced, having participated in numerous armed boardings since 1986. At that time the government had approved the arming of patrol vessels after a humiliating incident in which Fisheries officers were held against their will on a Spanish fishing boat that had fled to the Azores rather than obey orders to proceed to St. John's. A Canadian Forces frigate, the HMCS *Terra Nova*, was situated over the horizon in Canadian waters as backup.

I was present in the Fisheries operations centre to observe the operation. Lights were flashing on various consoles, and television sets programmed to news channels were blaring out news of the action on the Grand Banks. Duty officers sat grimly at their places, taking down blow-by-blow descriptions of the action from the skipper on the high seas. Testosterone filled the room as the skipper of the *Cape Roger* pursued his prey, the *Estai*, a seventy-foot Spanish trawler, in fog and drizzle through what for all members of the world community save Canada were international waters on the nose of the Grand Banks. Intoxicated by the excitement and mesmerized by the glittering lights, I entered into the spirit of the pursuit. In my imagination, Fisheries Minister Brian Tobin was Captain Ahab of *Moby-Dick* barking orders to his crew. He had harpooned the Great White Whale and was being dragged in his longboat through the seas.

The *Estai* had already cut its warps, the cables attaching fishing gear to the trawler, dropping its net into the sea and liberating itself to flee. It had fought off one armed party trying to climb aboard from a Zodiac boat by throwing the ladders into the water. Now it was heading eastward through thirteen-foot seas whipped up by winds of fifteen miles per hour. The *Cape Roger* was being helped by a surveillance aircraft and from some distance away by its sister ships. Five Spanish fishing vessels kept pace with pursued and pursuer, bringing moral support to their fellow countrymen on board the *Estai* and threatening the *Cape Roger* by crowding in close to her until they were driven off by water cannon. The one European Union inspection vessel in the area, the *Kommander Amalie*, stayed well clear of the action.

The minister asked the public servants present to sign a written order authorizing the skipper of the *Cape Roger* to fire warning shots over the bow; if the *Estai* didn't stop, he would be authorized to blow away the propellers. Even though my signature wasn't required to make the document legal, and I suspected that Tobin only wanted me to inscribe my name to implicate the prime minister in the decision in case matters turned out badly, passion overcame reason and I joined the others in signing. The order was issued and there was a short silence. The duty officer then announced that after four bursts of .50-calibre machine-gun fire, the *Estai* had come to a stop in the water. The easy part was over.

Act Three

The weather could not have been better for a fight on Easter weekend as the crisis came to a head. Winds were low, seas were moderate, and visibility was fair. As the Canadian and Spanish fleets faced off on the Grand

Banks, I called Ambassador Pardos to tell him Canada intended to arrest another Spanish fishing vessel the next morning, and should the Spanish patrol boats intervene, our frigates had orders to fire on them. Just before the deadline, Deep Throat, my secret contact inside the European Union, called me. During an all-night emergency meeting of European ambassadors in Brussels, the Spaniards had backed down. The fish war was over but Spain would make us pay the price by throwing roadblock after roadblock in the way of a free-trade deal with Canada for years to come.

40

Running the Gauntlet

For several frantic days in October 1995, the Canadian government's efforts to cultivate close ties with China were on the verge of collapse. Chinese Premier Li Peng was scheduled to make the first visit to Canada by a senior Chinese leader since the 1989 massacres in Beijing. There would be private talks in Ottawa with Prime Minister Chrétien, followed by a general meeting involving ministers and senior officials. In the afternoon the premier would depart for Montreal in his own aircraft for the highlight of the visit: a meeting with premiers to welcome him at a gala dinner, as well as a sentimental meeting with Pierre Trudeau, who had been prime minister when Canada established diplomatic relations with China. The premier would depart after the festivities for Dorval Airport to continue his world tour.

But Premier Li Peng, we discovered, wanted to be difficult. Less than two days before his scheduled arrival in Ottawa, a grim member of the People's Liberation Army, accompanied by the Chinese ambassador to Canada, came to my office to lay down the law. The uniformed officer snapped out his message: "I am here to tell you that if Premier Li sees so much as a single anti-China demonstrator, he will cancel his official visit to Canada and return home. Canada will suffer the consequences." Premier Li Peng, also known as "the butcher of Tiananmen" for his role in the brutal suppression of the pro-democracy movement in China in 1989, was in Mexico on the foreign tour that would take him to Canada and had taken umbrage when confronted by demonstrators in Mexico City. Determined to accept no further affronts to his country and to his personal dignity, he had sent ahead the army officer, a member of his personal retinue, to ensure there would be no demonstrators on the streets of Canada during his visit. The body language of the emissary and the disquiet in the eyes of the ambassador indicated this was no bluff.

I wanted to tell him that if the premier couldn't abide demonstrators, then he should skip Canada. Sometime earlier the ambassador of another friendly dictatorship had come to my office to ask in all seriousness that I give orders for the arrest of people planning a protest march against her regime. It had given me great pleasure to give her a lesson on the functioning of Canadian democracy and to show her the door. In this case, however, Premier Li was visiting Canada in response to a major Canadian trade mission to his country the previous November. Should the premier leave in a fit of pique, our opening to China would be set back. As a citizen and a public servant, I knew we couldn't agree to the Chinese demand, but a subtle form of diplomacy was required to convince the Chinese premier to come and, after arriving, not cut his visit short.

Foreign Minister André Ouellet invited me to his office to devise a plan to save the visit. It would, we decided, be guile against intransigence. We decided to enmesh the premier in the program in Ottawa to make it too difficult for him to turn around and leave when he eventually — and inevitably — encountered the reality of Canadian street democracy. To lure him into our trap we moved the scheduled talks from the Cabinet room in the Centre Block of Parliament — with its banks of windows open to the parliamentary lawn that was all too likely to be filled with chanting demonstrators — to rooms buried deep in the heart of the fortress-like Pearson Building on Sussex Drive. The demonstrators would be free to do their thing, but we bet that the premier wouldn't walk out when roars of the demonstrators filtered their way through the walls.

Twenty-four hours later a smiling Premier Li Peng descended the stairs from his aircraft, which was drawn up outside the tightly controlled hangar dedicated to the arrivals and departures of official visitors at Ottawa's airport. The crowd assembled in the hangar gave the premier a rousing welcome — unsurprisingly, since they were all staff and families from the Chinese embassy. A little girl handed over the obligatory bouquet of flowers, the leaders delivered their mandatory speeches, the customary national anthems were played, the standard smartly dressed guard of honour was inspected, and the motorcade formed up routinely. But in a departure from usual practice, the RCMP escort officers took the back roads into Ottawa. The first encounter our distinguished guest had with the Canadian public was thus with an enthusiastic group of foreign-service employees in the lobby of the Pearson Building, commandeered to leave their offices and applaud. Had the premier known, he would surely have approved — "rent-a-crowds" were the way dictatorships greeted visitors the world over. We, however, were compromising our virtue and inviting him into the Pearson Building under false pretenses to expose him to the face of Canadian democracy in the form of assembled ranks of protestors when he emerged.

A protocol officer escorted the Canadian prime minister and Chinese premier, accompanied only by their ambassadors and advisers, to a small, windowless room in the interior of the Pearson Building for the first meeting. It was, in fact, a meeting before a meeting to allow the leaders to become comfortable with each other before the beginning of official talks. All went well until the prime minister delicately tried to discuss demonstrators and democracies. Li Peng's affable smile turned into a scowl. By this time, the coalition of anti–Li Peng groups was, as expected, marching down Sussex Drive toward the Pearson Building. A distant roar could be heard in our inner sanctum, but the prime minister said that the noise must be from crowds cheering for Canada's distinguished guest. The premier replaced his scowl with a smile as the waiting protocol officer escorted us to a large conference room as far from the street as possible, where ministers and senior officials waited patiently. The meeting was over in short order — there were few substantive items on the agenda other than trade matters — and it was time to depart.

Emerging from the elevator on the ground floor, the premier walked through the rows of applauding foreign-service employees. Their acclamations were more than offset, however, by the howls of the banner-waving crowd outside, held back by Ottawa's finest. The RCMP and Chinese security officers decided not to risk trying to leave from the front entrance, where the crowd was concentrated, and led a by now deeply unhappy guest to the back exit in the basement. There, a group of public servant smokers was to be found, puffing furtively as always on the cigarettes banned from the working and public areas of the building.

This hardened group of outcasts wasn't about to applaud anyone, not even the head of government of a country of great importance to Canada, and they looked on with indifference as the premier was hustled into his car. The media and demonstrators were lying in wait as the RCMP driver gunned his car out the door. Several were knocked down by the accelerating vehicle, but no one was seriously hurt. Someone said afterward that it seemed like a movie about John Dillinger escaping after a bank robbery with the FBI on his tail.

The big question now was whether the premier would cancel the Montreal portion of the trip. The Canadian interpreter assigned to the premier and sitting forgotten in the front seat of the Canadian-supplied limousine that took him to his aircraft — who debriefed me later — was an invisible witness as the premier fulminated against the villainy of Canadians and debated whether he should carry out his threat to abandon his mission.

When I arrived at the hotel in Montreal that evening for the next event, I was given good and bad news. The good was that the premier had arrived; the bad was that he had been jostled by a group of "Free Tibet" protestors who had breached the lackadaisical Montreal police lines, forcing him to run the gauntlet from his car to the front door. Our gamble, nevertheless, seemed to be paying off. Now that he was in Montreal in the same hotel as the cluster of admiring premiers and business people, it would be hard for him to bolt for the airport.

There was one last dramatic act to be played in the farce. Prime Minister and Mrs. Chrétien went to fetch Premier Li Peng and his wife at their suite to take them up to the gala dinner. I followed as they took the escalators, located on a wall alongside huge windows, to the banquet floor. At the top, Canada's smiling premiers awaited. Outside, clearly visible to the prime minister's distinguished guests on the escalator, was a veritable wide-screen IMAX view of papier mâché tanks, imitation Statues of Liberty, huge banners painted with Chinese characters, and thousands of people screaming insults at Canada's honoured guest. Premier Li, glum at the beginning of the ride, was red-faced and furious by the end.

"I am departing immediately! Never have I or my country been so humiliated!"

"You have it all wrong," Prime Minister Chrétien quickly said. "They're mad at *me*. They do this all the time — not to worry."

Premier Li had no ready answer. But his face, and the visit, were saved.

Book Drive

I visited the schools in all 26 fly-in communities in a region larger than France. There were bookshelves in the libraries, but no books because no funding was provided by the federal government to buy them. Several had received cartons of welcome used books from service club organizations in the south, and the teachers and parents appealed to me to find some way to obtain enough to stock their shelves. Remembering the decisive influence books and reading had on me when I was a child, I set out to do exactly that.

With my good friend Grand Chief Stan Beardy in a school library devoid of books. *Office of the Lieutenant Governor.*

Eager young Indigenous volunteers from a Toronto First Nation school help me load books onto trucks bound for Attawapiskat and Constance Lake First Nations. *Office of the Lieutenant Governor.*

Canadian Forces Rangers unloading boxes of books at a remote First Nation school. *Office of the Lieutenant Governor.*

A Canadian Forces Hercules transport plane drops loads of books on frozen Severn River. I am explaining the airdrop process to a student from the nearby Fort Severn First Nation School, the most northerly and isolated in the province.. *Office of the Lieutenant Governor.*

Children at Fort Severn anxious to see books delivered by parachute. *Office of the Lieutenant Governor.*

Joy on the faces of the children as they stock the bare library shelves with gently used children's books. *Office of the Lieutenant Governor.*

Summer of Hope

In July and August 2005, five photographers working with Photosensitive, a non-profit organization of professional photojournalists, went north to take timeless photographs of my first five Summer of Hope literacy camps.

Andrew Stawicki, founder of Photosensitive, travelled to North Caribou Lake in northern Ontario: "I saw happiness in their expressions. I realized this change was the result of creating interest in their lives by focusing and improving their reading skills in a fun environment." *Photo by Andrew Stawicki.*

North Caribou Lake First Nation: the children and a counsellor make friends. *Photo by Andrew Stawicki.*

Someone prefers working by herself. *Photosensitive.*

Someone else could use a little help. *Photosensitive.*

Eager to learn. *Photosensitive.*

Eager to play. *Photosensitive.*

A dreamcatcher silhouetted against the Northern Ontario sky. Dreamcatchers symbolize the power of literacy and books to filter out bad dreams and allow positive ones to pass through. *Photo by Craig Chivers.*

41

The Referendum of 1995

The RCAF pilot, more used to handling fighter aircraft than ferrying his prime minister to international meetings, banked the Canadian Forces Challenger sharply one way and then the other to line it up with the runway before coming in for a hard, gut-jarring landing at New York's LaGuardia Airport. It was October 24, 1995, and I was accompanying Prime Minister Jean Chrétien to New York as his diplomatic adviser for the fiftieth anniversary celebrations of the founding of the United Nations. It was the weekend before the referendum in Quebec, and the prime minister was deeply worried. Lucien Bouchard — leader of the Bloc Québécois, a Lazarus resurrected after being written off for dead when stricken by flesh-eating disease a year before, and a messianic, telegenic firebrand speaker from the North — had captured the imagination of the Quebec public since he had emerged as leader of the "yes" side a scant two weeks earlier. The polls indicated that he just might succeed in destroying Canada. The strategy of the "no" forces was to have the prime minister maintain a low profile, given the modest popularity scores he had registered in polling in Quebec. Although no one had confided in me, I assumed that the communications specialists thought that it would be better for the prime minister to be seen playing a statesman's role outside Canada rather than campaigning on the ground in Quebec. If this were the case, they couldn't have been more wrong.

At the airport Canada's ambassador to the United Nations was waiting to escort us to the luxurious Pierre Hotel in midtown Manhattan, but we were in no mood to enjoy the surroundings. In his briefing, the ambassador reminded us that the United Nations was in a state of financial crisis. The Americans were refusing to pay their dues, and few of the 185 member states were meeting their obligations on time. Meanwhile, the end of the Cold War had led to an explosion of ethnic conflict in Africa and Europe. There had been genocide in Rwanda and state collapse in Zaire, Liberia, Somalia, and Angola. The wars in Bosnia and Croatia were coming to an end, but the United Nations' involvement over the years in these countries, both wrenched by violence out of the former Yugoslavia, was judged a failure. None of this was news either to the prime minister or me. Managing Canada's involvement in these and other crises, with their constant ups and downs, had been part of the prime minister's daily fare since the general elections that had brought him to power in November 1993.

The ambassador claimed that these catastrophes weren't the fault of the United Nations as an institution; rather, they were the result of pusillanimous governments' unwillingness to provide the organization with the means to carry out its mandate of "saving generations from the scourge of war," as spelled out in the charter adopted by its founders in 1945. The prime minister's presence in New York, he claimed, was an important vote of confidence in the United Nations by one of its strongest traditional supporters.

But vote of confidence or not, the next two days passed in a blur. We were all preoccupied with Quebec. My mind was only half on my work as I accompanied the prime minister on his calls. I heard but did not grasp the significance of the words of Yitzhak Rabin, the former hawkish Israeli defence minister who had become a fighter for peace as prime minister as he told us that a settlement with the Palestinians was within reach. The ruler of Kuwait, dressed from head to foot in white ceremonial desert robes, smiled enigmatically and promised to direct several major defence contracts to Canada as a sign of appreciation for our help in the 1991 Gulf War — and later reneged on his pledge. The prime minister of Norway shed crocodile tears as he bemoaned his fate in having to govern the coddled and demanding population of one of the richest countries in the world.

We left early for Ottawa, since the prime minister was determined to throw all his energies into the battle for Canada at the eleventh hour. I stayed out of his way, making the final arrangements for an extensive foreign tour to start shortly after the referendum — and planned months before when the experts were confident that winning the vote would be a piece of cake. Laurent, my son attending Queen's University, represented the Bartleman family in joining a tidal wave of Ontarians who went to a giant rally in Montreal to wave Canadian flags and appeal to Quebeckers to vote "no." Then, on Monday, October 30, I sat in my Ottawa office, my team around me, to watch the results come in. At the request of the Prime Minister's Office we had quietly prepared a contingency plan to cope with the international fallout should the separatists come out ahead. The nation then went through trauma as the referendum in Quebec was won by a whisker. Afterward, I gratefully sent my plan to file.

At the end of that week, on Saturday, November 4, I telephoned the prime minister's residence at 24 Sussex Drive and insisted that the household staff rouse Canada's leader from the sleep of the exhausted to speak to me. Prime Minister Rabin, I told a thoroughly shocked Jean Chrétien, had just been assassinated. We would have to move our scheduled departure on his foreign tour forward by two days to fly to Jerusalem for the funeral. Less than 24 hours later the prime minister boarded his aircraft in Ottawa, ashen-faced, to tell me that an intruder, armed with a knife, had broken into his residence in the early hours that same morning to confront his wife at the door to their bedroom. She slammed the door in his face, and the police, taking their time, eventually came to their rescue. The prime minister was shaken to the core. The near death of his nation had been followed by the assassination of a respected leader whom he had just met, and then by a close call in his own house.

The shocks were coming like hammer blows. Twenty-four hours later the prime minister was pushing his way through a chaotic crowd of world leaders and their bodyguards, jostling for position in the heat of the Middle Eastern sun around the grave of Israel's deceased prime minister on Jerusalem's Mount Herzl. With no time to rest, he boarded his aircraft to fly to his next international commitment — the Commonwealth summit in New Zealand. The flight eastward across the Indian Ocean was interminable, broken only by stopovers for fuel in the Maldives and for a brief rest in Perth, Australia. At the summit itself, allied with Nelson Mandela, he engaged in a desperate and ultimately futile and soul-destroying effort to persuade the corrupt Nigerian government to spare the life of human-rights and environmental activist Ken Saro-Wiwa. Thumbing their nose at the international community, the Nigerians hanged him just as Prime Minister Chrétien was meeting with Mr. Saro-Wiwa's son. With barely a pause for grief, it was then back to Australia for an official visit, this time to the capital, Canberra, before making the long flight to Osaka, Japan, for an Asia-Pacific Economic Cooperation summit.

And the world moved on — such is the nature of time and history. Staring out the window of the aircraft at the southern hemisphere's night sky on the long flight home with my travelling companions asleep, I realized that what was important to us when we started this trip — the referendum and the assassination of Rabin — had already begun to fade from the consciousness of the international community. I came to the conclusion that the breakup of Canada would matter deeply only to the United States and to France: the former because we were their largest trading partner; the latter because of the international political consequences of a unilingual French state in North America. Others would doubtless be sorry, but not viscerally. Their concern would be for the precedent separation would set for other multi-ethnic countries in a decade that had already witnessed the collapse of Yugoslavia and the Soviet Union. Our national unity problems were ours, and we would have to solve them for ourselves.

42

The Ambassador Goes Back

Terrorism was a standard feature of international relations long before Al Qaeda and ISIS appeared on the scene. On the evening of December 17, 1996, leftist guerrillas of the Túpac Amaru Revolutionary Movement attacked the residence of Japan's ambassador in Lima, Peru, during a reception. Taking hundreds of guests hostage, including Canadian Ambassador Anthony (Tony) Vincent and his wife, Lucie, they threatened to kill them if the Peruvian government didn't release the members of their organization held prisoner in jail. Around midnight, Gar Pardy, Foreign Affairs director general of consular affairs, telephoned me at home to give me the news. I told him the prime minister would want to be informed immediately. And he was, despite being roused from a sound sleep. It was the first time a Canadian ambassador had been taken hostage by terrorists, and he wanted to be involved. "Call me any time of the day or night," the prime minister told me.

Later on, Pardy telephoned to say the guerrillas had released Lucie and the wives of other diplomats but were holding their husbands prisoner. The next morning he called again to say Tony, with diplomats from France, Germany, and Greece, had been set free on condition they deliver messages to the government and return to the Japanese residence to resume their captivity. That was when Tony showed what he was made of. The other diplomats scampered for safety and didn't return. Tony, after speaking to the Peruvians, decided to fulfill his part of the bargain and return to the Japanese residence. I got Tony on the line. "Before you act I want you to speak to the prime minister."

The prime minister told him he was a brave man but didn't have to go back to a possible death. "But I gave my word, Prime Minister," Tony said. "Besides, by returning I can save lives. The guerrillas will want to use me as a negotiator."

In the following months, Tony, now trusted by the terrorists and the government, served as an intermediary carrying messages and witnessing talks between the two sides. When Tony came to Toronto in February 1997 to participate in talks between Peruvian President Alberto Fujimori and Japanese Prime Minister Ryutaro Hashimoto on the crisis, Prime Minister Chrétien took Tony aside and told him he was "a gutsy guy, someone we're all proud of."

Despite Tony's efforts, a peaceful resolution to the standoff wasn't possible. Peruvian security forces stormed the Japanese embassy, freeing the hostages and killing the terrorists. The Japanese prime minister called Prime Minister Chrétien to express his admiration and thanks for Tony's efforts, and Canada had another hero. In 1999, Tony passed away while serving as Canada's ambassador to Spain.

43

Russia: Tchaikovsky's Funeral March

In October 1997, I accompanied the prime minister on an official visit to Russia, this time to St. Petersburg as well as to Moscow. Jean Chrétien and Boris Yeltsin had developed a firm friendship, making a point of meeting bilaterally at the annual G7 summits and staying in touch by telephone. Like Chrétien, Yeltsin came from a humble background and was a populist. Yeltsin had been a stonemason and plasterer in his hometown of Sverdlovsk in the Urals. Canada's prime minister had worked in a paper mill in the summers during his university years. Yeltsin, like Chrétien, had entered politics at an early age, assuming a senior position in his region's Communist Party in 1968 before being plucked from obscurity by Mikhail Gorbachev and brought to Moscow to head the local Communist Party structure and begin his march to the top. He was a hero in August 1991 when he had led the resistance to Moscow reactionaries who had sought to return Russia to its old totalitarian communist ways, rallying the crowds from the top of a tank in the manner of Lenin during the 1917 revolution. He had displayed a ruthless streak in October 1993 when he had ordered Russian tanks and artillery to open fire on the Russian White House, at that time home to the Russian Duma or parliament, to quell dissent from Russian legislators. And despite a bad heart, bouts of major depression, and a binge-drinking habit, he had won election after election in the 1990s.

The previous twelve months had been bad ones for the president. In November 1996, he had undergone a difficult bypass operation. The following January he had dropped out of sight for a prolonged period, ostensibly suffering from the flu. After Yeltsin retired, he boasted that he had suffered from and covered up five heart attacks in his years in office. No one, however, had been fooled. The consensus of my counterparts in foreign capitals in those years was that Yeltsin would die before he completed his term of office. My staff quietly prepared plans (that I kept hidden in my office safe) for the prime minister to attend a state funeral in Moscow at short notice. Yeltsin, however, had proved everyone wrong, deciding to stop drinking, to take care of his health, and to pull himself together. It was therefore a very much alive if pale and subdued Russian president, accompanied by a watchful wife, who hosted the prime minister and his wife on their official visit to Russia in October 1997.

The first event was an informal Sunday lunch at the presidential dacha. Zavidovo, Joseph Stalin's former hunting lodge, stood in the middle of an immense forest, thirty minutes by helicopter from Moscow. We had arrived late the previous night from Ottawa and our tired bodies were still on Canadian time. One didn't, however, turn down a personal invitation to lunch from the president of Russia. Yeltsin originally wanted Chrétien to start the day with a bear-and-boar hunt, but the prime minister had begged off, saying that hunting wasn't his sport. That was true, but he probably also remembered the photos of Brian Mulroney posing with dead animals in the Zavidovo forest when he had accepted a similar offer to go hunting with the Russian president some years earlier. The howls of outrage from animal lovers in Canada had probably been heard in Moscow.

On our journey from Moscow, we flew over one impoverished village after another, joined together by two-lane pothole-filled roads. Scattered among them, like modern-day reincarnations of the estates of the aristocracy dispossessed of their holdings in the October Revolution, were huge Western-style mansions, many still under construction, the country homes of Russia's new capitalist class. It could have been a late fall day at the prime minister's country home at Harrington Lake in the Gatineau Hills at that time of the year. The trees, however, were birch and poplar rather than maple, oak, pine, and spruce. The leaves had fallen, just as they had in the Gatineau Hills, and the wet ground was golden on that grey October morning.

Approaching the dacha, we walked past chefs in military uniform, standing stoically in a light rain while manning an array of spluttering barbecues. Inside was warm Russian hospitality of a nature I imagined Joseph Stalin never offering to his guests, who might very well have departed for the Gulag after dessert. The Yeltsins were accompanied by an interpreter, a protocol officer, and my opposite number — the president's diplomatic adviser (the successor to the one I'd met in 1994). They greeted the Chrétiens, the prime minister's escort officer, a Canadian interpreter, and me at the door, then took us to one end of the combined living room–dining room for drinks beside a roaring fire. The president reached for sparkling water, saying that Mrs. Yeltsin had laid down the law — no more alcohol.

Then it was time for lunch. Yeltsin's table was laden with every type of Russian delicacy imaginable — three or four different sorts of caviar, salads, pickled eels, pâtés, and olives. The first course was a delicious borscht soup. There was then a succession of dishes. Barbecued food was borne in from outside all afternoon — pike, carp, eel, wild boar, pheasant, venison, and duck, as well as beef and pork. The four wineglasses in front of each guest were kept full with the best that Crimean vineyards had to offer. Too bad it was the middle of the night according to my internal clock — all I wanted to do was to climb back on the helicopter, return to the hotel, and go to bed.

Twenty courses and six hours later we took our leave and returned to Moscow. It had been a social afternoon and the discussion was on family and other personal matters. Nevertheless, the two leaders agreed to stage a meeting at the North Pole to highlight our common northern frontiers and to announce Russia's decision to send a delegation to Ottawa in December to sign the treaty banning anti-personnel mines. Neither would happen. The prime minister would discover that Canada didn't have aircraft capable of transporting and landing him safely at the North

Pole; the Russian president would learn that he didn't have the backing of his government to sign the treaty.

The next day, in a departure from past practice, the president offered us a choice of coffee or tea at the official talks — beer was no longer on the menu for these morning meetings. When the prime minister had visited Moscow in May 1995 for the fiftieth anniversary commemorations of the end of the Second World War, and again in April 1996 for the special summit on nuclear safety, Yeltsin had been mildly drunk. In fact, I had rarely seen him when he was completely sober. At the July 1994 G8 summit in Naples he had walked up to me at a reception to seize my hand in a rough, friendly grasp, not knowing and not caring who I was. He was heavily overweight and his face was blotched, florid, and swollen, giving the impression that he had just spent the night sleeping face down on the concrete in an alley with a group of drunks. The following year at the Halifax summit he had disgraced himself by drinking too much and had collapsed in a drunken stupor in an elevator in the presence of his mortified wife and his Canadian liaison officer.

The two leaders promised to do something to increase trade from its almost derisory levels and to develop closer ties on Arctic matters. Yeltsin, however, was dismissive of the prime minister's concerns about Russian mafia extortions against Canadian investors in Russia. He also reneged on his commitment, made less than twenty-four hours earlier, to sign the anti-personnel mines treaty. When the prime minister raised the issue, the Russian ministers of foreign affairs and finance interjected to flatly tell their leader that Russia shouldn't and couldn't afford to sign on. The Russian armed forces, they said, relied on anti-personnel mines to protect hundreds of nuclear weapons storage sites — there were neither troops nor resources available to provide an equal level of alternative security.

Yeltsin turned to the prime minister and said that if he could convince their mutual friend Bill Clinton to sign the treaty, then he, Boris Yeltsin, would override his ministers and ensure that Russia followed suit. He then shrugged and smiled as if to say: "You see, I would sign now if I could, but these people won't let me." The drunken Yeltsin, I thought, would never have allowed himself to be spoken to in this manner before foreign visitors and would have fired his ministers on the spot. And before the end of the decade it would become clear that Canadian hopes for a breakthrough in economic ties with Russia wouldn't be realized, frustrated by mafia shakedowns, a Wild West business atmosphere, and red tape.

After Moscow we boarded the Airbus to fly to St. Petersburg for the final part of the official visit. Riding at top speed in a motorcade with sirens wailing wasn't the best way to take the measure of a city. My field of vision was made worse by a cold fall rain and by the condensation that collected on the windows of our passenger van. I caught glimpses of magnificent cream-and-yellow eighteenth-century buildings, more Central European in architectural style than Russian, as we rolled down Nevsky Prospekt, the splendid boulevard in the heart of the city. Off in the fog, the driver told us, was the Peter and Paul Fortress used in tsarist times as a political prison for such notable inmates as Fyodor Dostoevsky, Leon Trotsky, and Maxim Gorky. In another direction was the Hermitage, one of the greatest museums of the world, incorporating within its wings the former Winter Palace of the tsars. Later, on a tour, I saw priceless treasures but couldn't help wondering how much sweat the peasants of old Russia had to expend to allow their feudal overlords to purchase them.

The next day we stopped at the Piskaryovskoye Memorial Cemetery for the war dead to pay our respects. Some decades earlier I had read Harrison Salisbury's non-fiction classic description of the siege of the city, then known as Leningrad. In *The 900 Days* he describes in poignant detail the incredible fortitude of the people who endured starvation rations, German shelling, disease, and secret police brutality from August 28, 1941, to January 27, 1944. Almost a million people, he reports, had perished in the siege, and I had found it difficult to come to terms with death on such a scale. Once at the cemetery, I began to understand. I followed behind as Mr. and Mrs. Chrétien walked down a pathway through mounds of heaped earth, each holding the remains of hundreds of thousands of civilians. The snow was lightly falling. From off in the distance, I could hear Tchaikovsky's funeral march. Young soldiers in ceremonial dress, their fur hats and uniforms slowly turning white, goose-stepped in a Russian army ceremonial march down the walk ahead of the official party and stood at attention while the prime minister laid a wreath at the monument to the dead.

I would remember Piskaryovskoye long after dirty snow in Red Square, official talks in Moscow and St. Petersburg, lunch in Zavidovo, elegant Kremlin drawing rooms, splendour in the Hermitage, Lenin in his mausoleum, KGB dirty tricks, and the rough-hewn Yeltsin started to fade from my memory.

44

Cuba: My Secret Mission

In August 1996, thirteen years after I had left Cuba, I returned to Havana as an emissary of Prime Minister Jean Chrétien. My mission was to persuade President Fidel Castro to introduce market and human-rights reforms into Cuba. At that time Cuba was isolated in the region and in desperate economic shape. Over the previous decade, all the countries in Cuba's neighbourhood in Latin America and the Caribbean had adopted liberal democratic governments. Farther afield, Cuba's former communist partners, with the exception of China, Laos, and Vietnam (who themselves were introducing market reforms), and the hermit country of North Korea, had turned to Western-style forms of government. There was reason to assume that the crumbling of communism in Central and Eastern Europe would soon be followed by its collapse in Cuba. The only question seemed to be whether change, when it came, would be peaceful as in Poland, Hungary, and the former Czechoslovakia, or whether it would be brutally rapid and violent as in Romania, where Nicolae Ceauşescu and his wife had been stood up against a wall and summarily shot after a drumhead trial on Christmas Eve 1989.

The Cubans had been abandoned by their former partners. Soviet aid, equivalent to more than $3 billion per year throughout the 1980s, was cut back beginning in 1989 and ending completely in 1992. Trade with the Soviet Union and its satellite states totalling 87 percent of all Cuban imports and exports in 1988 collapsed with the collapse of the Soviet Empire in 1991. Castro had desperately hung on, permitting farmers to sell a limited amount of their output in private markets, loosening controls on small entrepreneurs, permitting foreign investment under tight controls, and legalizing the use of dollars in special shops where Cubans could spend remittances from family members abroad.

Canada's ambassador to Cuba at the time told me that conditions had reached their nadir in the summer of 1993, by which time the Cuban economy had contracted by 60 percent. When he had arrived in Havana in July of that year, not a car was to be seen in the streets, people walked or rode bicycles to work, there were long lineups of people desperate to obtain food outside ration shops, and there were frequent cuts in electricity. True, conditions had slowly improved in 1994 and 1995, but life for the average Cuban was harsh. Castro had become more apocalyptical than usual in his public pronouncements, talking about socialism or death and rushing from trouble spot to trouble spot to calm the people. The full panoply of totalitarian measures, including intimidation by neighbours and the secret police, was deployed to keep order among a population increasingly more demoralized than disaffected.

Logic dictated that Castro might take advantage of a Canadian initiative to save at least part of his revolution before the deluge. After all, he had already introduced some market reforms, in particular allowing foreign investment by Canadian, Spanish, Italian, and Mexican companies. However, Castro was a dedicated revolutionary, and it would go contrary to everything he had fought for to make the sort of changes I'd been authorized to propose. His speeches, broadcast live by Radio Havana Libre around the world, were as implacably anti-American as ever and reflected a determination to protect the revolution in Cuba to the end. And despite a growing dissent movement of a size and nature that would have been unthinkable during my years in Havana, Castro himself seemed to have retained popularity among a population proud of the accomplishments of their revolution in health and medical research, in education, and in sports.

Prime Minister Chrétien didn't have a romantic view of the revolution, but wanted to help Cuba achieve a soft landing in the post–Cold War era and to increase the odds that the transition to liberal democracy, when it came, would be peaceful. Throughout 1995 and 1996, contacts between Canada and Cuba were stepped up, with high-level meetings between foreign ministers, parliamentary visits, and greater Canadian International Development Agency (CIDA) activity. The Cuban government took a further series of modest measures to open its economy to foreign investment and to give greater freedom for small entrepreneurs. Meanwhile, the Cuban economy stagnated and Cuba watchers in Miami and elsewhere were saying that Castro, who was in poor health, might be willing to open up the economy and introduce democratic reforms to save something of the revolution before the entire system collapsed.

The dinner with Castro went as well as could be expected. He greeted me warmly at the door, putting his arm around my shoulder, and moved without prompting to his favourite chair in the living room. I had the impression before the discussion began that he knew the purpose of my visit, probably from the listening devices planted by the Cuban Ministry of the Interior in the walls of the residence, and was in no hurry to talk business. In contrast to the monologues he had engaged in during his visits to the residence in the past era, the president asked me questions and seemed genuinely interested in what was going on in the wider world. However, he seemed to be groping in the dark to find answers that would fit his ideological view of the world. What, for example, had caused the collapse of communism in Eastern Europe? What had given rise to a one-superpower world and rendered his revolution irrelevant? When I sought to engage him on the subject of my visit, he gently said that he could get into that the next day over lunch. He was more interested in knowing what I wanted for lunch than in the purpose of my visit and smiled when I told him I would like to have a traditional Cuban meal of roast pork, beans, and rice. The president departed early, walking slowly to the door like a tired old grandfather who had done his duty in receiving respectful visitors and now just wanted to go to bed. I preferred the old Castro, full of himself and raging against the injustices of the world.

The next day the ambassador, an official from Ottawa, and I met with Castro in his office from ten in the morning until five in the afternoon, with lunch served at the conference table. Introducing my message indirectly, I said Canada's prime minister wanted to see Canada-Cuba relations strengthened. Ties had been reinforced since his government had come to power in 1993. An unprecedented number of contacts between Canadian ministers and Cuban officials had taken place. We were helping Cuba modernize its national banking and tax collection system, and there had been parliamentarian exchanges. More, however, could be done. Canadians realized that Cubans had gone through difficult times, but all countries and not just Cuba had to adapt their economic, and even in some cases their political structures, to face the new reality of globalization. As well, all countries of the Americas except Cuba were now liberal democracies. The prime minister wanted Canada to help Cuba continue with its process of adaptation.

I then handed over a list of possible areas for future collaboration, including dialogue on human rights. This latter subject was sensitive, but it was of great importance to the Canadian government and people. Canada was holding constructive exchanges with countries as diverse as China and Indonesia and wanted to initiate a similar process with Cuba. Castro avoided replying and launched into a diatribe against the United States, which, he said, was forcing Cuba to maintain a state of siege, with controls over its population to protect itself against American aggression. He then began a lengthy monologue lasting the rest of the morning on his achievements of the past thirty-seven years, recounting in great and painful detail the entire course of Cuba's involvement in Africa. With a hint of bitterness, he said that more than 2,000 Cuban soldiers had died fighting for the independence of Angola and Namibia. Carrying on in the same vein, he observed that today the Namibian government wouldn't even allow Cuban ships to fish in its waters. He also wryly observed that Cubans had been forced to make compromises in the past for the greater cause. Cuban troops in Angola, for example, found themselves protecting the oil wells of American oil companies that provided the foreign exchange used by the Angolan government to pay Cuba to fight its domestic enemies, who in turn were in the pay of the CIA and the South African government.

Growing morose, Castro admitted that Cuba had lost the ideological war against the United States in the Third World. He gave the impression of being a beaten man who was uncertain what direction he should take his country. He had trouble concentrating, often losing the thread of his thought. In the afternoon session, I tried to put the conversation back on the rails by noting that Canada was master of its foreign-policy agenda with Cuba and would pursue it independently of the United States. I also repeated my message that the world had changed and that countries that didn't open their borders to the free flow of people, ideas, and trade would become marginalized.

The president made several efforts to reply to substantive points in the paper I'd handed over, but drew back each time. Finally, he said that he would review our conversation and the Canadian paper with his Council of Ministers. He would then send a special envoy to Canada in due course with Cuba's response. Three weeks later the Cuban ambassador called on the prime minister in Ottawa to convey a message from Castro that he thought the discussions in Havana had been fruitful. Several weeks later a personal envoy of the president, the vice-president, made a follow-up call on the prime minister to say that Cuba accepted our offer to deepen relations and was prepared to begin a serious dialogue on human rights.

45

Cuba: Chrétien Versus Castro

In follow-on talks to implement the action program, the Cubans focused on concluding deals in which they could obtain material benefit and access to Canadian food aid, but whenever the Canadian negotiators raised human-rights issues there was no meeting of minds. The Cubans repeated the Cold War double talk that the Communist Party reflected the will of the people and that democratic elections and liberties in the developed world were smokescreens for the interests of capitalists. They insisted that social and economic rights of the group took precedence over the political rights of the individual.

Pope John Paul II then paid a highly publicized visit to Havana during which Fidel Castro freed a number of political prisoners. The prime minister sent me to Rome to find out if the Vatican thought Castro was now ready to adopt a more open approach to human rights in general. Archbishop Tauran, foreign minister of the Vatican, told me not to expect any change in Castro's repressive policies. A visit by the Canadian prime minister, he said, wouldn't lead to any dramatic change in the nature of the Cuban state, but would encourage reformers and hearten those Cubans hoping for eventual democratic reform.

Back in Ottawa, I told the prime minister that it was unlikely Castro would follow through with his commitment to engage in a serious dialogue. But a visit to Havana might well help consolidate the opening made by the pope. The Cuban vice-president then reappeared in Ottawa to renew a longstanding invitation from his president to the prime minister to visit Cuba. He argued that sufficient progress had been made in Canada/Cuban talks in the past year to justify a visit. The prime minister, who knew better, was noncommittal but agreed to send me once again to Cuba for another session with the president.

Accompanied this time by the Foreign Affairs assistant deputy minister for the Americas, I returned to Havana in February 1998. At a meeting with the Cuban vice-president before calling on the president, I said Canada's prime minister was prepared to make a low-key visit to Cuba but had conditions. Castro didn't like my message. When we met with him that evening, he was in a foul mood. The mellow, reflective Castro I'd met in my previous visit was gone. In his place was a weakened old lion, so thin his shirt hung loosely on his ribs. His mood was one of intense irritation. When he sat down, his right leg pulsated in an up-and-down motion and his left arm twitched. He held his left arm with his right to try to still it and leaned toward me.

"I'm tired of visitors who come asking the impossible," he said.

Looking into the president's eyes, I thought of Zaka, our family pet poisoned by Cuban Interior Ministry thugs in 1983. I was certain Castro had given his approval and wondered how one of the most charismatic leaders of the twentieth century, who had devoted his life to seeking justice for the downtrodden, could behave so callously. To him, animals and people were just pawns to be pushed around in the service of a by-now discredited ideal.

Castro snorted and started a long monologue, not tolerating the slightest interruption for about four hours. His views, in contrast to those of our encounter in 1996, were clear and decided. He described at great length the visit of the pope, who had obviously made an enormous impression on him. Castro moved so close that his spittle splattered my face. I had the impression that he wasn't really addressing me. He was engaged in a stream-of-consciousness dialogue with himself. My sense was that he had forgotten why we'd come to see him. He seemed to be drawing conclusions from the visit of the pope and was unhappy that he had, perhaps in a fit of enthusiasm, accorded too much freedom to the local Catholic Church.

Around two o'clock in the morning an old retainer signalled to the president that dinner was ready. I then made my move. When the president was temporarily distracted from his monologue by having to struggle to his feet and lead us to the table in an adjoining room, I told him that Prime Minister Chrétien had sent me to say that he would like to pay a working visit to Cuba in April. Some progress, I said, had been accomplished in the bilateral talks in the past year, but more could have been done on human rights. Cuba's release of political prisoners following the pope's visit had been a step in the right direction. Could not more be done in the context of the prime minister's visit, such as releasing other higher-profile prisoners and undertaking to sign the U.N. Covenant on Economic, Social, and Cultural Rights? I emphasized that human-rights issues were of great importance to the Canadian people and to the prime minister personally, and that continued progress would lead to even closer Canada-Cuban relations.

Castro's eyes flashed, but he made no reply. Instead, on sitting down, he began another long, meandering account describing the role of Catholicism and African folk religions in Cuban history. This was followed by several hours on Cuba's role in Africa, repeating what he'd told me during my previous visit. This time there was no self-pity. History would show that Cuba had played a noble and crucial role in the struggle for decolonization and had no regrets. The old retainer silently passed around the food and kept our water glasses filled, obviously well versed in providing simple businesslike meals in the middle of the night.

Around 6:00 a.m., with the morning light starting to penetrate the room, Castro asked me to repeat the message from the prime minister, which I did. But instead of giving me his answer, he launched into a tortuously long, often confusing, and detailed analysis of globalization. Then, just before 8:00 a.m., the president, by now relaxed and smiling, with his guests barely conscious, made his pronouncement. He wanted the Canadian prime minister to visit, but Cuba wasn't prepared to make concessions. "Don't ask Cuba to do anything that would damage it, and Cuba won't ask Canada to do anything that would embarrass it," he said.

* * *

After I reported back to the Prime Minister Chrétien, he decided to proceed with a working visit on April 27 and 28. The prime minister was under no illusion that Castro wanted our help to ease the transition of his country to a market economy or making human-rights reforms. But a visit might give heart to the dissident community and consolidate the reforms the pope had obtained for the Catholic Church. The prime minister also wanted to take the measure of Castro the man and the historical figure.

Thus began the first official visit to Cuba by a Canadian prime minister since that of Pierre Trudeau in 1976. From the start it was a clash of different personalities with diametrically opposing visions of the future. The jousting started at the airport arrival ceremony, broadcast live on all Cuban radio and television channels. Castro, radiating newfound vigour, welcomed the Canadian prime minister by delivering a vicious anti-American diatribe during which he pledged fidelity to the principles of the revolution.

The prime minister replied with a calm, measured speech containing the messages he would convey to Castro repeatedly over the next thirty hours. "The winds of change are blowing through our hemisphere … and we must all adapt…. This is an expression of confidence … to a more dynamic, more democratic, and more prosperous hemisphere … that is becoming a family with shared goals, shared values, shared hopes and dreams…. We are committed to working to achieve greater social, economic, and political justice throughout the region." The two leaders then got into Castro's big Soviet-era limousine and set out for the newly restored National, a beautiful pre-revolutionary hotel overlooking the sea on Havana's famous Malecón Drive.

The official talks began later in the morning, with the prime minister and me on one side of the table and Castro and his vice-president on the other. The winds of history, great ideas, and the principles of the Cuban revolution were the themes of Castro's opening remarks. I think he assumed that the prime minister would be overwhelmed with the brilliance of his analysis and allow him to dominate the discussion. The prime minister, however, stopped the president in full rhetorical flight. "I want," the prime minister said, "to discuss substance. Could a civilian complaints commission be empowered to investigate human-rights complaints? Could foreign non-governmental organizations be granted greater freedom of action? Would Cuba sign the U.N. Covenant on Social and Economic Rights?" He then passed over a list of four high-profile dissidents languishing in a Cuban jail for the past year without being charged and asked Castro to release them.

Castro's face betrayed all manner of emotion, passing from astonishment to anger and to bitterness. He said nothing for some time, picking up and throwing down distractedly the index card with the names of the four dissidents scrawled in my barely legible handwriting. "I've never been so humiliated," he said in a barely audible voice. He would have walked out the door, I believe, had he not been in his own office.

The dialogue never recovered, though the leaders remained at the table for more than two hours. The president had been prepared to release three low-level prisoners as a sort of human-rights gift, but the prime minister had just raised the stakes. It was at this point that Castro probably decided that the policy of constructive engagement with Canada had reached the limits of its usefulness. The Canadians were taking human rights far too seriously.

Although other bilateral and international issues were then discussed, there was no meeting of minds. The prime minister mentioned that Canada had been happy to resume our aid program. To commemorate his visit to Havana, CIDA intended to announce that it would provide funding to allow Cuba to provide new textbooks and scribblers for its schoolchildren for a year. Castro and the vice-president sat silent and tight-lipped. They weren't about to say thanks to a visitor who hadn't listened to Castro's thoughts on the future of humanity. Eventually, after stroking his beard attentively, always a sign that he was thinking hard, Castro turned to Haiti and proposed that Canada fund a program to pay Cuban doctors to administer to the desperately poor in that country. While not rejecting Castro's suggestion, the prime minister made one of his own. Why shouldn't Canada and Cuba collaborate in clearing anti-personnel mines in Angola and Mozambique? Cuban forces had operated there for over a decade. Canada could fund a program and Cuban soldiers could remove the mines.

Castro looked absolutely devastated. He would later tell a national Cuban television audience that he'd never heard a more imperialist proposal. Imagine! Canada suggesting that Cubans do the dirty work in the minefields while Canadians sat off to one side garnering the credit! Castro glanced at me angrily from time to time as the ill-fated talks progressed, as if I were to blame for his game plan going wrong. Finally, the meeting dragged to a conclusion, and as the prime minister and I made our way to the door, I felt the hands of the president on my shoulders from behind, squeezing hard and shaking me.

"I hope you're satisfied, Bartleman!" He hissed out the words in Spanish, his voice cold, high-pitched, yet low enough not to attract the attention of Prime Minister Chrétien, who was already striding rapidly ahead to meet the assembled Canadian press contingent. I had no idea why Castro was so mad at me. Perhaps he felt I hadn't conveyed his message to the prime minister not to ask Cuba to do anything during his visit that could damage it. Whatever the reason, the fury in his eyes made me glad I was a Canadian able to depart with the prime minister, rather than a Cuban who would have felt the full wrath of an unhappy leader in a police state! I also thought his sentiments were a touch unkind to someone who had spent a night with him so recently.

The next morning Castro, by then in a better mood, said goodbye to Prime Minister and Mrs. Chrétien at the airport. As I said goodbye to him, he drew me to him. "Your prime minister and I had a good discussion in my car on the way to airport. And do you know why, Bartleman?"

I said that I had no idea and smiled expectantly, hoping he had overcome his fit of pique at me of the day before. But I had no such luck.

"Because you weren't there, Bartleman, that's why!" He was probably right.

46

Mother Teresa

The news of Mother Teresa's passing on September 5, 1997, arrived at the height of the public hysteria over the death of Princess Diana earlier that same week. What irony! One young, a divorcée, touched by scandal, and secular; the other old, a living saint, Nobel Peace Prize laureate, and the embodiment of deeply conservative religious values. Both were, however, dedicated to the poor and marginalized. And both were victims of depression and feelings of inadequacy at low points in their lives that they overcame to become role models for millions.

The funeral was in Calcutta, but it was a city far different to the one I'd known as a young diplomat based in Bangladesh when I had visited it on business or holiday. The local authorities had cleared the refuse and human wrecks from the side of the road coming in from the airport; now advertising billboards honouring Mother Teresa — and selling Indian automobiles, baby food, and electronic goods — decorated the route. An indoor sports stadium seating 12,000 had been fitted up for the funeral service. The majority of the official guests were ladies in black mourning, as if the wives of world leaders had conspired to make the event an all-women happening. Hillary Rodham Clinton, Bernadette Chirac, and Sonia Gandhi joined Mrs. Chrétien in the places of honour.

At one point, as the distinguished guests stood chatting, the British high commissioner bore down on the group in his role as the modern-day representative of the Raj. "Make way! Make way for the Duchess of Kent! May way for the Duchess of Kent!" he proclaimed, but no one paid him any attention, and the duchess had to fend for herself.

The funeral began when soldiers in a death march without drum rolls entered, carrying Mother Teresa on an open bier — a person whose soul had departed, and whose flesh was all too mortal. There was a smell of decay, incense, mosquito repellent, and sweat, and I found it hard to keep my eyes off the hands on her chest — large, full, work-scarred, and clutching a rosary. The service began: hymns, sacraments, speeches, wreath-laying, popularity contests, flashbulbs, jostling press, and bemused looks on the faces of the phalanx of assembled bishops, archbishops, and cardinals as they listened to the eulogies from representatives of other faiths — Hindu, Parsi, Muslim, Buddhist, and Protestant. Individuals whose lives she had touched — a leper, a former criminal, a handicapped person — came forward with offerings that included a painting of the Sacred Heart of Jesus and flowers. The official guests approached the bier for a final farewell. The cortège then departed, led by altar boys with crucifixes and candles, followed by a guard of honour in full-dress uniforms and turbans, moving with an air of destiny like a squad of mechanical soldiers. A crowd of Sisters of Charity, clergy, and representatives of the poor and sick followed.

India thus honoured a foreign-born nun of the tradition and spirit of St. Francis of Assisi with military honours and pomp remote from her lifestyle. It was a ceremony appropriated by the state for the purposes of the state, by the church for the purposes of the church, and by the mourners for the purposes of the mourners. And yet, in the Indian context, there was no sense of inappropriateness. All of us, myself included, wanted to pay tribute to her, were conscious that we were saying farewell to one of the giants of the twentieth century, and shared a desire to be present as history was made.

Part Five

Burying the Past, 1998–2002

Hamilton Spectator Wire Services, Cape Town, South Africa, February 6, 1999: Canadian Envoy Recovers. A packed South African Parliament heard President Nelson Mandela laud his government's achievements including fighting crime yesterday, but Canada's ambassador [*sic*] missed the speech. Canadian High Commissioner James Bartleman was nursing injuries from an attack by an intruder who stunned him, tied him up and robbed him in his hotel room. Bartleman, 59, was attacked … after a man gained entrance pretending to be a hotel employee. Foreign Affairs spokesman Sean Rowan said the ambassador [*sic*] suffered a fractured nose and an injured foot in the attack.

47
The Beating

I first became aware that something was wrong in December 1995, about two years after I started working for Prime Minister Chrétien. I had just returned from the Francophonie summit held at Cotonou, the malaria-ravaged capital of Benin in West Africa, suffering from wild nightmares, high anxiety, and severe stomach pains. It would be years before I'd learn that I might have been one of the unlucky few who suffered from the side effects of mefloquine, the anti-malarial medication I'd been prescribed prior to departure. Apparently, this particular medication could bring about deep and hard-to-treat depression and thoughts of suicide.

Thinking that it was a simple stomach upset, I visited our family doctor seeking a quick fix. Asked to describe my work schedule, I proudly related all the "important" things I'd been doing, saying that I kept up a similar pace year-round. The doctor ordered an extensive series of tests that indicated I had no physical problems. "But your body," he told me, "is telling you to change your job." That was advice I didn't want to hear. I loved what I was doing, embracing stress, working twelve hours daily from Monday to Friday, spending the weekends on the telephone, and regularly forgoing statutory holidays and annual vacations. By the spring of 1998, however, I had become so ill that carrying on was no longer an option. I asked to return to Foreign Affairs and a less stressful job. The prime minister respected my choice and wished me well.

In August 1998, I left with Marie-Jeanne, eight-year-old Alain, and Stella, our lovable mutt from the Gatineau Hills, to take up a posting as high commissioner to South Africa. We picked South Africa because Marie-Jeanne, who had been born in the Belgian Congo, wanted to return to the continent of her birth, and I was interested in the country of Nelson Mandela. The posting, we thought, would last four years, after which we would return to Canada and I would retire. We would, in fact, remain abroad four years but would serve in three posts on three separate continents, not getting to know any one of them in the depth it deserved.

As if by magic, the debilitating physical pain stopped on the flight to South Africa. Although my depression continued, life was worth living again. Once settled in Pretoria, my professional instincts were aroused by managing a multi-purpose mission with trade, immigration, consular, aid, and public-affairs programs. Marie-Jeanne rediscovered immense daytime skies, starlit heavens, fierce thunderstorms, red earth, eucalyptus and acacia trees, birds with gorgeous plumage, and the flowers of her youth. Alain loved his school, made friends, and bonded with the household staff. We did things as a family for the first time in years, visiting the game parks in South Africa, exploring the cold deserts of Namibia, and swimming in the Indian Ocean.

But at night my nightmares continued. I dreamed I was a marginalized Aboriginal kid living in poverty in the small Muskoka village of Port Carling who had become a diplomat and had successfully faced challenge after challenge to rise to the top of his profession. And then my dream would turn into a nightmare. Locked within my nightmare, I'd find myself back in Muskoka, once again the Aboriginal kid on the fringes of society, a failure unwilling to leave the village and confront the outside world. I would wake up uneasily, the dream still vivid, but the memory of it would fade and I would get on with life. Every so often, however, no matter what I was doing or where I was, the memory would reappear. I would wonder whether I was living inside or outside my dream. This would lead me to ask myself: Why me?

On February 5, 1999, matters came to a head. After a career punctuated by close calls, my luck ran out. I left the residence in Pretoria in the late afternoon and flew to Cape Town where I was to attend a speech given by President Mandela. A car and driver from the local Canadian consulate picked me up and drove me to a hotel downtown on the seafront where I had reservations. By that time the sun was setting over the Cape Mountains and I felt privileged to spend some time in one of the world's most beautiful cities, but I didn't feel that way for long after checking in.

As soon as I was in my room on the third floor, I made myself comfortable, removing my shoes and changing from suit into shorts and golf shirt before picking up the telephone and calling my wife in Pretoria to let her know I'd arrived safely. As we were talking, someone knocked on the door. Assuming it was a hotel employee coming to turn down the bed, I told my wife I'd call her back and went to open the door to be greeted by a smiling, neatly dressed, heavily muscled individual who told me he was from maintenance. "The front desk has asked me to check the condition of your overhead fan," he said, pointing at the ceiling behind me. When I turned my head to see if there was a problem, my visitor shoved me inside, pulled out a taser, and pulled the trigger. But I didn't collapse as I should have after absorbing the charge of electricity. If I'd had time to think, I wouldn't have resisted and just told him to take whatever he wanted and go. After all, those were the instructions all Foreign Service employees were supposed to follow when being mugged to avoid being injured or killed.

My assailant stepped back, his finger still on the trigger. I stared at the gun, hypnotized by the crackling sparks of electricity. I was feeling no pain, but my body was tingling just as it had when I foolishly stuck a fork into the slot of a toaster to free a piece of burnt toast decades earlier. In my imagination it had turned into the moray eel that bared its teeth at me after I disturbed it while snorkelling on a reef years before in Cuba.

I stepped back and kicked the thief as hard as I could. Pain engulfed my now-broken foot, rendering it useless in the coming fight. He dropped to his knees, and as he staggered back to his feet, I hit him as hard as I could with my fist. His head was as hard as a block of concrete. Agonizing pain shot up my arm, and I was no longer able to continue the fight. In retrospect — and I have refought this unequal combat hundreds if not thousands of times in my nightmares over the past fifteen years — I should have made a run for it when he was still down. After all, at the age of fifty-nine, I was too old for this sort of nonsense.

My visitor didn't blink, but smashed his fist against my jaw, cutting open my lip and jarring my teeth. None broke. As I backed away, throwing ineffectual punches, I heard myself screaming, as if the cries were coming from someone else. Surely, I thought, the private guards the hotel claimed were stationed on every floor to protect the guests would hear me and come to the rescue. Then my assailant knocked me over a night table, and when I scrambled to my feet, he punched me down onto the bed. When I got up again, he delivered a blow that broke my nose, triggering a cascade of blood over my body, onto him, and over the rug and bedroom furniture. But the fight, if a one-sided beating can be described as such, continued. After giving me a thorough thrashing, punctuated with loud cries and appeals for help from me, he eventually stopped pounding me to say that if I didn't shut up he would kill me. "I've got a gun, "he said, "and I'm not afraid to use it." Given the reputed low value South African criminals placed on the lives of their victims, I believed him.

So I shut up and meekly told him to take what he wanted and leave.

Aware that I was now under his control, he left me to try on my clothes in the closet, returning with two ties, one to bind my arms behind me, the other to do the same with my legs. He then pushed me backward onto the bed and went about searching my briefcase and suitcase at leisure. All he could find was $300 in South African currency. He became even nastier, slapping me around and demanding to know where I'd hidden the money. He had seen me arrive by chauffeur-driven limousine, dressed in an expensive suit. Obviously, I was a rich man. He didn't understand my explanation that as a diplomat I received a clothing allowance but was just a civil servant, and in my country, civil servants, including diplomats, weren't particularly well paid.

My captor paced back and forth, talking on a cellphone to an accomplice elsewhere in the building or out on the street. While I didn't understand what he was saying, I guessed he was reluctant to leave with such a paltry haul after taking the risk of penetrating one of Cape Town's better hotels. Every few minutes he would turn his attention to me, demanding as in a class-B movie that I tell him where the money was hidden. At last he decided it was time to go and jammed a piece of my underclothing into my mouth. He wanted to be sure I wouldn't raise an alarm as he made his getaway.

I was caught up in a frantic attempt to stay alive. My broken nose was filled with congealing blood and I couldn't breathe. I would die a horrible death by suffocation unless I removed the gag, but my hands were tied. Desperately trying to remain calm, I managed to spit it out. My persecutor was starting to stuff it back in when I began to beg for my life. I told him I would surely die if he forced the gag down my throat. I had a wife back in Pretoria who would be widowed and children who would be left without a father. I would make no noise as he made his departure. Why not simply tie me to an armchair? He could trust me.

He looked me in the eye, perhaps seeing for the first time that I was a fellow human being and not just a faceless stranger fit only to be robbed. Then, shrugging and grimacing, he resumed his pacing, twisting the gag in a distracted manner as he decided my fate. I continued to try to reach him on a personal level, telling him that my sports coat and tie that he had stolen from the closet suited him and that the watch he'd wrenched from my wrist and put on his wrist went well with his new clothes.

Suddenly, he stopped, approached me with a scowl, and told me he was going to take my word that I wouldn't call out as he left. But if I did, or if I provided the police with any details about what had happened, members of his gang — called, he said, the Gestapo — would go to Pretoria and kill my wife and family. He bound me to an armchair so tightly that the marks on my arms and legs took almost a month to disappear, then walked to the door. Turning around, he came back, still scowling. I thought he'd changed his mind and it was the end. Instead, he said, "I'm sorry," and slipped out of the room.

I was devastated. This petty thief, after brutalizing, humiliating, and robbing me, was now seeking to deny me the right to hate him.

Shifting my position as far as I could to the right, hunched over, and helped by a rush of adrenaline, I pressed my arm downward and to the side until the armrest snapped. It was then relatively easy to use my now-liberated right hand to free my left arm from its armrest and move on to untie my legs. Afraid that the thief might change his mind and return to finish me off, I stumbled to the door and locked it, but I thought I could hear his footsteps in the hall coming back toward my room. Calling the useless people at the front desk, who for all I knew could have been in cahoots with the intruder, wouldn't do me any good. By the time they sent someone to rescue me, I would already be dead.

I looked around for some means of protecting myself and saw a large glass pitcher of water and two glasses on the dresser beside the television. Seizing it, I intended to smash it against the wall and use the shards attached to the handle to shove into my assailant's face if he decided to force his way through the locked door. But at the last second, overwhelmed by an unbearable thirst brought on by my yelling for help and pleading for mercy, I changed my mind, poured myself a glass of water, and gulped it down in a swallow. Then I poured myself another drink, but before I emptied the glass, I once again heard footsteps in the hall. I picked up the pitcher, ready to defend myself, but the steps continued on by. It was a scene from an Alfred Hitchcock thriller, and I wanted out of there fast. I set down the pitcher close to me, in case I needed it, and dialled reception. The hard part now began.

The next few days passed in a blur. The departmental press officer called me in my hospital room to remind me of the unwritten code Canadian diplomats who were victims of crime when posted abroad must follow: play down the gravity of the incident to avoid offending the host government. I complied. President Mandela called Prime Minister Chrétien but not me to say he was sorry. The story became headline news in Canada and South Africa for a few days but was quickly forgotten. Prime Minister Chrétien called to express his shock and to tell me he would cancel my posting to South Africa and send me elsewhere to recover if I thought that would help. "Talk to your wife and call me back," he said. I said I would.

My nightmare now appeared every night and intruded into the daylight hours with its message of hopelessness. Soon I was afraid to go to bed. It was as if the grovelling I'd to do to survive had destroyed my self-esteem and sense of identity and resurrected old struggles over existential issues that I'd come to terms with as a child and youth. Flashbacks, not of the beating but of the nightmare, invaded my life. I was terrified I would wake up and find myself marooned in the Port Carling of the late 1940s. Life tasted of ashes. My nightmare now came in Technicolor rather than black and white, and I stumbled around the office in a daze, upsetting my co-workers.

Why, I wondered, did people get depressed? Unaware at that time of the possible side effects of mefloquine, the anti-malarial medication I'd taken before and after my visit to West Africa three years before, I wondered why I was continuing my slide downward. I could understand why I'd become depressed when I was working for the prime minister: I had become a workaholic and paid the price. But why here in South Africa where my workload wasn't abnormal? Were the neurotransmitters of my brain wired to degenerate when they reached a certain age? Had the racism I'd faced as a boy somehow scarred my brain? Was it a mid-life crisis, with its corrosive nostalgia for youth and adventures never to be relived? Was it mourning for a career in the fast lane that I no longer wanted but missed just the same?

Was it the whiff of oncoming mortality and ensuing eternal oblivion? Intuitively, I knew that all of these reasons were to blame. My beloved grandmother, had she still been alive, would have reflected the attitudes of her generation and told me I was a hypochondriac and to get a grip. I was, however, simply sick and getting sicker, even if my illness was mental and not physical. In the meantime, all I could think about was killing myself, something I blamed on the Gothic experience with death that I'd witnessed during my earliest years in the village.

* * *

For suicide, it seemed, was the death of choice of the people in my village, with prominent residents doing themselves in by drowning, carbon monoxide poisoning, and self-inflicted gunshot wounds. Usually, we children would learn of suicides from death notices framed in black taped to the front door of the general store or prominently displayed on the wall of the post office. These notices always sent a chill down my spine. All activity in the normally rowdy schoolyard would halt as the cortèges passed by on the way to one of the three churches from which flowed the mournful pealing of bells before and after the funeral services.

Our house had its own macabre history. Soon after we moved in our parents told us that several years earlier the next-door neighbour had hanged himself on an apple tree in what was to be our new backyard. Within months of our arrival, the neighbour on the other side of our house shot himself with a hunting rifle. My mother, like every other villager, quickly learned of the death and asked the widow what she could do to help. She was told that the best service would be for me to keep her youngest child busy while the family tried to cope, so I was sent out to play with the son, who was only one year younger than I was. Neither one of us knew that his father was dead, and we watched with curiosity as the steady flow of village ladies arrived with offerings of home-baked goods to comfort the family. We both guessed that something momentous was happening and suspected from the grim looks on the faces of the ladies that the news, when someone would eventually tell us what had happened, wouldn't be good.

The family, bereft of a breadwinner, plunged into poverty. My companion, devastated by the death of his father, rebelled against the injustice of it all by walking out into the busy traffic and lying down on the road, daring drivers to run him over. He also stole from tourist cottages and, while still a child, was sent to a reformatory for delinquent boys. He once escaped and made it home. A posse of heavily armed villagers swept down to search for him in his mother's backyard before turning their attention to ours. It was a black moonless night, and from within our house I heard the voices of the villagers, as excited as if they were hunting some dangerous wild animal rather than a frightened child. They tramped through our rhubarb patch and searched our outdoor privy. My father chased them away, threatening to set our dogs on them if they didn't get off our property. I will never forget my friend's screams when they caught him, calling for his mother as the police pushed him into the back of a cruiser, its red rooftop light flashing. He was returned to reform school, initiating a cycle of incarceration that didn't end until he also killed himself.

This early exposure to suicide meant that I sometimes wondered how it was possible for people to take their own lives. What drove people, whether young marginalized Aboriginals or middle-class white villagers, to kill themselves? Albert Camus, the Nobel Prize–winning author, said that suicide was the central philosophical issue that all people had to address sooner or later, but that didn't make sense to me. Neither could I accept the declaration of Arthur Koestler, author of *Darkness at Noon*, who claimed it was only natural to do oneself in when life became unbearable. I paid more attention when Ernest Hemingway shot himself, noting that his father had done the same; I wondered if the father's behaviour had influenced the son.

My attitude changed after I was mugged. No longer was it a question for philosophical or psychological musing. I fell into a deep post-traumatic depression. A weight, heavier and more penetrating than anything purely physiological, pressed down on my chest, destroying my will to live. I told Marie-Jeanne to throw my ashes into the Indian River during the spring runoff from the dam below the Indian Camp at Port Carling. I sensed that the mixing of my ashes with the water of this river, so important to my Indian ancestors and to the early white pioneers, would reconcile the Indian and white natures of my being and bring closure to my existence.

I sought the help of a doctor in Pretoria, who told me I should take a long walk every day and all would be well. I didn't believe him and consulted a therapist recommended by a South African friend. That didn't work out. I found it hard to tell my problems to a stranger, and she seemed intimidated by the fact that I was a high commissioner. Urgent action was required. Marie-Jeanne found another doctor for me, and he started me on antidepressants. The side effects were horrible. I walked around in a daze, once getting lost in an airport. Most disappointing of all, my nightmares continued, mocking my efforts to get better. Marie-Jeanne, the hero of this story, was non-judgmental and found another doctor. He changed my medication, which helped immensely. I then called the prime minister to accept his offer to cancel my posting to South Africa and go elsewhere.

In April 1999, Foreign Affairs proposed and I accepted its offer to send me to Australia as high commissioner. At our cottage in Canada that summer I started to write the memoirs of my boyhood and youth, focusing on life as a half-breed in a small Ontario community when overt racism was an accepted part of Canadian society. Without at first being conscious of the effect of my actions, I felt the therapeutic magic of the pen start to kick in. Writing, as a form of self-discovery, was helping me recover. And as I began to pull myself together, I started writing other books, some diplomatic memoirs, others social justice novels with Indigenous protagonists, some becoming bestsellers, some complete flops, and all continuing the healing process.

After an all too short posting of one year in Canberra, I was cross-posted in the summer of 2000 to the European Union in Brussels as Canada's ambassador. More than a year later, over the 2001 Christmas holidays, Marie-Jeanne, Alain, and I spent a week in Senegal. It was the first time we had set foot in Africa since our escape from South Africa after the mugging. I wanted to see if I'd put those events, irrationally associated with Africa, behind me.

It was a good visit. We saw a different Africa. Senegal might have been one of the world's poorest nations, but its people embodied a rich, confident, coherent fusion of francophone culture and language with Indigenous African values. It was also safe — at least in Dakar where we stayed. I also had the sense that the people had come to terms with the injustices of their colonial past. On a day's outing to Gorée Island, a former notorious embarkation point for slaves and now a UNESCO Heritage Site, we saw Americans with tears in their eyes. Their ancestors had left this region hundreds of years ago in chains and now they, their descendants, were back, trying to come to terms with the harsh reality of their roots. Meanwhile, the locals gossiped; children frolicked in the sea; young men dived for coins tossed by middle-aged European tourists from the docks; hawkers sold crudely carved statuettes of African fertility gods, sunglasses, soft drinks, and colourful shirts; and property developers offered gentrified houses of former slave owners to members of the jet set. Life carried on oblivious to the distress of American pilgrims trying to ascribe meaning to a massive historical injustice and to a former Canadian high commissioner still brooding on an obscure incident in a Cape Town hotel room. The time was overdue for me to bury the past and move on.

In early 2002, the telephone was ringing as we entered the residence on our return to Brussels. Prime Minister Chrétien wanted me to be Ontario's next lieutenant governor. With Marie-Jeanne's encouragement, I accepted. At an age when most people were retiring and taking it easy, I was being given the opportunity to make a fresh start in life.

Part Six

The Queen's Representative in Ontario, 2002–2007

48

Giving Back

It was as if everything I'd done in life had been a preparation for my new role: the summer living near the dump in Port Carling when I learned to read from comic books; my introduction to the Port Carling library at an early age where I borrowed six books a week and dreamed of a better life; the early racism that blighted the lives of my mother and brother and me to a lesser extent; discovering the good side of the people from the village; the deep attachment I formed for the land of my ancestors in Muskoka; my year in Europe where I listened to Martin Luther King deliver his message of reconciliation; being accepted as a member of my mother's First Nation; and the thirty-five years spent working in Ottawa and at diplomatic missions on six continents as a Foreign Service officer.

I loved being lieutenant governor. I enjoyed meeting people and hearing their life stories, listening to their jokes, and giving them a shoulder to cry on. Public speaking, which I had never enjoyed as a public servant when I had to adhere to the line of whatever government was in power, I embraced when I could speak frankly about social causes important to me, especially the plight of Indigenous children.

I participated in 2,500 events and delivered some 2,000 speeches, about half at Queen's Park and the others outside the office. I visited cities, towns, and villages in all 103 electoral districts, calling on local mayors and officials, visiting seniors' residences, speaking at schools, handing out honours and awards, meeting the local press. I served as Chancellor of the Order of Ontario, Honorary Chair of the Ontario Medal for Good Citizenship, and Honorary Chair of the Medal for Young Volunteers Advisory Council. I was Ontario's official host, offering dinners and luncheons to the Queen and members of the Royal Family; to the royal families of Belgium, Japan, Sweden, and Norway; and the heads of state and government of South Africa, Vietnam, Czech Republic, Mongolia, Latvia, Hungary, and many more. I welcomed distinguished statesmen and stateswomen to the province such as Bill Clinton, Mikhail Gorbachev, the Dalai Lama, and Archbishop Desmond Tutu.

I summoned the legislature into session under three governments and outlined legislative agendas in Speeches from the Throne. I appointed premiers and swore in cabinet ministers after elections. I signed Orders-in-Council formalizing Cabinet decisions and signed off on appointments to give them the force of law. I sent greetings to some 6,000 Ontarians celebrating birthdays of ninety years or older and wedding anniversaries of fifty years or more. I sent 3,000 special-event messages. I extended patronage to some 100 organizations such as the Canadian Cancer Society, the Red Cross, the Good Neighbours' Club, and the Heart and Stroke Foundation, hosting events for them at Queen's Park. Since I had never completely shaken off the depression that had dogged me for years, I joined the fight against the stigma of mental illness. And I carried the message about the corrosive effect of racism in my visits to schools.

The second insert describes these core responsibilities. The final chapter and third photo insert express what I consider to be my chief accomplishments as lieutenant governor: promoting literacy, the love of reading, and the embrace of books among Indigenous children.

49

The Plight of First Nation Children

Even from the far-off places where my wife and I were living, I was aware of the reports of desperate poverty, terrible housing, boil-water advisories, disappeared and murdered women, drug abuse, criminality, violence, and Third World conditions that prevailed on the northern reserves. I wanted to know if matters were as bad on the southern ones where the kids had access to good provincial schools and where work was to be had in neighbouring white towns and cities. In visits to Curve Lake, Hiawatha, Beausoleil, Georgina Island, Wasauksing, Shawanaga, Wahta, New Credit, Walpole Island, Kettle and Stoney Point, and Tyendinaga, I found First Nations with pockets of poverty but which were flourishing.

Of course, I knew about conditions on my own First Nation, the Chippewas of Rama, a few miles from my birthplace in Orillia in Central Ontario. I'd been visiting relatives and friends there for years and had witnessed its transformation from a rural slum in the days when my grandfather was still alive to a vibrant, progressive community with an industrial park, marina, and eventually a casino employing the largest number of Indigenous people of any enterprise in Canada. I was proud of the fact that increasing numbers of its young people were going to college or university, a trend that continues to this day. In 2014, for example, well over 100 young people, out of a total on- and off-reserve population of 1,600, supported financially by the community, were attending institutions of higher learning.

I had a lot to learn about conditions in the North, however, and on the advice of friends in the Indigenous community, I called on Stan Beardy, at that time grand chief of the Nishnawbe Aski Nation (NAN), in his office in Thunder Bay to seek his guidance on how I could best be useful in helping the children and youth. Stan briefed me on NAN, telling me it was a grouping of forty-nine First Nations whose traditional lands occupied more than 60 percent of the area of Ontario, running from the height of land to the James Bay and Hudson Bay coasts and from Manitoba to the Quebec borders. He said it was the only part of the province occupied to this day largely by Indigenous people — in the boreal forest by the Anishinabe (Ojibwa) and their close cultural cousins the Anishininimouwin (Oji-Cree), and along the Hudson Bay and James Bay Lowlands by their good friends, the Omushkegowak (Swampy Cree). Being so isolated, few people on the outside were aware of the extent of the suffering of the people, especially the children.

"Go see for yourself and make up your own mind," he told me. "And then come back and help the children."

* * *

On a hot July day in 2002, four months after I was sworn in as lieutenant governor, I flew north to Kashechewan First Nation, a Cree community on James Bay at the mouth of the Albany River. As the Government of Ontario King Air 350 turboprop circled the airport, I saw an aircraft taxiing down the runway preparing to take off, and a large group of people on the ground.

"What's going on?" I asked the chief I met a few minutes later in the terminal building.

"A thirteen-year-old-girl killed herself by injecting melted-down medications into her veins until she died," he said. "Her body's being flown out for an autopsy, and the community came out to say goodbye."

When I recovered from the shock, I asked the chief why she had done it. He told me that she'd had no hope.

Two months later, just after the opening of school, the chief of the Oji-Cree community of Wunnumin Lake called to tell me three grade eight kids had killed themselves by hanging, including a girl who had climbed a tree in front of the school, tied a cord around her neck, and jumped as her classmates made their way to school in the morning. "Please come and help us grieve," he said, and so I went and met the families of the dead, the chief and council, and the children in the school. It was the hardest thing I had ever done. The children remaining in the grade eight class, reduced to about a dozen students, appeared to be in a state of terminal depression. They all wore hoodies, resolutely stared at their desks, and refused to look up or say anything as I joined the chief in an effort to get them to express their grief in words. Afterward, the chief told me the three children had been members of a suicide pact and had killed themselves because, he said, they'd had no hope. In due course I would learn that from 1985 to 2008 there had been more than 3,000 attempted suicides and some 400 completed ones in an epidemic of death ignored by mainstream society that continues to this day.

Working with Stan, who became a close friend, I set out to help the children. Making use of an Ontario government aircraft, I went on fact-finding missions to every fly-in First Nation in the province, some many times over. I called on chiefs and councillors; met with elders and alcohol and drug workers; held discussions with the staffs of nursing stations; visited the homes of the people; and, most important, went to the schools and talked to the kids. I was well received and made many friends. Eventually, the community members invited me to attend funerals for young people who had taken their lives, to sit in healing circles, and to participate in large anti-suicide and family wellness conferences organized to deal with the alienation and death wishes of their young.

What I learned was heartbreaking. I found children living in desperate poverty; crammed into shoddily built houses; eating the unhealthy food of the poor (when it was available); suffering the diabetes, obesity, and tuberculosis of the marginalized; drinking water that had to be boiled before use; attending substandard schools; and being taught by inexperienced teachers. I discovered that Indigenous communities received only 80 percent of the funding provided to non-Indigenous children attending provincial schools. There was no money for special-education teachers, library books, and sports equipment, or for that matter for new schools when buildings rotted and fell down. The children lived in a world similar to the American South before the civil-rights movement of the 1950s and 1960s — a world where the education for Indigenous children, just as it was for black children in that unjust era, was separate but not equal. I wondered what Martin Luther King would have thought had he been alive.

But that wasn't all. When the children travelled with their parents on the winter roads to Timmins, Sudbury, and Thunder Bay, they discovered that despite being First Peoples, they were the outsiders. No wonder they were many years behind their non-Indigenous peers in educational achievement and few of them graduated from high school. Most damaging of all, the children suffered from the intergeneration impact of the residential school experience of their parents and grandparents. For almost a century, starting in the late nineteenth century, the Canadian government had engaged in a massive and cruel social engineering project in which Indigenous children were removed, often by force, from their parents and sent off to barracks-like institutions where their caregivers were mandated to turn them into brown-skinned white Canadians. The racist program was a disaster. Raised without the love of their families, sexually assaulted by non-accountable teachers and clergy, generation after generation of Indigenous children came to maturity not knowing how to raise children, and when they married and had children, they brutalized them as they had been brutalized — and the cycle of familial destruction continues to this day.

The last residential school run by the federal government in Ontario closed its doors in 1974, but that just set the stage for further suffering. Beginning in the 1960s and continuing into the 1980s, provincial welfare authorities took enormous numbers of babies and children from their mothers and gave them to white families to raise. At the same time the people in these remote regions moved off the land into settlements and were abruptly confronted with the challenges of life in the modern globalized world.

With their parents, grandparents, and great-grandparents before them traumatized by their residential school experiences, the youth had no one to turn to in their families for love and support as they faced these monumental shocks, so they turned inward and began to kill themselves. Initially, I was naively unaware of the depth of anti-Aboriginal racism that coloured mainstream attitudes. I had expected that officials would have been as shocked as I was at my findings. But they just shrugged, as if to say, "The people are so poor, unemployment is so great, violence is so widespread, corruption is so ingrained, health determinants are so terrible, racism is so pervasive, drug use and criminality so widespread, and the education system is so broken, there's no point in doing anything." Unwilling to give up, I turned to people of goodwill to help me address childhood literacy among Indigenous children, a problem I knew something about from my own childhood experiences.

In two massive book drives, we filled empty library shelves with a million and a half used books in schools on First Nations across Ontario, in northern Quebec, and in Nunavut. I then appealed to the public for donations to establish a book club of 5,000 children called Club Amick for all grades one to six students in the fly-in communities, with each child receiving a new book every four months to establish his or her own personal library. At my suggestion Ontario's premier established creative writing awards for First Nation, Inuit, and Métis students aged six to sixteen, with prizes of $2,500 for the winners.

I'm most proud of my role in creating Summer of Hope reading camps on Ontario's northern First Nations. I began by obtaining the support of the First Nations themselves and used a grant from the Ontario government to fund five pilot projects. Scouts Canada, the YMCA, and Frontier College (Canada's oldest literacy organization) worked together to run them in the summer of 2005. The 200 campers and fifty staff loved the program, but at $100,000 per camp, costs in my opinion were too high and joint management by the three organizations too cumbersome. I thus came up with a model that cost no more than $33,000 per camp and turned the initiative over to Frontier College to run. I then obtained funding from universities, teacher federations, trade unions, banks, power companies, and charitable foundations to support a five-year program in all twenty-six fly-in communities in the province. Frontier College did such a good job managing the program that the money I raised paid for six instead of five years of operation.

After I retired in 2007, Frontier College expanded operations across the country as First Nations everywhere embraced the program. In 2014, 6,000 campers in eighty-seven camps read an estimated eleven books each, 93 percent of teachers noted strengthened social skills, 89 percent noted improved academic skills, and 89 percent of parents said their children read more because of camp. In 2015, 10,000 campers attended ninety-nine camps. Although summer reading camps cannot fill the gaps in programs provided by the federal government, they offer children the chance to dream dreams of a better life, just as I dreamed my dreams when exposed to the magic world of books when I was a kid.

Afterword

For more than seventy years, I have tried to understand why people and governments have treated Indigenous people so badly. Was it because white society was burdened with a sense of collective guilt for taking of their land? Was it because the guilt had been transformed into disappointment that Indigenous people had not quietly disappeared from history as predicted by eminent historians like Donald Creighton? Was it raw racism? I eventually came to the conclusion that these answers were incomplete. The main reason, in my view, is that many members of the mainstream Canadian public, like those in settler societies around the world, harbour doubts that Indigenous people are as fully human as they are. Let me explain.

In chapter nine, I tell a story called "Six Choir Boys" about the death of my mother's infant brother in the late 1920s, while living at the family shack at the Indian Camp in Port Carling. Carpenters from the boat works built him a tiny coffin, the Anglican priest organized a dignified funeral, six adolescent boys stepped forward to serve as pallbearers, and a local man dug the grave. The late Lloyd Cope, who was one of the pallbearers, wrote to me after reading one of my books.

> You mention six choir boys being pall-bearers at his funeral. I was one of those boys (about 10 years old) and this was the first time I was exposed to death, and the fact that other than the white race had feelings. I feel confident in saying that many of the residents of Port Carling similarly had a change of thought as a result of Mr. Smedley, the Anglican Minister, and his wife taking the initiative in providing burial procedures for the infant child.

Lloyd's letter is one of compassion and understanding. If only the same sort of compassion and understanding had been shown by white society to the Indigenous people over the past century and a half, perhaps governments would not have sent their children to residential schools, starved them, sterilized their women, conducted medical experiments on their children, scooped up their children and sent them off to be raised by white families, underfunded their education, ignored the murders of Native women and girls, and continue to ignore the epidemic of suicide among Indigenous boys and girls who feel, with reason, abandoned by everyone — the list is well known and there is no need for me to repeat it.

What is to be done? Implementing the recommendations of the Truth and Reconciliation Commission would be a giant step forward, especially the recommendation to teach Indigenous history in schools, involvement of the non-government world in initiatives like school and community twinning, and supporting Frontier College's Aboriginal summer reading camps. Exposure to literature, especially novels, short stories, and poems, can also bring people together. A novel takes the reader inside the heads of its characters, and when a character laughs the reader laughs, when the character suffers the reader suffers, when a character rages against injustices of humankind and divine providence the reader does likewise, and so on. Most important, the novel leads the reader to make connections and links between the fortunes of the protagonists and him or herself and thus broadens his or her understanding of the big issues we often think about only after midnight with our heads under the covers. Non-fiction, even creative non-fiction, can't do that. Writers such as Richard Wagamese, Joseph Boyden, Thomas King, and Drew Hayden Taylor are already building bridges through their writings. I do what I can through mine. There are ways to fight racism if there is a will.

Acknowledgements

I thank the members of my family and the following individuals who helped me along the way: Sam Williams, former chief of Rama, for his lessons on wisdom and peace of mind; Stan Beardy, chief of Muskrat Dam First Nation, for his friendship and guidance on how best to help Native children; William Williams, for his stories of trench warfare on the Western Front and his love of writing, and Ruth Gibson, who had more faith in my abilities than I did; teachers at the Port Carling Continuation School in the 1950s; Antoinette Gillies and Madeline Roddick, teachers at London Central Collegiate who urged me to get a university education; Jim Cassidy, a mentor when I was a teacher at Lambton Central Collegiate in Petrolia; Angus Mahon, caretaker for whom I worked at Black Forest Island on Lake Joseph, who told me to stay in school; Bob McCulley, a star athlete in Port Carling, who always had a kind word for me when I was a kid; Jerry Mahon, my best friend in boyhood; Reg Stephens, lockmaster at Port Carling, who wanted me to become a United Church minister; my friend Russell Eaton, for whom I worked in the 1950s digging ditches, cutting wood, and painting cottages, who died homeless on the streets of Toronto; My friend Vern York, member of the Shawanaga First Nation, who lived year round at the Indian Camp, with whom I played countless games of checkers as a boy and who showed me the best fishing spots on the Muskoka Lakes before dying homeless on the streets of Toronto; Dorothy Duke, my Sunday School teacher, who taught me life lessons; Robert Clause of Sewickley, Pennsylvania, who funded my grade thirteen and university education; Arthur Menzies, my ambassador during my first tour of duty at NATO, who became a close friend after he retired; Dick Gorham, my boss — with an incredible *joie de vivre* and store of absolutely filthy jokes — when I was a director at headquarters; and Raymond Chrétien, a friend and the closest I would ever have to mentor in the Department; Gwen Boniface, former OPP commissioner, and Bill Blair, former chief of the Toronto Police services, who mobilized their organizations to collect hundreds of thousands of books to establish libraries on remote reserves; Avi Bennett and Paul MacPherson, who generously provided the key funding to launch Club Amick for Young Aboriginal Readers; Dalton McGuinty and Bev Mathews, who took a personal interest in the literacy programs; Sherry Campbell, president of Frontier College, who turned my Summers of Hope Reading camps into a nationwide program; Lincoln Alexander, my vice-regal mentor and friend; Sandy Cameron, Anthony Hilton, and Vania Ceccia from the office of the lieutenant governor; and, above all, former-prime minister Jean Chrétien.

I thank Penumbra Press for permission to draw on *Out of Muskoka* and Dundurn for allowing me to include a modified excerpt from *The Redemption of Oscar Wolf*. I thank McClelland and Stewart for agreement to use excerpts from *Raisin Wine: A Boyhood in a Different Muskoka*, *Rollercoaster: My Hectic Years as Jean Chrétien's Diplomatic Advisor, 1994–1998*, and *On Six Continents, A Life in Canada's Foreign Service 1966–2002*.

Thank you to the photographers of Photosensitive, a Canadian non-profit organization, for permission to use their black-and-white photos of Indigenous children attending aboriginal children's summer reading camps and for the cover photograph. Thank you to Don Smith, author of *Sacred Feathers: The Reverend Peter Jones and the Mississauga*

Indians and *Mississauga Portraits: Ojibwe Voices from Nineteenth Century Canada* for sending me extracts of letters he obtained from the National Archives about one of my ancestors. And, finally, thank you to Dundurn, especially Kirk Howard and Patrick Boyer for suggesting I write this book, and to Kathryn Lane, Karen McMullin, and Michael Carroll for making it happen.

Index

Page numbers in italics refer to photographs.

Also by James Bartleman

The Redemption of Oscar Wolf

In the early 1930s, Oscar Wolf, a 13-year-old Native from the Chippewas of Rama Indian Reserve, sets fire to the business section of his village north of Toronto in a fit of misguided rage against white society, inadvertently killing his grandfather and a young maid. Tortured by guilt and fearful of divine retribution, Oscar sets out on a lifetime quest for redemption.

His journey takes him to California where he works as a fruit picker and prizefighter during the Great Depression, to the Second World War where he becomes a decorated soldier, to university where he excels as a student and athlete, and to the diplomatic service in the postwar era where he causes a stir at the United Nations in New York and in Colombia and Australia.

Beset by an all-too-human knack for making doubtful choices, Oscar discovers that peace of mind is indeed hard to find in this saga of mid-20th-century aboriginal life in Canada and abroad that will appeal to readers of all backgrounds and ages.

Exceptional Circumstances

Autumn, 1970: Hostage-taking separatists in Quebec abduct a foreign diplomat and a cabinet minister and threaten violence across the country. As fear sets in, the government turns to Luc Cadotte, a specialist on international terrorism and veteran of the clandestine struggles in Latin America.

From the jungles of Colombia to Montreal under siege, former diplomat James Bartleman plots a turbulent thriller based on events he witnessed first-hand. Swerving between fanatical ideologues and crass careerists with bloody hands, Cadotte has to choose sides when they all seem dirty, and put everything on the line in a crisis that puts all that he stands for to the test.

Available at your favourite bookseller

VISIT US AT

Dundurn.com
@dundurnpress
Facebook.com/dundurnpress
Pinterest.com/dundurnpress